D1598606

Managing Sports

Managing Sports

and Risk Management Strategies

Herb Appenzeller

79680

Carolina Academic Press
Durham, North Carolina

To my beloved grandchildren
Justin, Kristy, Elizabeth, Kelly,
Thomas, Barrett, David, Luke, and Sarah
who put gold in my golden years.

ISBN: 0-089089-504-X
LCCN: 92-72046

Carolina Academic Press
700 Kent Street
Durham, NC 27701
(919) 489-7486

Printed in the United States of America

92-72046

79680

Contents

2 7. 61

Preface

I accepted my first job in a small rural high school totally unaware that I lacked the experience and expertise to accomplish the tasks at hand. The positives were energy, enthusiasm, and a love for students. These factors enabled me to survive and succeed in my work. Today the field of sports administration has changed so dramatically that I would be fortunate to be hired for the same position I entered years ago. Sports administrators now work and live in a world that routinely features computers, zero-base budgets, personnel administration, sports medicine services, fund-raisers, and risk management strategies.

Annie Clements, a leader in sports law and sports management, describes the role of sports administrators in the years ahead:

> Successful sport managers will be sensitive to trends and events, will welcome change, will anticipate the needs of society, and will develop new programs when requested . . . Sport management will be challenging and an exciting career if you are sensitive to the people and world around you, eager to dream, and willing to be a diligent planner and a demanding evaluator. . . . [S]port managers of the future will be limited by the extent of their imagination (Parks and Zanger, 1990, 257, 264).

Centuries ago, Quintilian, a Roman educator, wrote that "education is not what you are able to remember but the things you can't forget." This book is about the things I can't forget after 44 years in teaching, coaching, and administration. This book is intended for everyone in sports administration and those who aspire to such positions. It is my hope that students in colleges and universities will profit by the material in this text. This book reflects a practical approach to sports administration for the decision maker in need of appropriate information to facilitate decisions and policies that are both educationally and legally sound. The text is not intended to be an exhaustive treatise of the sports administration field, but is an attempt to emphasize the areas that need attention.

This book is different. It was designed that way. It uses meaningful examples from the on-the-job experience of the author. Anecdotes and personal stories of actual situations experienced by the author fill the pages.

Thomas Peters and Nancy Austin note in their bestseller *A Passion for Excellence* that stories, as nothing else, reveal what is important to an institution. They believe, as does this author, that stories convey the mistakes and successes of the past so that others can profit from them. Bob Gingher, a book editor for the *Greensboro News and Record*, writes that "no one develops learning tools by rote, but again by examples and by the story." He concludes, "stories are the indispensable tools of teachers and students; without them, there's no such thing as 'moral imagination.' " One final note—in the 1950s, I attended a football clinic and got one idea and play from the late Jim Tatum, coach at the University of North Carolina at Chapel Hill. That one idea and play won the final game of the year and enabled us to complete the only undefeated season in our school's long history. I believe that even one idea derived from a clinic, workshop, conference, or text makes it worthwhile. It is my hope that *Managing Sports and Risk Management Strategies* will provide not just one idea, but many, for the sports administrators who face challenges every day in their chosen profession.

Acknowledgments

The mere listing of names is inadequate for the valuable contributions many individuals made toward this endeavor, but I hope they realize how important they are and how grateful I am for their help. I especially appreciate four colleagues for major contributions to this book: Ronald L. Baron, Executive Director, The Center For Sports Law and Risk Management, Dallas Texas; Jerald D. Hawkins, Professor of Exercise Science, Lander College, Greenwood, South Carolina; Ann Terrill Johnson, Vice President for Institutional Advancement, Greensboro College, Greensboro, North Carolina; and J. Phillip Roach, Professor, Director of Athletics, Intramurals, and Physical Education, Rollins College, Winter Park, Florida.

Significant contributors include: H. Thomas Appenzeller, William Beale, Mary Broos, Kris Chamberlain, Mike Clopton, Wayne Edwards, Lynne Gaskins, Dennis Haglan, Wat Keys, Debbie Lazorik, Guy Lewis, David Martin, Steven McCollum, Philip Menzies, John Morley, Dickson Shaefer, Don Selby, Dennis Smith, United Educators Insurance Risk Retention Group, Inc., Robert Turner, and Michael Welch.

I am grateful for the many athletics directors, coaches, student-athletes, sports management majors, and colleagues who made sports administration exciting, challenging, rewarding, and, best of all, fun.

Part 1
Managing People

1
The Sports Administrator

1.1 The Changing Role of the Sports Administrator

I entered the sports profession in 1948 with an unusual background for coaching and administrative duties—a major in Latin and a minor in English. I felt comfortable coaching because I played football and ran track in high school and college. My duties as athletics director were limited to scheduling, purchasing, and maintaining equipment. There were no formal requirements for administering a sports program, no methodology to guide me. I followed John Dewey's educational theory of "learn by doing," as did most athletics directors on the secondary, collegiate, and university levels in those days.

Until the late 1970s, most National Collegiate Athletic Association (NCAA) Division I and II and National Association of Intercollegiate Athletics (NAIA) athletics directors were former head coaches in football and basketball (and occasionally baseball) promoted on the basis of service and merit. In some instances, however, they were coaches unable to win, but whose services enabled them to gain a higher reward. Others such as Paul "Bear" Bryant (Alabama), Clarence "Big House" Gaines (Winston-Salem State), and James Valvano (N.C. State) held dual roles as coaches and athletics directors. Today, coaches who hold dual positions are becoming a rarity. In 1991, George Perles, who held the position of athletics director and head football coach at Michigan State University threatened to file suit when the president argued that "having one person hold both jobs would provide insufficient oversight over the football program." As a result, the trustees developed new criteria for evaluating Perles as a coach and athletics director. Perles's attorney remarked that his client would consider legal action to "fight the new criteria." Perles was removed as athletics director following

the 1991 football season but was retained as football coach. President
John B. Di Baggio said, "the jobs are separate and distinct, and a mistake
was made when they were joined over my objections" (*The Chronicle
of Higher Education* 1991). The Board of Governors of the University
System of North Carolina adopted a policy prohibiting dual roles for
coaches and athletics directors, a possible trend throughout the nation.

Today's outstanding coaches often elect roles other than athletics
directors. Dean Smith, renowned basketball coach at the University
of North Carolina at Chapel Hill, has a fifteen-year contract with an
annual salary review. In 1989 Smith received $113,382 with added
financial incentives that included a bonus for postseason play. Smith
has the option to give up his coaching responsibilities for realigned
duties, with a guaranteed salary "at least equal to that of the then
athletics director of the university, including fringe benefits . . . until
2001" (*Greensboro News and Record*, 15 Dec. 1990).

Irwin Smallwood, former sports editor of the *Greensboro News and
Record*, observed that in the 1970s athletics directors at many major
colleges and universities had duties that were "about as ceremonial as
they were functional" (Smallwood 1987). Smallwood noted that the
day of athletics directors playing golf with influential alumni is over
as "bright young men in three-piece suits whose credentials lean more
toward the Harvard School of Business are the norm rather than coaches
who won conference championships or bowl games" (*Greensboro
News and Record*, 3 June 1984). Athletics directors now have training
or expertise in sports administration. Smallwood points to John Swofford, a graduate of the University of North Carolina who pursued a
masters degree in sports administration at Ohio University, as the
prototype of the new breed of sports administrator who is as schooled
in "finance, marketing, time management, and networking as they are
in punts, passes, and training tables" (*Greensboro News and Record*,
30 May 1991). Swofford, who directs a staff of over twelve people and
administers a budget that has grown from $3.4 million in 1976 to $11
million in 1986, describes his job as "just like operating any other
major business except mine is in the academic setting." Swofford received $97,000 in 1989, with an expense account of $15,000 and a
bonus of one-twelfth of his salary whenever his football team partic-
ipates in postseason bowl games or the basketball team enters NCAA
postseason play.

Tim Gleason, assistant director of the National Association of Collegiate Directors of Athletics (NACDA), reaffirms this trend:

> No longer are coaching skills and/or backgrounds in physical ed-
> ucation suffice to the complex roles of today's athletics director.
> The 'ol coach' simply cannot take over as AD, as once was the
> case. The job requires a myriad of marketing skills, computer
> knowledge and sharp business acumen, more so than ever before.
> (Gleason 1983)

In *Management of Sport: Its Foundation and Application*, the authors comment on the role of the sports administrator at a major profit-oriented institution emphasizing the importance of individual and team accomplishments.

Some of the job titles in this setting include athletics director, associate and assistant director, sports information director, promotion or marketing director, academic advising coordinator, ticket manager, and facilities and/or event manager. . . . The athletics director is responsible for the overall operation of the collegiate athletics department. Part of that responsibility includes fund-raising, as well as substance abuse identification, treatment, and policy development. . . . (Parkhouse 1991, 21)

Gene Hooks, former Wake Forest University athletics director, agrees with the concept of sports management training as a prerequisite to the job, but adds:

You need to keep your ego in check. It's your job to keep other people pumped up. In this job you catch a lot of hell when things go wrong and receive very little credit when they go right and with coaches, you're probably dealing with as much ego as you're ever going to find. (*Greensboro News and Record* 3 June 1984)

I have always believed that the best administrators do not care who gets credit when their programs achieve success. These administrators work behind the scenes to ensure a smooth operation for coaches and athletes alike. When General H. Norman Schwarzkopf, Jr. was asked to name his heroes, he named his father, who was also a general, Civil War Generals Ulysses S. Grant and William Tecumseh Sherman, and World War II and Vietnam General Creighton Abrams. His reason—all were "muddy-boot soldiers . . . " and "none of them ever worried about who got the credit. They just worried about getting the job done" (*Parade*, Aug. 4 1991).

I remember hearing from one of my colleagues who left the coaching ranks to become an assistant athletics director at an NCAA Division I institution that he was very frustrated over his distance from the athletes and the challenge of competition. He asked me as a veteran administrator, "When does the excitement begin?" I assured him that in time he would experience satisfaction with success. When the football team scored a major upset against its biggest rival—his question was answered—all details behind the scenes were handled efficiently and on that day he saw clearly his role as an administrator. He wrote me the following day and simply said, "You were right, the excitement and reward were all there yesterday."

Going back to Gene Hooks and his explanation of the "back of the scenes" role of the athletics administrator, consider the following for a minute. Can you name the basketball coaches at the University of

Nevada-Las Vegas, Duke University, University of North Carolina at Chapel Hill, and Indiana? Can you name the football coach at Penn State or Notre Dame? Now, can you name the athletics directors at the same institutions? Better yet, name the presidents or chancellors of each. I routinely ask my students to take this exercise and it never fails; they name Jerry Tarkanian, Mike Krzyzewski, Dean Smith, and Bobby Knight. They respond quickly to Joe Paterno and Lou Holtz, but they all pass on athletics directors and presidents.

1.2 Women and Minorities

There is little doubt that the role of today's administrator has changed, but the opportunities for minorities and women are still in question. For twelve years, R. Vivian Acosta and Linda J. Carpenter, professors of physical education at Brooklyn College, have conducted studies of minorities and women in intercollegiate sports. In a 1986–87 study, they found that only one out of five minorities are involved in intercollegiate sports on the administrative level. Their statistics include athletics directors, associate and assistant athletics directors, and sports information directors. Their study reveals the following:

- Black—0.156 per school (about 123 total in NCAA schools)
- Hispanic—0.018 per school (about 14 total in NCAA schools)
- Asian—0.012 per school (about 9 total in NCAA schools)
- Indian (Native American)—0.018 per school (about 14 total in NCAA schools)
- Near Eastern—0.006 per school (about 4 total in NCAA schools) (Acosta and Carpenter 1986)

Regarding women in intercollegiate sport, Acosta and Carpenter report that Title IX opened the door for women to compete in sports, but the number of women coaches and administrators declined. They noted that while *Grove City v. Bell* made Title IX a victim and led to discrimination against women after 1984, the Civil Rights Restoration Act of 1989 revived it. G. Ann Uhlir, Dean of Health, Physical Education, Recreation, and Dance at Texas Women's University, agrees that "opportunities for elite women athletes have improved, but total participation slots available for women have declined" (Uhlir 1987). She notes that in 1972 "virtually all athletics programs for women were directed by women. . . . By 1979–80 over 80 percent of all collegiate athletics administrations were merged and 90 percent of the merged administrations had men at the helm." She commented that the woman who was replaced by a man had better qualifications, a higher degree, more experience, academic tenure, and rank.

Uhlir cautions that the "delegation of decisions about bats and balls only to those who direct the locker rooms will inevitably lead to episodes that move from the sports page to the front page of our newspapers." She sees hope through faculty and faculty committees whose advocacy can have an impact on the institution's environment.

Anita De Franz, a former Olympic athlete, writes in *Sports Illustrated* about the status of African-American women in sports in the 1990s. De Franz lists some disturbing facts:

- A survey of 106 Division I schools that field women's basketball teams found that only 11 are coached by black women.
- In those 106 schools, there is only 1 athletics director who is an African-American woman.
- There are no black women among the executive directors who lead the fifty governing bodies for United States Olympic sports.
- There has never been a black woman on any United States Olympic coaching staff.

De Franz describes the lack of female coaches, black or white, when she says:

Even worse, in U.S. amateur sport, there are fewer female coaches today, black or white, than there were only 10 years ago. Decisions on women's staff and spending used to be the province of the female administrators who were responsible for women's athletics. Now decisions are usually made by white male athletic directors, whose imperatives are football and the bottom line.

De Franz concludes by saying that "Today's African-American women are ready and able to contribute to this nation through sports. But only if given the opportunity, only if given the chance" (De Franz 12 Aug. 1991, 77).

Today there is hope for the future as NCAA Division I institutions are hiring women athletics directors. Progress was made when Barbara Hedges was named athletics director at the University of Washington. Hedges becomes the second woman in history to be named athletics director at a university with a big-time football program. The other woman who administered an NCAA Division I-A program with football was Mary Alice Hill at San Diego State University, who was subsequently fired for personal difficulties in administering the athletics program.

Hedges has agreed to a three-year contract at $110,000 per year. She joins five Division I-A athletics directors who have major basketball programs but not football. These women include Eve Atkinson at Lafayette College, Judith Davidson at Central Connecticut State University, Judy Rose at the University of North Carolina at Charlotte, Janice Shelton at East Tennessee State University, and Deborah Yow at Saint Louis University (who received great reviews after less than one year on the job). Judith Sweet, athletics director at the University of California-San Diego, has been selected president of the NCAA; a first, and one that sets a precedent for the NCAA. Title IX guidelines should once again lead to growth in opportunities in sports for women, including athletics administration.

Those who are making concerted efforts to train minorities and women for administrative positions in sports include Dr. Leroy Walker, former United States Olympic track and field coach and retired chancellor at North Carolina Central University, who conducts a summer institute for minorities and women who aspire to sports-related administrative positions. The next decade should also see more minorities joining the sports administration field.

John Naisbitt and Patricia Auburdene make an enlightening prediction concerning women in all fields of business and management in *Megatrends 2000*:

> Although we do not realize it yet, men and women are on equal playing fields in corporate America. Women may even hold a slight advantage since they need not unlearn old authoritarian behavior to run their departments or companies. (Naisbitt and Auburdene 1982, 240)

If *Megatrends 2000* is an accurate predictor of things to come, the caucasian male may become an "endangered species" in management positions in the twenty-first century. Naisbitt and Auburdene conclude with a revealing statement on the future accomplishments of women:

> In the first decades of the third millennium, we and our children will look back at the later half of the twentieth century and remark on how quaint were the days when women were excluded from the top echelons of business and political leadership, much as we recall when women could not vote. How naive were the men and women of the 1980s we will say, those people who believed in something called a 'glass ceiling' and thought it would forever exclude women from the top.

1.3 Administrative Duties

Sports administrators will have different expectations in the 1990s and the twenty-first century. They will have a knowledge of personnel and time management, financial affairs, scheduling, sports medicine services, crowd control, marketing, event management, equipment and facility control, public relations, computer applications, fund-raising and promotion, and legal management, including risk management planning.

It is essential that sports administrators on every level have a job description that outlines their responsibilities and specific duties. Lee Johnson, principal of Logan High School in Logan, Utah, speaking at the Western States Conference for Secondary School Athletics Directors said:

Athletic competition furnishes opportunities for character building and sound emotional development which cannot be found anywhere else in the educational experience. Who then is the best qualified to promote this fact of the program? Who but the athletics director. He and the head coaches are the keys to success in this vital area.

Johnson lists the requirements and duties for secondary school athletics directors:

- Public relations expert
- Counselor
- Selects coaches according to objectives developed by the athletics director
- Encourages professional growth—aware of national trends
- Represents department on faculty council—helps determine salaries for personnel in the department.
- Accountable for business management of athletics activities
- Helps coaches select and order equipment and supplies
- Coordinates all details of athletic contests including facilities for visiting teams
- Interprets regional and national policies and regulations
- Responsible for physical examinations and welfare of athletes throughout season
- Responsible for transportation of team members to contests away from home
- Helps build schedules of various sports
- Responsible for game management. (Johnson 1970)

Robert Purdy, author of *The Successful High School Athletic Program*, writes that "athletics at every level should be conducted by professionally prepared personnel of unquestionable integrity who are dedicated to the task of developing their charges to the highest degree possible—mentally, physically, and morally" (Purdy 1973, 21).

On the collegiate level, Guilford College outlined its expectations for the athletics director:

The Athletics Director is the chief administrator of the athletics program. The position gives primary leadership in articulating and implementing the mission of the intercollegiate sports program of the college. That mission is to enhance the development of student-athletes within an overall program of academic growth, personal health and exercise, the development of personal character and concentration, the support of team effort and competition, and the enhancement of habits that lead to lifelong well-being. (*Guilford College Athletics Handbook* 1986)

The responsibilities and duties of the athletics director include the following:

- Supervises the coaching staff and teams
- Supervises the budget and system of requisitions
- Works cooperatively with coaches in scheduling of their sports to utilize coordination of travel and facilities
- Issues contracts for home contests
- Plans the Hall of Fame banquet
- Checks on the eligibility of all athletes and maintains records
- Checks on physical examinations of athletes and maintains records
- Checks on insurance coverage of all athletes
- Responsible for crowd behavior and operation of intercollegiate events
- Fund-raiser for the booster club and athletics program
- Schedules booster club meetings and is ex-officio member of every booster club committee
- Works cooperatively with the director of sports studies and the director of intramurals to coordinate programs
- Supervises the athletic advisory council as an advisor in their monthly meetings
- Ex-officio member of the faculty athletics committee
- Supervises the sports information director
- Maintains a program of publications with the various groups that involve the athletics program
- Attends professional meetings, workshops, and clinics
- Encourages the professional growth of the staff members
- Conducts weekly athletics staff meetings
- Closely supervises all sports programs

1.4 Mission Statement

Most job descriptions for athletics directors emphasize compliance with the mission statement for the program. James Mason, recognized as the "father of sports administration" for starting such a program at Ohio University in 1967, and Jim Paul, a leader in professional baseball, discuss the importance of a mission statement in a sports program:

At the beginning of the planning process, organizations need to develop a mission statement. Although such a statement has some of the characteristics of a goal, the mission statement is more comprehensive. It is the ultimate statement made by an organization regarding its purpose. It is the guideline for plans and decisions and encompasses the strategies and policies for the organization. Thus it is vital that the mission statement be carefully and thoughtfully developed. (Mason and Paul 1988, 6)

An example of a mission statement comes from the University of Lowell (Massachusetts):

The mission of the Department of Athletics is to contribute to the University's commitment to excellence and to the enhancement of its School of Choice goals by: (1) developing a comprehensive program of intercollegiate, recreational, and non-credit instructional sports opportunities designed to enhance the physical, emotional, and social well-being of all members of the University community; (2) encouraging a positive perception and enhance public awareness of the University; and (3) providing quality spectator opportunities for members of the University community and the region. (*University of Lowell Athletics Handbook* 1989)

1.5 Organizational Structure

It is important that an organizational chart describe everyone's role in the administrative and operational aspects of the program. Athletics directors often complain that staff members frequently bypass their immediate supervisor, opting instead to go around that person to someone of authority for special requests or complaints. I remember how frustrated a colleague of mine would get because his football coach ignored the organizational plan, never reporting to him or seeking his help, choosing instead to go directly to the president for extra funds or any matter on his agenda. He would go to local business and industry, in addition to influential alumni and individuals, to solicit funds without permission or notification of the athletics director.

It is important that personnel in the program observe the structure of the organizational chart and adhere to it. My style was always to seek mutual understanding and loyalty. I stressed going through proper channels, not bypassing those in authority, encouraging staff members and coaches to come to me when problems were developing rather than after they had happened. Most coaches alerted me to potential problems, but one coach preferred to keep them to himself until they had happened because he only wanted to tell me of successful ventures. I told our personnel that they could talk with administrative officers, but, as a courtesy, I would appreciate their checking with me first. In forty years, I had very few requests from staff members for permission to talk with the president. The requests were always granted. I remember only one time when one of the coaches wrote a letter of dissent about her budget and alleged discrimination of her program. She was an excellent coach and extremely loyal to the program and me, thus, the letter was a complete surprise and quite unfortunate in its allegations. When I pointed out the errors in her letter she realized her mistake, offering to go to the president's secretary to retrieve the letter. I told her to let it go, we could discuss it with the president. This was the only time this happened and she realized she made a mistake. We hired a new president who, having been a collegiate wrestler, wanted to start an intercollegiate wrestling program. I agreed to find a part-time coach until the president told me he had already hired a friend and a former college team member to coach. I remember expressing my displeasure, asking if the new coach would report to the president since he was a presidential appointee. I was assured this was not the case.

The volunteer coach was outstanding, accepted no pay, and in fact, spent his own money to upgrade the program. He moved the heavy mats from the basement to the main floor (no small task) before every match, and washed uniforms in his home laundry. He worked within the organizational structure as a valuable asset to the program. I could not have found a better individual to lead the wrestling program. A year later, I thanked the president for hiring such a person. "Whew," was his reply, "I have worried since you told me I was out of order when I hired him."

Schools have different structures, but most organizational charts are similar in design. See Appendix A for sample organizational charts.

1.6 Reporting Structure

For years I reported directly to the president. Later, when the president changed the system so I reported to the provost who represented athletics on the administrative council, communication became a problem. The provost did not inform me of meetings with the budget committee. After I missed meetings for a third year, the chairman asked if I was "above the law." The provost replied when I asked him why I was not notified of the meetings, that trustees were responsible for athletics, not a committee. In situations involving budget preparation and insurance matters, the provost often procrastinated, causing additional problems. When the provost's position was eliminated, I reported to the president again, with improved communication. I favor a reporting system where the athletics director reports directly to the president.

The University of Lowell (Massachusetts) has a unique reporting system that appears workable. They note on their organizational chart that the "Director of Athletics reports to the President on matters relevant to intercollegiate athletics, and to the Vice President for University Life on matters relevant to intramural, recreation, or club sports" (*University of Lowell Athletics Handbook* 1989). This structure expands the lines of communication and is worthy of consideration.

The University of Oklahoma has a line and staff organizational structure that is unusual in that it has an organizational chart for governing authorities, departmental staff, revenue and nonrevenue sports, programs, academics, and internal and public affairs. It is an excellent model for large institutions.

1.7 Manager versus Leader

Warren Bennis, Distinguished Professor of Business Administration at the University of Southern California asks, "Where have all our leaders gone?" Bennis, author of several books on leadership writes: "There is an unconscious conspiracy in contemporary society, one that prevents leaders no matter what their original vision from taking charge and making change" (Bennis 1989, xii).

Bennis deplores the fact that the United States has lost and not replaced leaders such as Franklin D. Roosevelt, Martin Luther King, Jr., and John and Robert Kennedy, all of whom challenged us to overcome fear and prejudice and dream about what we could do as individuals and as a nation. Bennis regrets our lack of leadership, but notes that it is also a worldwide problem because no one has come forward to replace the leadership of Winston Churchill (World War II leader), Albert Schweitzer, Albert Einstein, Golda Meier, Anwar Sadat, and Mahatma Gandhi.

I agree with Bennis when he says that "leaders are people who do the right thing; managers are people who do things right." Modern sports administrators have the opportunity to fill the leadership void by drawing people to them and leading people to places they have not been before. Bennis joins experts in the field of leadership in insisting that leaders are made not born: "If the basic desire to learn to lead exists, the major capacities and competencies of leadership can be learned" (Bennis 1989, 37).

David P. Campbell, an expert on leadership, developed the Campbell Leadership Index (CLI). Campbell, a member of the staff of the Center for Creative Leadership defines leadership as "actions which focus resources to create desirable opportunities" (Campbell 1991). Campbell describes actions of leadership as "planning, organizing, managing, deciding, speaking, writing, producing, cajoling, motivating, creating, economizing, inspiring, disciplining, politicking, persuading, compromising, confronting, perhaps even litigating." Resources are defined as "people, money, time, space, and materials but also nebulous assets such as public opinion, legislative power, unique talents, opportunistic accidents (for instance, disasters that can be turned to some useful end), geographic disadvantages, and personal contacts."

Campbell specifies that there are seven tasks that must be achieved if leadership is to occur. They include "vision, management, empowerment, politics, feedback, entrepreneurship, and personal style." Regarding one of the tasks—personal style—Campbell emphasizes:

> The leader is the most visible individual in the organization and, consequently, influences the spirit of everyone else. If the leader is competent, optimistic, and trustworthy, a positive spirit will usually pervade the organization. If, in contrast, the leader is in-

competent, meanspirited, or unethical, a less productive atmosphere will likely result.

Authorities on leadership such as Campbell and Bennis stress the importance of developing leaders rather than managers and set a high standard for the modern sports administrator to attain.

1.8 Characteristics of Leaders

In my experience in administration, I have observed certain characteristics and qualities of leadership in other administrators. Outstanding leaders possess most of the following eight characteristics.

1. The ability to relate to people—Getting along with people is absolutely essential for success. Sports management is truly a people industry and sports administrators who avoid people are in the wrong profession. Research reveals that more administrators lose their jobs not from a lack of knowledge of the industry, but from their inability to get along with people.

2. A sense of caring—For years I asked student-athletes to describe a sports administrator who they felt stood out favorably in their minds. Without exception every group described a leader that touched their lives as someone who cared about them. Genuine caring can never be disguised, and students from nursery to graduate school cannot be fooled. Caring means respecting the self-worth and dignity of a person.

3. A sense of humor—I find that a sense of humor, the ability to laugh and not take oneself too seriously, is one of the most important qualities of an athletics director.

4. Self-discipline—I was coaching football at Chowan Junior College in eastern North Carolina. On the first day of football practice, I was disappointed with the physical condition of the squad. I received a telephone call from Earle Edwards, head coach of the N.C. State Wolfpack inviting the team to a postseason game against his talented freshman team. I declined, telling him we would not be a match for his outstanding players. I relayed my conversation to the team and their reaction was immediate: "Call back and agree that you will check with him later in the season before you turn it down." I said I wanted them to be in top condition by practicing self-discipline—stopping any cigarette smoking and drinking, and failing to keep good hours. Several weeks later, the co-captains reported that all but three men had stopped smoking. A week later the captains reported that 100 percent were observing all training rules. Through self-discipline, the team had the first and only undefeated season, and true to our agreement, we played the N.C. State freshmen on Thanksgiving Day.

5. Accepting responsibility—It is easy to talk about responsibility, but accepting it is often a different story. When I look for leadership

in any group, I look for people who are willing to accept responsibility and carry it out.

6. The ability to make decisions—This characteristic is so important that it separates the outstanding from the average sports administrator. President Harry Truman, one of my favorite leaders, made famous the phrases, "The buck stops here" and "If you can't stand the heat, get out of the kitchen." When historians judge our past presidents they use a certain guide: In time of crisis, did he have the ability to make decisions? Certainly Truman did with his controversial decision to use the atomic bomb and the firing of General Douglas MacArthur.

During my years as a sports administrator, I worked with many who had different leadership styles. When I teach sports administration courses, I require the students to read *The Achiever* in which Gerald Bell discusses six leadership styles: commander, attacker, avoider, pleaser, performer, and achiever. (Bell 1973 15) Students aspiring to leadership roles in sports particularly appreciate the book. Most administrators I know are mixtures of the six characteristics, but the successful ones have the ability to make decisions. I find that coaches may not always agree with the decisions of an administrator, but they admire the person who can and will make a decision.

Tom Butters, athletics director at Duke University, described a situation that reveals the type of job a sports administrator holds. A security man approached him just as Duke was about to start the NCAA's Final Four basketball game against Kentucky, informing him that a threat had just been made against the life of starting forward Gene Banks. Butters had literally seconds to make a difficult decision. He made it. Minutes later a member of the Iron Dukes Booster Club tapped him on the shoulder clutching a hot dog and said, "This is the last damn time I'm going to stand for these cold hot dogs." Butters said, "This is what's great about the job. There can be a crisis in the morning and something absurd in the afternoon." (*Greensboro News and Record*, 3 June 1984) Dante in *The Inferno* said it best, "The hottest fires in Hell are reserved for those who in time of moral crisis maintain their neutrality."

7. Courage—When I was a junior in college, I received a call from the local high school asking me to officiate a football game that afternoon. The teams were bitter rivals and the game had barely started when I made my first mistake. I turned to a man who called me an S.O.B. and said that I would meet him after the game. Without hesitation he said, "You're on!" What a foolish thing for me to do, but as a 20-year-old college student you often react when you should think and use good judgment. After the game, the visiting fans, convinced that I caused the loss, surrounded me, ready to fight. I could find no friendly face in the crowd when suddenly a familiar face appeared, a fraternity brother elbowed his way toward me. To my surprise, he turned to the man facing me and said: "Herb's my friend, and no one

except this person in front of him better tangle with him. If anyone does, he will deal with me." There was something in his voice that commanded respect and, unbelievable but true, everyone in the crowd left without a word spoken. I later learned that my friend had been a Navy Ace in the Pacific Theatre in World War II. From that day on, I realized what one person, willing to stand alone could do. Monk Critcher, the Navy Ace, influenced my life and gave me the inspiration to speak out on unpopular issues even if it meant standing alone. On my desk is a plaque that quotes President Andrew Jackson: "One person with courage makes a majority." By the nature of the job, sports administrators will continue to face challenges almost daily—courage to stand alone can be one of the finest attributes of leadership.

8. The ability to empower others—Upon retirement, a chief executive officer of a prominent national corporation was asked what he would do differently if he started over. He replied that he lacked the ability or willingness to delegate duties because he thought that no one could do the job but him. In my opinion, the ability to empower others to assist you in your work is the effective use of leadership skills. I witnessed the good work empowerment accomplished on our staff. Many of our alumni coaches had outstanding coaching records in football with Top 10 teams in the of the states of Virginia, North Carolina, and South Carolina. For some reason we were not getting our quota of the alumni coach's players. I knew they loved the college and the football program but something was definitely wrong. When I raised the question the answers were all the same, your present coaches do not seem to want our student-athletes. On the other hand, the coaches said they did not have the scholarship money other schools had to recruit the blue-chip players.

I asked the coaches to consider an annual alumni football clinic on campus with alumni coaches serving as clinicians. This would be a great public relations venture between alumni coaches and staff. An assistant coach loved the idea and volunteered to run the entire operation. The head coach was reluctant to empower the assistant coach but finally gave him the authority. The alumni clinic became so successful that major universities would call to check the dates so their clinics would not conflict with ours. The alumni clinics accomplished more than I ever hoped, with the assistant receiving attention from coaches and college officials who recognized his outstanding work. I am certain it led to his advancement as head coach at a very fine institution.

In the process of empowerment, athletics directors need to make individuals feel that they can make a difference. It has been said that empowerment enables administrators to somehow encourage ordinary people to do the work of superior people. Bennis, in his book *Why Leaders Can't Lead*, writes that in leadership empowerment of others is more important than power. (Bennis 1989)

1.9 A Five-Year Plan
by J. Phillip Roach

David P. Campbell, writing in *Issues and Observations*, believes that even the leader who is dictatorial, working in an autocratic setting, needs to involve others in the planning process. He reasons that

> whether the leader is acting consensually or unilaterally, the leadership process must produce a vision for the future that all concerned can, and will, use for guidance. (Campbell 1991, 2)

Developing a five-year plan for an athletics department will serve as a baseline for the administrator. A five-year plan will be useful in the following areas:

- Coordinating—informing, communicating, providing, and assisting in implementing the tasks and responsibilities outlined in the plan.
- Planning—to envision, validate, prioritize, develop a database, and establish a work flow and a plan of action.
- Organizing—using suitable people for defined tasks, allocating appropriate money for specific programs, delegating, and establishing relationships.
- Directing—making decisions, knowing when to initiate, and determining strategies, timing, and logistics.
- Evaluating—one can better regulate and redirect with an instrument, such as a five-year plan, to judge one's own performance and that of various programs regarding objectives, roles, and standards.

When developing a five-year plan the athletics director should involve staff members, making them responsible for a particular program. The athletics director should keep in mind the mission of the institution when asking each program head to develop the five-year plan. This is a beginning. The administrator can take individual program plans and integrate them into a synergistic plan for the entire department. It is helpful to pair a veteran coach with a newer staff member to work through the process for better insight.

After the plans have been merged, project the needs and respond to them in a systematic manner. A five-year plan will help the administrator focus on the central mission of the athletics program. Too often administrators base their decisions on pressures from alumni, coaches, or other administrators, or on budget constraints rather than on what is best over the long term for the institution and, specifically, for the athletics program.

The following things should be considered when a five-year plan is developed:

- The mission of the athletics department,

- A description of the current resources (facilities, budget, and staff) of the athletics department,
- An assessment of the current strengths and weaknesses of the athletics program, and
- A statement regarding the future direction and needs of the athletics program.

A five-year plan should include

- *Participants*—the number of male and female student athletes the institution expects will be a part of the athletics program on a yearly basis.
- *Facilities*—the needs and changes, including costs, of the various program facilities on a yearly basis.
- *Equipment*—a systematic approach to planned purchase and repair of major equipment.
- *Staffing*—if the number of participants increases or diminishes staffing will be affected. Adding a sport may require additional staff members. Part-time coaches often reduce the quality of the program.
- *Budgeting*—the standard cost-of-living index and a historical review are the best indicators of future budget costs.

The five-year plan should set a date to originate the plan or fulfill the need along with a completion date. Once the plan is developed it should be widely distributed within the institution and endorsed by proper committees and administrative personnel. Each institution is different; therefore, the people who accept the plan will be determined by the uniqueness of the institution. Such people should include the person to whom the athletics administrator reports, the director of facilities, the business manager, the director of buildings and grounds, and those responsible for budgeting. If athletics staff is involved in the academic program, the chairperson for that area and the academic dean should be included in the process. A sample five-year plan developed for Marietta College is found in Appendix B.

1.10 Public Relations

Jeaneane Williams, a public relations consultant, writing in *Successful Sports Management*, said that

> public relations in sports management is an all-encompassing term. Taken in its simplest form, it means the positive relationship of the organization/institution and its *total* personnel complement with *all* of its public constituencies. (Lewis and Appenzeller 1985, 177)

Williams comments that, unfortunately, public relations is neglected in too many organizations. Too often public relations is considered an easy job that anyone can do.

It is true that everyone within an organization does public relations—good or bad. From the receptionist who answers the phone
to the trainer, the coach, the team doctor, the ticket taker, the
activities coordinator, the star quarterback, the promoter, the mas-
cot, the manager (athletics director)—the public is building an
impression of your organization based in part on the people who
work within it. (Lewis and Appenzeller 1985, 184)

I learned about public relations, particularly internal public relations,
by communicating with people with whom I worked. I enjoyed success
at my first job, coaching baseball and basketball, teaching, and administering the sports program at a small, rural high school. The teams
won two championships in baseball and two in basketball those two
years. I left reluctantly because I wanted to coach football. When the
principal at the second high school paid me the highest coaching supplement in the history of the county schools, I never questioned the
source of the supplement, I just accepted it. All teachers and support
staff were required to work at the annual Halloween Carnival for two
nights. It was obvious they dreaded it. When I innocently asked two
teachers where the money was going, they looked at me in amazement
and said, "You really don't know, do you?" Then the bombshell: "It's
going to pay your supplement." So much for getting off to a good start
with my colleagues. I knew my work was cut out for me to develop a
positive relationship.

When I was hired to teach, coach, and administer the athletics programs at two colleges, I found an antiathletics attitude among many
faculty and administrators. I thought I was the answer to all the problems in the athletics department. After all, a trustee agreed to build a
residence hall if I came, and I was given a full professorship and a salary
above the majority of the professors, many of whom had given years
of service. I felt little pressure to win because this was a school that
revered an athletics director who coached football and basketball to a
combined six-year record of 6–109–3. The trustees, faculty, administration, and student body stood solidly behind this man and even made
excuses for his dismal record. However, I soon felt the resentment
when I learned that three outstanding professors offered to resign if I
took the job. I realized that I had to build a solid public relations
program if the athletics program was to survive and grow.

1.11 Internal Public Relations

I decided to develop a positive image by involving students, athletes,
staff members and coaches, and members of the faculty, administration, and trustees. It was not an easy task but one that was essential.
Some of the things I did included

• Letters to each group (personal, not form letters)

- Talks with students in assembly and in residence halls,
- Brochures,
- Open houses,
- A sport-art contest on campus,
- A twelfth-person award (see below),
- Bulletin board displays in selected areas of the campus,
- An Athletic Advisory Council,
- Meet-the-team night on campus,
- Invitations to sports banquets, and
- Complimentary tickets.

In addition, the staff and coaches were urged to attend as many campus functions as possible. How could we expect campus support unless we gave it. Our staff and coaches attended faculty meetings to show interest in academic matters. Other attempts to foster a favorable image included

- A student-staff breakfast and lunch;
- A sports Hall of Fame;
- Clinics featuring alumni coaches;
- Letters to parents explaining policies that dealt with physical examinations and insurance, and a sports newsletter;
- A newsletter to faculty, administrators, trustees, and alumni;
- Parents weekend for various sports;
- Invitations to meet with faculty and college support staff to answer any questions and concerns.

Twelfth-Person Award

Jackie Sherrill captured the imagination of Texas A&M by inviting walk-ons to join his scholarship athletes on the football team. He used these highly motivated students on the Aggie kickoff team and gained tremendous support for the team.

I had a different version that I called the Twelfth-Man Award until the potential arrived for a female recipient; hence, the Twelfth-Person Award. Each season the members of our football team would nominate faculty, support staff, administrators, maintenance, or food service personnel to travel on away games. Two were selected for each trip as the guests of the team. These guests would travel and do everything with the team—eat, sleep, attend pregame meetings, walk the sidelines during the game, celebrate a victory, and commiserate in defeat. It was amazing how much this experience improved relations and appreciation between the guests and the members of the team. At the end of the season, team members voted on the recipient of the Twelfth-Person Award, a person who they felt gave outstanding support to the football program. The recipient of the award was not always a guest on trips, but one who gave strong support. The Twelfth-Person Award became a cherished award and did much to improve the image of the program.

I recommend an award such as this to improve and enhance public relations for any sports program.

Information to the President

I recommend to all administrators this simple but effective procedure. Every two weeks I alerted the president about the performances of the sports teams in season. When a member of our women's tennis team, a first-year student from Finland, was 10–0, I informed the president in writing about her accomplishments. I kept him posted on her progress—20–0, 28–0, and finally 32–0 and a national champion. These brief comments were helpful to the president in many ways and kept him current on the teams' progress or lack of it. One year he kept up with four nationally ranked teams, feeling comfortable answering inquiries from various sources. On the other hand, I felt obligated to alert him to potential problems, such as the time I had calls from parents demanding that I immediately fire one of the coaches. I informed the president about the calls, and that I had plans to correct the situation. When he received telephone calls from the irate parents, the president was on top of the situation and was not "hit from the blind side."

Campus Newsletter

Gene Hart, an outstanding athletics director at Rockhurst College in Kansas City, Missouri, observed that we often think that everyone on campus knows what a sports program is doing. Because nothing could be further from the truth, Hart made sure that a news release went out each day to administrators, faculty, and support staff. He developed a Rockhurst Daily News Sheet (RDN) and said of it:

> I can't think of anything that really helped communications on our campus more than this piece. The students looked through this sheet every morning. We strategically placed it around campus—about 25 spots where they can pick it up. That gives us the chance to call in anything we want to advertise to our students or the faculty or administration of what's going on the next day or the next week. (Hart 1983)

In my opinion, the sports administrator needs to develop a strong internal program before going public. It is crucial that attention be given to public relations at staff meetings because one person in the organization can undo all the good that others have done to build a positive image of the program. Good public relations will not just happen; it takes time and effort to impress on staff and coaches the need to build a positive image. Effective public relations need continued emphasis by the department's athletics director.

1.12 External Public Relations

A suggestion is in order regarding favorable media coverage. Avoid the use of "No comment!" This can be the worst thing you can say.

Just read the newspapers and listen to radio and television interviews after something goes wrong in a program. Over and over those in charge will inevitably say, "No comment." It is better to say, "We are looking into the situation, and we will get back to you with the details as soon as possible." However, when you say this, make sure you do it. Media sources will appreciate your honesty and effort and reward you for it (Lewis and Appenzeller 1985, 179).

Jeaneane Williams gives good advice to the sports administrator when she writes:

> In really serious instances, when something major has happened and it is certain that the media will pick it up, don't wait for a call. Do the organization, public, and media a service by reacting proactively. "Control" of the media is impossible and should not be attempted. The worst thing that can happen following an incident is to refuse to see or talk with the media and leave them in the dilemma of trying to provide proper information to the public. If a reporter must resort to interviewing anyone available for on-the-spot comments, don't expect an accurate account to appear in the media. (Lewis and Appenzeller 1985, 179)

Through the years I found that you cannot expect only favorable coverage from the media unless you are willing to be honest and report information that isn't favorable. I found that the media will actually try to put things in the best possible light if you are open and honest with them. We took this approach and felt that it came back, not to haunt us, but to help us in the long run.

One final suggestion. It can be expeditious to select a spokesperson for the institution. This person can collect available information, check sources, and then represent the institution to the media. I strongly recommend this and feel your program will be well served if one person deals directly with media sources.

1.13 Sports Hall of Fame

In 1970 I started a Sports Hall of Fame. The first event was almost a disaster, but out of the mistakes it became a strong, exciting event. The school produced an unusually large number of outstanding athletes. With so many outstanding men and women in the college's sports history, we attempted to select too many, too fast. The first Hall of Fame inducted twelve people. A mistake that could have ended it that night. Each presenter and inductee agreed to limit their talk to five minutes but the emotion of the moment overcame some, and we knew we were in trouble, time wise, when the first three presentations went on and on. We felt that no one in attendance would ever return to another Hall of Fame.

We now limit the number of inductees to four and find the program is much better for all concerned. At first we chose the presenter, but later we gave the inductees the opportunity to choose the presenter. This works well. Some suggest that inductees select a previous member of the Hall of Fame to be presenter, but again, this is a matter of choice for the institution's Hall of Fame committee. The Hall of Fame committee has representation from all eras in the school's sports history to ensure that worthy candidates are not overlooked. The committee has coaches, active alumni, administrators, the sports information director, and a representative of alumni. The committee invites people to send names of possible candidates by notifications in alumni publications and booster club newsletters. The committee meets in the spring to consider the nominees according to the criteria listed below. At least two are selected as alternates in the event a person does not accept the nomination or is unable to attend the banquet. The presentations are made on Homecoming weekend, which is a prime time for this special event. The Hall of Fame induction procedures guidelines are as follows.

• Outstanding performance as a student-athlete.
• Outstanding service to the athletics program as a coach or in other areas of significant service.
• Student-athletes to be chosen from those who have either been out of college at least ten years or who are deceased. Athletes should have attended college at least two years.
• Coaches should have served at least five years.
• Candidate must be of good character and reflect credit upon the college.
• Candidates need not be graduates of the college, but must have left the college in good standing and in the good graces of its officials.
• Nominees each year will be limited to four living members with the number of deceased members left to the discretion of the committee.
• Nominees should reflect a balance in the sports program and in class year.
• If nominees are unable to attend the induction ceremony, their names are to be carried over to the next year and an alternate selected.
• Nominees should be chosen by consensus of the Hall of Fame committee.
• All nominees by the committee must be endorsed by the booster club board of directors before the action is final.

The committee suggests that the board of directors consider appointing the Hall of Fame committee in keeping with the principle of having at least nine members for a period of three years, rotating three members off each year and adding three new members each year. The committee also prefers that the following criteria prevail at the Hall of Fame Banquet:

- The banquet will be held on campus at an appropriate time to be determined by the board of directors.
- Each presenter is asked to limit their remarks to five minutes.

Mike Palmisano, a primary organizer for the Michigan Hall of Fame, makes several important suggestions regarding a sports Hall of Fame:

- A nominating committee selects the candidates, but there are no specific rules for nominating people; committee members are free to "submit names as they see fit."
- A small selection committee decides on the candidates.
- Select no more than six inductees the first years, and then include anywhere from four to eight.
- Group the candidates in lists of 10-year periods (1900–1910, 1910–1929).
- Consider one honoree posthumously each year.
- No age restriction or number of years must have passed for consideration but candidates are usually in their mid-to late forties. (Palmisano 1990)

Michigan schedules their event on a Friday evening of a home football weekend. The Hall of Fame event is called the "Hall of Honor." Palmisano notes that they vary the master of ceremonies who "introduces each inductee by reading the person's biography featured in the event program." A short film clip of five to six slides precedes the presentation and the inductee. Each inductee may respond, but in five minutes or less. A medallion is then placed around the inductee's neck by the athletics director. In addition, the inductee receives a plaque. A duplicate is placed in the trophy case of the Crisler Arena. The Hall of Fame event can be a fund-raiser with profits going to a scholarship fund or some special project. A Hall of Fame can play a significant role in building and maintaining the tradition of a college athletics department. It can generate tremendous good will for the athletics program, bring alumni and former athletes closer to the department, and serve as a motivation for current athletes to excel. Any college or university can develop an Athletic Hall of Fame with a little investment and that investment will reap large dividends down the road (Palmisano 1990).

1.14 Athletics Committee

I was not involved with an athletics committee during my four years as a secondary school sports administrator or as the athletics director of a junior college. However, the athletics committee was an integral part of the athletics program at Guilford College. I had just about every type of committee imaginable—some workable, others more of a hindrance than a help.

Let me give an example of total frustration. When I arrived at Guilford College as head football coach and athletics director, I had a situation that needed changing. The college was a member of the North State Conference, but could not compete for a championship in football because we did not play the required number of teams to be eligible for the title. The athletics committee suggested I contact the following persons: the president, the business manager, the academic dean, the dean of students, and three influential alumni.

The request was simple: add East Carolina and Western Carolina universities to the schedule to be eligible for the conference championship. In addition, start preseason training September 1, like all other institutions, instead of September 13. You can't imagine my dilemma. Each nonalumni had a different opinion of the situation. I finally got approval of the request after trips totaling 760 miles. I asked the president to let me administer the program. I agreed that I would not develop policy without the approval of the athletics committee. If I did not do as expected, he could fire me. He agreed to this procedure which continued over a 31-year period.

- Committee I—A five member committee. The chairman was the most respected faculty member on campus. His philosophy was simple: run the athletics program; you are the professional; and don't call a meeting unless you need help. He was practical and sound and always a source of strength.
- Committee II— A new chairman took over. We had more meetings than Committee I. I still had freedom to run the program, but I always checked on policy matters with the committee.
- Committee III—A disaster! We had more than twelve members. It was much too large. Eight were antiathletics while four were interested in a sound athletics/academic program. Two of these athletics members never showed up, making things difficult for me. At times, this committee met at a member's home without my knowledge and developed rules that I opposed. One such rule was to award grants-in-aid only to athletes with predicted averages of 2.0. A member of an Ivy League school could get a grant with a 1.6 predicted average, but our athletes had to have a 2.0 predicted average to get a grant. We compared ourselves academically to Duke, Davidson, UNC-Chapel Hill, and Wake Forest, but to get a grant in athletics required a higher predictive average than those academically strong institutions.
- Committee IV—We realized that twelve committee members were just too many to accomplish what we wanted because it was almost impossible to get them together on a regular basis. Committee IV consisted of three regular members, with the ath-

letics director designated ex-officio. This small committee represented various academic disciplines such as biology, management, English, physics, and psychology. The three-person committee worked very efficiently and had high credibility among the faculty. The group became a sounding board for policy.

One year, we called various institutions throughout the nation to determine the memberships on their athletics committees. We found many with large, unwieldy committees, while others were composed of coaches and physical education teachers. I recommend a small, workable committee representing the various academic disciplines. This model works, and I recommend it highly.

The chairman of the athletics committee was very helpful to the program. At the annual conference meeting, he persuaded all athletics directors and faculty chairpersons not to schedule conference championship events in any sports during exam week. The members agreed to send all examination dates to the conference commissioner. For the first time ever, conference tournaments were non scheduled so that all could compete during nonexam or nongraduation dates.

When the chairman reported on the athletics department at faculty meetings, he used graphs and slides to show the progress of the athletics department in academic and athletic achievement. As a professor of physics, he could boast of our accomplishments better than I ever could as athletics director.

The athletics committee, if properly constructed, can be a tremendous asset to any athletics director. Some institutions do not have an athletics committee, preferring to let the athletics director develop and implement policy with the consent of the president or chancellor. This might be the easiest to operate for the athletics director, but in the long run, it can create as many problems as it initially avoids.

Dr. Gary Frederick, athletics director at Central Washington University, notes that today's sports administrator faces demanding problems that include

> reduced budgets; the need for increased fund-raising; pressure to delete various sports; numerous scandals concerning the issuance of money to athletes beyond the allotted amounts; altering transcripts; and numerous other complications. (Frederick 1983, 19)

Frederick observes that the athletics committee is important to the athletics director, but it varies in importance from little to great. The ability of the committee to assist in the process of governance as an advisory group depends on the administration and the athletics director.

For two years, Frederick writes, the athletics committee worked on numerous projects such as a statement of university athletics philosophy and ethics; standardization of eligibility requirements for men and women athletes; the reexamination of national and conference

affiliation; addition and deletion of programs; budget recommendations; financial aid policies for student-athletes; investigation of the
graduation ratio of student-athletes in comparison to the total student
body; investigation of the frequency of course withdrawal by student-
athletes after the end of the playing season in comparison to the total
student body; reevaluation and recommendations concerning Title IX
requirements; reevaluation of hiring procedures for the coaching staff
and an examination of the requirements for coaches to advance on a
salary schedule; and reevaluation and recommendations concerning
current fund-raising and planned fund-raising.

The Central Washington University athletics committee includes
the athletics director, five faculty members, the faculty athletics representative, and three students. The committee can only recommend
and advise, with final decisions being the responsibility of the athletics
director and the university's administration. Frederick comments that
the athletics committee at his institution has "definitely become the
athletics director's conscience" (Frederick 1983, 20).

When I announced my intention to retire as athletics director, the
athletics committee did a very positive thing to enable everyone on
campus to have an input into the athletics program, including the
duties and responsibilities of a new athletics director. A questionnaire
was sent to students, faculty, administrators, coaches, staff members,
and parents. After the questionnaires were returned, open meetings
were held for all groups. We were considering a change in direction
from an NAIA Division I scholarship program to a possible NCAA
program. All groups were invited to share ideas and opinions. In addition, one question concerned the responsibilities of the athletics director, and each respondent was asked to rank the responsibilities of
the athletics director in descending order of importance. I recommend
the questionnaire for all who contemplate a change or reevaluation of
their sports program. It is a valuable instrument for institutions search-
ing for an athletics director. (See Appendix C for a copy of the
questionnaire.)

1.15 Booster Clubs

I have seen both good and bad regarding booster clubs on the high
school and collegiate level. I remember the firing of a successful coach
when he refused to buy his groceries from a store owned by a powerful
member of the high school's booster club. I have witnessed the firing
of coaches who were excellent teachers and role models, but failed to
post winning records. Members of booster clubs can exert heavy pressure on administrators and school board members. The potential for
good is present. I have witnessed many acts by booster clubs that
provided positive support for student athletes, coaches, and
administrators.

When I began my tenure at Guilford College in 1956, I started the Quaker Club. The college had existed for 132 years without an athletics booster club and many on campus preferred it that way. From a modest beginning, the Quaker Club became a vital factor in the successful operation of the athletics program. It is a club that supports, not interferes, with the operation of the program, never attempting to influence the hiring or firing of a coach. Through the years, the attitude has been that it exists for the sole purpose of helping young people prepare for careers and life. Some of its activities include

- Hosting tailgate parties at home football games for parents, faculty, and friends;
- Selecting members of the sports Hall of Fame and sponsoring the induction banquet;
- Hosting receptions at selected home basketball games for men's and women's teams;
- Sponsoring the leadership awards banquet;
- Distributing a quarterly newsletter;
- Sponsoring the end-of-year awards banquet, and providing awards for individual athletes, coaches, and teams;
- Assisting the college in financing special projects such as purchasing video equipment, renovating the field house, and purchasing a soccer/lacrosse scoreboard;
- Renovating the athletics and weight training rooms;
- Raising endowment funds for future program enhancement; and
- Helping with and hosting various athletics events.

With such altruistic projects, one wonders why booster clubs get such criticism. The answer seems to be in the illegal conduct of overzealous alumni and fans who will do almost anything to have a winning program. A coach who was fired for getting his institution on probation is so popular with members of the booster club that he receives a new automobile each year and a stipend that corresponds to his former salary.

In another situation, a booster club was paying the salaries of four coaches at one time. Three of them had been fired, but they had years left on their contracts. Many coaches are fired each year and accept their fate as the institution pays the remaining years of their contracts. The problem lies with perquisites promised by booster clubs. Several lawsuits have revealed that some coaches are promised membership in three or four country clubs, a new car each year, and other attractive perks. The coaches often sue for the perks promised by the booster club. The end result is usually a financial settlement.

In the early days the funds raised were placed in a Quaker Club account in a local bank. The goal was to have control of the funds, and we tried to safeguard the program by requiring three signatures before a check could be written. This process was cumbersome; but, more than that, it caused people to become suspicious of fund usage.

When I was asked to oversee the total operation of the Quaker Club, including finances, I agreed on one condition: all booster club funds had to go through college channels. When we had needs, the request would go from the athletics director to the business manager for approval. An important addition was that all funds would be audited by the college auditors. This system works and eliminates adverse perceptions about the use of funds.

I was flattered when three athletics directors called to inquire about the booster club. Each reported that the club had been singled out as a model and they wanted to copy the guidelines. All went well until I explained the financial arrangement we followed. They replied that they, not the school, wanted to have control over their funds and would use local banks for that reason. That was twenty years ago, and isn't it interesting that the Knight Foundation published its report in March 1991 with one of its concerns being the financial structure of booster clubs. The report recommends the following:

> All funds raised and spent in connection with intercollegiate programs will be channeled through the institution's general treasury, not through independent groups, whether internal or external. The athletics budget will be developed and monitored in accordance with general budgeting procedures on campus. (*The Knight Report* 1991)

While this recommendation is one of the best, it may be the most difficult to implement.

For all those who have a booster club or plan to start one, a copy of the Quaker Club Constitution may be of interest. The document was prepared by an attorney along with a special committee. It is thorough, legally sound, and concise, and can serve as a model and be modified to meet each institution's particular needs (Appendix D).

1.16 Handbook

Early in my career I learned a valuable lesson. We had a veteran staff; teachers and coaches with an average tenure of twelve years who surely knew established policies and the rules of the department. For this reason, I felt no sense of urgency or need to develop a handbook. Unfortunately, the number of years on a job does not automatically guarantee an understanding of rules, regulations, policies, and procedures.

One of the coaches informed members of his team that all sports-related injuries would be covered in full by an accident/injury medical policy. Soon after, a member of the team drove to the basket for a lay-up, ran into an unpadded wall, and as a result of the collision lost two front teeth. An oral surgeon met the injured student at the hospital emergency room to implant his teeth. This was the good news. The bad news came later when the surgeon's bill arrived for $2,000. The limit on the dental policy was $200 per healthy tooth, leaving a balance of $1,600. We were faced with a serious dilemma. On the one hand, the coach had promised full medical coverage; on the other hand, we were setting a potentially costly precedent if we paid the remainder of the bill. If another student was injured, the balance could be $16,000 or even $160,000 and we could be obligated to pay. The dentist realized the predicament and came to our rescue by forgiving the balance as a donation. Another dentist or physician, however, might not be as generous and understanding. It was clear we needed a handbook that would set specific guidelines so that this type of thing would not happen again. Isn't it interesting how I became proactive rather than reactive?

After I developed the handbook, I discussed it at several staff meetings. Some of the most stimulating and productive staff meetings involved the interpretation of the contents of the handbook. Each staff member was then required to sign that they understood the contents of the handbook and accepted responsibility for its material. Staff members now understood that medical costs for sports-related injuries were covered *up to the limits of the policy.* The coaches knew that they could be liable for payment of the bill if they misinformed their team members concerning insurance coverage. Each year the handbook should be reviewed and revised.

Peter Levine, writing in *American Sport: A Documentary History,* points out the need for written policy: "There is a critical need for the development of a written policy and objective statement so that the resources of the Athletics Department may be marshalled effectively" (Levine 1989, 122). Levine notes that a lack of written policy is among the current problems in administration:

> At the policy making level, neither the Athletics Council nor the President has developed a statement of policy or objectives which provide guidance for the program as a whole. Without such a statement the Athletics Director, is placed in a weakened and relatively dangerous posture. At the Athletics Director's level, there seems to be no statement of policy for ongoing operations of critical importance, e.g., ticket assignment priority, responsibility for public information releases, job descriptions and responsibilities. (Levine 1989)

A table of contents for a handbook can be found in Appendix E.

2
The Staff Member

2.1 The Employment Process

I have held four positions during my teaching, coaching, and administrative career; two in secondary schools and two in college. I had four unique hiring experiences. There were only two jobs available when I graduated in midyear, and I chose a small rural school over a larger city school many miles from the college. I agreed to coach boy's baseball and basketball and assume the duties of athletics director. The principal had one opening in teaching, the eighth grade, which he emphatically stated would be absolutely no problem for me. When I reported, I found that I would teach in a self-contained classroom (which meant that I would teach thirty students all day). The subjects I would teach included English, mathematics, science, North Carolina history, music, art, and physical education. I was overwhelmed with the assignment, but things went well and I learned so much more than the students. Our baseball and basketball teams won conference titles both years, getting me off to a good start.

I was offered a job at a larger school just ten miles from the job I had. My job description was similar, with the addition of football to my coaching duties, and I would teach history and Latin in high school. The principal was aggressive and did all the negotiations, but the county superintendent would make the final decision. He tried to persuade me to consider a job at the largest school in the county, a good distance from my first school. He felt there could be hard feelings between communities if I chose the one so near my first job. At his suggestion, I visited the school he recommended and immediately realized that something was wrong. The principal talked with me for less than ten minutes and sent me to the local drugstore to meet the chairman of the school board, who emphasized the number of talented athletes available to coach, the financial benefits, and outstanding facilities. It was clear that the offer was lucrative, but I must WIN, WIN,

32 Managing Sports

and WIN BIG. I chose the smaller school with limited resources but with a supportive principal who would not expect or demand miracles. It was ironic that the football team had a record my second year of 7–1 and we played the final game against the school I turned down. We had a dilemma because injuries had reduced the squad to sixteen players, with no quarterback to direct the team. The opponent still had a squad of fifty-five. Somehow the team rose to the occasion and the hard fought game ended in a 6–6 tie. Our fans were excited and pleased, but their fans were unhappy. Several weeks later the other school fired a very good coach, and I knew I had made the right decision.

I did not use good judgment when I was rewarded with a sizable salary after my second year. I planned to enter the business world and resigned, confident I could easily get a job anywhere. How wrong I was! I changed my plans and decided late in August to return to teaching, coaching, and administration. I learned, however, that it is extremely difficult to get a job if you do not have one. After each interview, the principal or superintendent would casually ask, "You are under contract, aren't you?" When I said "No," eyebrows were raised, and I am sure they felt that I had been fired for whatever reason and the job offer never came. Ever since that day, and from observations of similar situations with others, I try to impress students and colleagues to keep their present jobs until they have another job. Trust me, this is sound advice!

Someone wrote that coincidence is God's way of accomplishing miracles anonymously. I had given up on a coaching job; it was late August and things looked dismal. A visiting professor, who was executive director for all the Baptist colleges in North Carolina, walked by me as I waited to defend my master's thesis. He stopped, came back, and asked if I would be interested in a position at a junior college in eastern North Carolina. I accepted on the spot, sight unseen. He advised me to go through the process of an interview with the president of the college who was vacationing at the beach. The subsequent interview was short and bizarre. The president was in his bathing suit when I arrived. He invited me to come into a room and asked if I smoked, drank, and went to church. Satisfied with my responses, he fell to his knees in prayer, shook my hand and said, "You're hired." This was an unusual hiring process, but it led to five unbelievably good years. I was happy during those years at the junior college, decided I wanted to stay, and built a home.

One telephone call changed my plans. A powerful trustee at a liberal arts college in Piedmont North Carolina lived in the town where I coached and taught. As athletics director, I had visited him when I was fund-raising. He said the time was right for me to move to Guilford College and he encouraged me to accept the position of professor of physical education, athletics director, and head football coach. That was it; for all intent, I was hired. I went through a series of interviews, but I was really the only candidate. I coached football for six years and continued as athletics director for 31 years, resigning the administrative position to accept an endowed sports management professorship.

My job interviews were different and they do not represent hiring procedures in the 1990s. High schools and colleges today operate on different systems and have set policies on hiring procedures.

Today, the procedure for hiring full-time staff members begins when the athletics director develops a job description and, when authorized, sends the job description to the appropriate state, regional, and national publications. When there is a fixed salary with little or no room for negotiations, the salary is included in the advertisement. It is important for potential candidates to understand up front the salary that will be offered.

A search committee is selected from a diverse group on campus. As far as possible, those people who represent the areas with whom the candidates interact are invited to join the search committee. Ideally, six people are on the search committee. Applications are sent to the chairperson, who documents all applications for government purposes. The chairperson immediately acknowledges receipt of the application.

The committee meets prior to the reading of the applications to discuss procedures. Each member of the search committee comes to a central place to read the applications and rank them. The committee discusses the candidates selected for review by its members and discusses the evaluation sheets so that it can select several for interviews on campus. At times, after references are validated, the committee may attempt to save funds by conducting the initial screening via conference calls with top candidates. In many instances, such calls eliminate candidates. The committee members decide on the procedure for the on-campus interviews, such as who will meet the candidate at the airport or on campus when they arrive, and who will go to breakfast, lunch, and dinner with the candidate. Representatives of various constituencies are invited to meet the candidates and interviews are set up with coaches, the vice-president for student development, the academic dean (if the position includes teaching), representatives of the booster club, the director of sports medicine, and the field house director. Representatives of the captain's council meet also, as they represent the athletes.

Following each interview, each person is expected to turn in an evaluation sheet to the chairperson of the search committee. When all those persons invited to campus are ranked, the committee meets to select a candidate. The chairperson of the search committee calls the candidate selected by the group after receiving approval from the president, who is the last to meet each of the top three or four candidates on campus. The selected candidate has a period of time to accept and the others who were invited are put on hold in the event the one chosen declines to accept the position.

After the candidate accepts, a news release is prepared for the media. Unfortunately, many schools let the pool of candidates read or hear about the selection. Our policy is simple and it works. The athletics director calls those people who were interviewed on campus to report the selection, and the remaining applicants who were not interviewed are notified by mail of the selection. After time passes in which our notification has been made, the formal announcement of the new addition to our staff is made. In my opinion, this is common courtesy and good policy. The procedure listed above has worked well for me and I recommend it highly.

One of our coaches, who accepted a position as a college athletics director, asked me what he needed to know to succeed in his new job. My answer was immediate: "Hire the best people you possibly can, and don't ever be afraid to hire someone you feel could threaten your position." In some instances, I feel that some administrators hire people with lesser qualifications to avoid feeling threatened.

I am convinced that you succeed when you hire the best possible coach. When they win, you win, and the entire program prospers. In my opinion, this is a top priority for the athletics director who wants a successful program.

2.2 Management by Objectives

Soon after the staff is in place a meeting should be scheduled between the athletics director and staff members to develop management by objectives. I was a member of a sports commission composed of outstanding community leaders when an executive director was hired. The search committee had a detailed job description for the newly hired director, but they became confused when I suggested that the chairperson of the sports commission meet with the director to develop a management by objectives (MBO) strategy. I am still not certain the commission members understood the MBO.

As athletics director, I met with each coach and member of the sports staff prior to the opening of school. Each individual would set their goals for the upcoming season with plans for achieving them. At times I set goals that were possibly too high. The staff member and I would discuss the objectives and reach agreement on what we believed to be reasonable goals. For example, I believed the sports information director (SID) was capable of raising $10,000 in revenue from the football program. This included advertisements, sponsorships, and sales of the program at games. The SID correctly pointed out that the home games were down to four, with none against traditional rivals. Homecoming could help make the proposed goal; however, it had rained the previous four years. We renegotiated a figure of $6,000 and agreed to review the situation in October and at the end of the season. We agreed in the MBO to review the progress toward the objectives at the end of the football season, in March, and again in May. At these review sessions, we would look carefully at extenuating circumstances that might cause the SID to fail to meet objectives.

At the end of the year, the SID would prepare a report that listed both positive and negative situations, with an overall statement of accomplished objectives and what had been achieved. The self-appraisal would be discussed, and if goals were not met the reasons were reviewed and a new set of objectives were prepared for the upcoming year. An MBO helps the administrator direct staff members toward a common goal and effectively helps each member set objectives to reach that goal.

2.3 Job Description

It is crucial that both employer and employee understand the duties and responsibilities of a particular job so there is no confusion or lack of clarity with either party. I remember needing a lacrosse coach after our year had started. I asked an assistant football coach with a lacrosse background if he would agree to coach the sport. He reluctantly agreed to coach but told his colleagues that he was unhappy because "head lacrosse coach wasn't in his contract." I remedied that the following year by adding a sentence that read, "and any duties the athletics director assigns." It satisfied our coach, but in all honesty, I realized it was too vague and overbroad a job description and one that probably would not hold up in court, if challenged. I do not recommend such a catchall sentence and after one year I removed it.

A word of caution may be in order regarding job descriptions. Richard Bell replaced Jim Carlen as head football coach at the University of South Carolina at a salary of $50,000 per year. His first-year record at South Carolina was 4–7, including a loss to archrival Clemson. Robert Marcum, the athletics director, instructed Bell to fire his assistant coaches. Bell refused and was fired. Bell sued the university for his remaining three-years salary of $150,000 and included Marcum and the university in a $1 million defamation of character suit. At trial, one of the key issues involved the question of who had the responsibility for firing assistant coaches.

Grant Teaff (Baylor), Bill Curry (Kentucky), and Frank Broyles, (Arkansas) testified on Bell's behalf by asserting that the head football coach, not the athletics director, had the authority to fire the assistant coaches. Broyles stated:

> Everyone familiar with football knows it is paramount that a head coach has total control over his staff. When it is violated it destroys the abilities of any coach to be effective. (Appenzeller 1985, 96)

Bell was paid his salary for the remaining three years of his contract, but the defamation suit was dismissed by the court. When Joe Morrison replaced Bell as head football coach, school officials reportedly changed the wording in his contract so that the athletics director had more authority in both hiring and firing of assistant coaches. If an athletics director plans to be a part of the hiring and firing process, this action should be included in the contract (job description) so that a situation similar to this one can be avoided. An example of a job description for a soccer coach is as follows:

A. Responsibilities

Administer, organize, and coach the varsity women's soccer program. Manage all aspects of the soccer team including student academic progress, practice planning, scheduling, travel, budget control, player safety, recruiting, promotion, and staffing responsibilities (*Guilford College Athletics Handbook* 1990.)

B. Specific Administrative Duties

1. Responsible for recruitment of quality student athletes who can contribute to a competitive soccer program.

2. Promote the soccer program and its participants with on-campus and off-campus activities.

3. Prepare an annual budget and function within its parameters. This includes developing a five-year purchasing plan.

4. Collaborate with the sports information director (SID) in making information available in a timely fashion and in promoting the soccer program.

5. Organize all travel arrangements.

6. Organize practice, preparation, and intercollegiate competition.

7. Promote the physical and mental well-being of all program participants.

8. Maintain communication and cooperate with the head athletics trainer and student trainers regarding injuries and the health of players.

9. Teach the skills of soccer from the basic fundamentals to the techniques of solid team play.

10. Order, inventory, care for, and fit all equipment.

11. Participate in booster club activities.

12. File insurance forms and eligibility lists in a timely fashion.

C. Reporting Channel

The head women's soccer coach reports to the athletics director.

D. Length of Responsibility

The head women's soccer coaching position begins employment on 1 August prior to the opening of school and finishes one week after graduation. This is a full-time position (ten months) with other duties as assigned by the athletics director. Included with the job description for individual coaches is a general statement regarding the expectations for the conduct of staff members.

2.4 Staff Qualifications

There had been a series of highly publicized injuries to cheerleaders across the nation in which outstanding gymnasts on cheerleading squads sustained injuries that caused paralysis and even death. Because of the concern, I spoke to a group of secondary school administrators, cheerleading advisors, and members of cheerleading squads. I stressed many aspects of safe cheerleading, but really talked about the urgent need for qualified cheerleading coaches. At the end of the session, an assistant superintendent told me I was not practical. He said it was impossible to find competent coaches or teachers to coach various sports. "In fact," he said, "we had three sports which were unable to hire competent coaches." Imagine my surprise when he said the sports were football, wrestling, and gymnastics. Unbelievable, but true! I responded that I would rather eliminate any activity, particularly a high-risk activity, if I could not employ competent coaches rather than risk a catastrophic injury to a participant. My response obviously agitated him and he stated that I "wasn't in the real world. Parents demand that we offer these sports and we must accede to their wishes." The assistant superintendent, by giving in to the demands of parents to offer high-risk activities without qualified personnel, walks a dangerous line.

An example of how this attitude can backfire is seen in a young man who was rendered quadriplegic. Officials at a military school in Tennessee announced that the wrestling coach had resigned and curtailed the wrestling program. However, one of the faculty members volunteered to help although he had no experience coaching wrestling (*Stehn v. Bernarr* 1970). When an eighth-grade boy received crippling injuries during a wrestling match that was part of the required physical education program, a jury returned a verdict in favor of the paralyzed boy for $385,000. This was the largest award by a federal court in Tennessee in more than a decade.

The Center for Sports Law and Risk Management recommends these guidelines to help school administrators comply with safe practices and successfully defend a lawsuit brought under the theory of negligent hiring or improper training:

1. Require job descriptions for all personnel.

2. Document staff qualifications that include training, degrees, certifications, and other legal requirements in a particular state, especially for high-risk activities.

3. Conduct periodic performance evaluations of all personnel.

4. Conduct regular staff meetings and in-service programs on a variety of topics.

5. Supervise and work closely with inexperienced personnel in high-risk activities.

6. Develop policy manuals for students, coaches, athletics trainers and teachers.

7. Keep staff members informed of rule changes, equipment changes, and other pertinent material. (Baron and Appenzeller 1990)

2.5 Employment Contracts

United Educators Insurance Risk Retention Group, Inc., developed an "Athletics Liability: Self-Assessment Audit." The audit notes that contractual disputes have become the source of lawsuits and that the sports administrator needs information on the institution's personnel policies. The audit raises five questions relevant to the situation:

1. Are the contracts for all coaching positions reviewed by the institution's counsel?
2. Are contracts for coaches subject to the institution's procedures concerning termination and appeal?
3. Are assistant coaches apprised of any clauses or agreements in the head coach's contract that allow for their termination at will?
4. Do contracts clearly specify perks, such as the use of owned or loaned vehicles, permission to operate summer camps as independent contractors, etc.?
5. Are athletics department personnel routinely advised of the institution's personnel policies and procedures? (United Educators 1991, 9)

2.6 Staff Responsibilities and Work Loads

On the secondary school level, job descriptions vary. In some school systems, particularly the large ones, athletics directors often teach or coach a sport. In some instances, the athletics director teaches as many as three or four classes. In other instances, the school may assign administrative responsibilities in athletics and other areas by naming the athletics director as assistant principal.

On the major college level, coaches rarely teach in the academic program. However, on the small college level and in major colleges where some coaches do teach, the question of staff work loads becomes an important issue. During my years at Guilford College, all the full-time coaches had other responsibilities. In some instances their duties included teaching, while at other times coaches assumed the responsibilities of the sports information director or supervisor of the weight room. The work load on campus for faculty was twenty-four hours; therefore, we used twenty-four hours as a standard for the athletics staff, assigning specific hours to various sports.

2.7 Staff Meetings

When I reviewed the athletics program for a very fine college, a consistent complaint from the members of the staff was that the athletics director had scheduled only one staff meeting that year. The staff was composed of teachers and coaches with one and two years experience at this institution and, with the absence of a policy manual, few knew the rules, regulations, policies, and procedures. The staff members felt that too much was left to chance and the administrator's discretion. Several staff offices were in buildings other than the gymnasium and this meant the staff rarely saw each other or talked about issues.

I held regular staff meetings when there was business, but I did not hold meetings for the sake of meeting. When several new coaches joined the staff, I met regularly for the year. We scheduled meetings three days per month from 10:00 A.M. to 11:00 A.M., with an agenda sent four days prior to the meeting to prepare the staff for items that would be discussed. At times, several members would find nothing listed on the agenda that affected them and they were excused from attending. At the staff meetings, several individuals talked too long on one item and accomplished little. A way to remedy that without offending anyone is to list the time allotted for each item and adhere to the schedule. The following topics appeared on the annual schedule of staff meetings. While not an exhaustive list, it can serve as a guideline.

- Organization of the athletics department—chain of command, philosophy of the institution, and job descriptions of members of the athletics department.
- Business operations—budget procedures, purchasing, requisitions, expense accounts, and per diem policies; invite the vice-president for finance to discuss policies and procedures and answer questions from the staff.
- Sports medicine policies—coaches, athletes, and student trainers; training room policies; head trainer should discuss the role of the coaches and athletes regarding the sports medicine program.
- Insurance—general information, parents letter, insurance forms, and the role of the staff in implementing insurance policies.
- Policies and procedures for use of athletic facilities—general information regarding procedures, scheduling priorities, use by outside camps, athletic field request form, and gymnasium request form.
- Equipment policies—laundry, physical education, and recreation use; indoor and outdoor use; identification of equipment and the policy regarding issuing equipment; standardization of uniforms.

- Cafeteria policy—policy prior to opening of school, holidays, and postseason; Meal hours, exchange of meals with opposing schools, and special parties, banquets, and dinners.
- Travel policy—scheduling and use of vans, credit card use, maintenance, accident and vehicle damage, registration and insurance, and emergency procedures.
- Booster club—role of coaches and staff in relation to booster club.
- General rules for athletes—physical examinations, eligibility rules, college rules, class attendance, practice rules, classes missed for travel, good conduct rules, due process procedures, and individual team rules.
- Risk assessment and reduction—areas of concern, role of athletic staff in identifying unsafe conditions, and report of the safety committee.
- Postseason play—policies and procedures.
- Eligibility requirements—college, conference, and national regulations.
- Faculty athletics committee—meet with chairperson to discuss the role of athletics staff with the faculty athletics committee.
- Awards—select award recipients.

The suggested agenda can be prioritized by the athletics director according to each institution's needs.

2.8 Staff Morale

I once asked a college president how morale was on his campus, particularly among faculty and members of the athletics department. I must have struck a nerve because the answer was immediate and not at all what I expected. He said, "I could care less what their morale is. Faculty are hired to teach, coaches are hired to coach and not run the school." He then shouted, "If they don't do their jobs, they can leave, but they better not try to be administrators." Certainly that is one way to look at it, but I disagree because good morale among staff and departments is important in creating a healthy community.

Athletics directors should encourage and promote staff morale by supporting coaches as they carry out their responsibilities. During my years as a sports administrator, I attempted to handle many routine details so coaches could devote time to their important role. I involved coaches with the budgeting process and made scheduling a joint effort. One of the coaches did not want to schedule a school that, frankly, was the very type of institution that our faculty, administration, and alumni wanted us to play. We discussed the scheduling on several occasions until I finally had to answer yes or no to the school. The coach agreed to the series and we had great results. I did all the scheduling for every sport until I was hospitalized one year and had to let each coach schedule during my absence. I realized that they did a much better job than I did because they knew the makeup of their teams and they knew when certain opponents should be scheduled. From then on, I asked the coaches to draw up a tentative schedule that I would go over with them for final approval.

At times, the younger coaches needed guidance and direction in scheduling and, in almost every instance, appreciated suggestions on the development of a balanced schedule. As an example, one of the younger coaches scheduled the two toughest conference opponents the week after we returned from fall break. The team would be gone for ten days (without formal practice) and return to play the two most important games on the schedule. We discussed this and adjusted the schedule. Another young coach scheduled three long trips with non-conference teams that had absolutely no bearing on the conference or district records the week prior to examinations. From experience, I knew that the faculty was extremely demanding at this critical time of the year, requiring research papers and class presentations, among other things. Once again, we made important changes in the schedule.

A morale booster is the opportunity for coaches already on the staff to be considered for head coaching positions when they become available. Assistant coaches "pay their dues" and are more of a known quantity than those on the outside. Giving present staff members opportunities to advance helps morale. Providing expenses for clinics and conventions is important. Because I wanted coaches to become active in coaching associations, I did all I could to encourage and promote attendance and participation at meetings. Developing an equitable work load for those coaches who teach also affects morale. The athletics director needs to represent the interests of the coaches, attempting to speak on their behalf. I know of no better way to develop morale than to let coaches know you are behind them in their efforts. I found that every coach I knew appreciated my occasional attendance at practice, following the theory of "management by wandering around" (MBWA).

One of the things that brought high marks was my custom of attending games away from campus. I made it part of my job to set aside several dates on each sport's schedule to travel to see the teams play. Not only did it reveal interest in a particular sport, it gave me an opportunity to visit other athletics directors, observe event management, and enjoy a contest with a rival school. The student-athletes also appreciated my effort and always let it be known to me.

It is important to recognize staff members whenever possible and alert the campus community to their accomplishments. Who can do this better than the athletics director? I learned a valuable lesson that helped me as an administrator from the principal of the second school in which I worked. He made it a practice to tell everyone he met in the community about his staff. I was stopped by a man at a service station who told me how pleased people were because they heard great things from the principal about the new coach. As a result, I then tried hard to live up to his expectations—he certainly boosted my morale. On the other hand, negative statements travel even faster than positive ones and such talk will certainly damage the morale of staff. It is trite but true that if you can't say something nice about a person, don't say anything at all.

I find that listening to people is an art—it is so easy as an administrator to talk instead of listen. Mark McCormack, in *What They Don't Teach You At The Harvard Business School*, makes listening a priority. He emphasizes letting the other person talk because that person will reveal important things if allowed to speak (McCormack 1986, 8). I can support this. When I was offered a job at a Division I school, the person mentioned a salary that so surprised me I could not respond. He took my silence as a negative response and said, "OK, then how about $15,000 more?" Although I did not accept the position, which was at more than twice the salary I was making, I learned that silence (at times) can truly be golden!

2.9 Good Conduct Rules

I remember well the heated argument at an athletics director's conference when one of the speakers warned those in attendance that the very fiber of sports as we knew it would be gone if his school lost its court case. The case took place in California and involved hair length among members of the high school's track team. "The regulation required each athlete to be neat and well-groomed, clean shaven, with the hair kept off the collar and at a reasonable length." Violation of the rule would lead to suspension from the team. Members of the track team felt that the rule was unnecessary and too stringent and unreasonable. Community feeling ran high and the coaches at Redwood High School believed the rule was necessary for "team morale, spirit, and discipline." In this case, one of 104 cases litigated in court, the court upheld the athletics department regulation when it stated that:

> In these perilous, troubled times, when discipline in certain quarters appears to be an ugly word, it should not be considered unreasonable nor regarded as an impingement of constitutional prerogatives, to require plaintiffs to bring themselves within the spirit, purpose and intendments of the questioned rule. (*Neuhaus v. Torrey* 1970)

On the other hand, a Vermont court took the opposite view of a case involving hair length for members of the boy's tennis team. The Vermont court made several interesting comments:

> Billy Kidd, the world famous skier, Joe Pepitone and Ken Harrelson, two colorful and popular major league players, would be unable to

make their teams. Ron Hill, who won the Boston Marathon on April 19 of this year would not even be permitted to try out for the track team if he had to obey the hair code. (*Dunham v. Pulsifer* 1970)

The court upheld the students' complaint and said:

• The Constitution does not stop at the public schools like a puppy waiting for its master, but instead, it follows the student through the corridors, into the classroom and onto the athletic field. (*Dunham v. Pulsifer* 1970)

Evidence that courts vary on similar issues is apparent in the 104 cases involving hairstyles in sports when the courts upheld schools in 58 cases and the students in 46 instances.

During my forty years as a sports administrator, good conduct codes were always an issue between coaches and student-athletes. At one time a basketball player came into my office to ask what more he could do to his hair to satisfy his coach. "This is my third haircut today and I still haven't passed the test," he said. One of our outstanding coaches disagreed when I asked that each coach put good conduct rules in writing. "I want to be a benevolent dictator," he replied, "so I can decide on each case." He explained that he might have a different standard for a blue-chip athlete and another for a reserve. Later, however, he did put his rules in writing and things worked out well. Another coach proudly told me that he was giving a special committee, composed of two seniors, a junior, a sophomore, and a freshman, the opportunity to draw up training rules for the football team. This was progress and I was interested in the outcome. When I asked the results of the meeting, he replied, "I don't plan to use them since I don't agree with them." He honestly thought the students would suggest tougher rules than his, but disregarded them when they recommended students be allowed to drink two beers on the weekend. So much for the democratic approach!

Another coach presented her rules to me for approval. One rule stated that there would be no drinking of alcoholic beverages twenty-four hours before a contest. In other words, a team member could drink as much as desired as long as it wasn't twenty-four hours prior to competition. Another rule involved athletes who became pregnant. The proposed rule would allow a pregnant person to keep an athletic grant if able to play. However, if the individual could not participate, the grant was withdrawn. In my opinion, although not the intent of the rule, it could encourage a student to have an abortion so she could play and keep the grant. After serious discussion, both rules were changed.

From my experience, I suggest that each team have basic requirements that the institution promulgates for all students. In addition, each coach should submit good conduct rules to the athletics director.

After mutual agreement is reached, the rules should be put in written form and approved by the faculty committee. If the rules are challenged, they have the support of the athletics administration and faculty committee to put the coach and athletics director in a strong position.

One final recommendation. Van Alstyne, who has written extensively on student rights, suggests certain requisites be followed to protect the rights of individuals in disciplinary matters. In "The Students as University Residents," he recommends:

> Serious disciplinary action may not be taken in the absence of published rules which:
> a) Are not so vague that men of common intelligence must necessarily guess at its meaning and differ as to its application, and
> b) Do not depend upon the qualified discretion of a particular administrator for their application. (Appenzeller 1975, 43)

The staff member, in concert with the sports administrator, should be careful to draft good conduct rules that are not arbitrary and unreasonable. If the rules are reasonable and fair, courts will generally uphold them in litigation. A Georgia court summed up the attitude of the court toward good conduct rules when it said:

> Among the things a student is supposed to learn at school . . . is a sense of discipline. Of course, rules cannot be made by authorities for the sake of making them but they should possess considerable leeway in promulgating regulations for the proper conduct of students. . . . Courts should uphold them where there is any rational basis for the questioned rule. All that is necessary is a reasonable connection of the rule with the proper operation of the school. (*Stevenson v. Wheeler* 1969)

The late Bobby Dodd of Georgia Tech had a simple one-sentence good conduct code for his football team that read, "Be a gentleman and go to church." Two examples, one of a brief good conduct code and another more detailed are in Appendix F.

2.10 Evaluative Criteria

I have found that coaches and other staff appreciate knowing where they stand with assessment of their effectiveness. My style was to meet periodically with staff members one-on-one. If I was dissatisfied with their performance, I would discuss it behind closed doors, never in public. I would then follow up with a memorandum that would start out with, "Pursuant to our conversation yesterday, we agreed that. . . ." A colleague of mine had a different approach. He would send memos to staff members whose offices were next to his. I preferred to talk things out and then send a memo confirming the details of the meeting.

When a person or coach is hired and goes through a management by objectives plan, evaluations are a necessary part. A questionnaire is given to members of each sports team, assistant coaches, and the athletics director. Coaches review the results of the questionnaires and have the opportunity to respond to them. The coach then fills out the evaluation form provided by the athletics director and an agreement is reached acknowledging strong points and the steps to be followed to strengthen areas that need improvement. A questionnaire that is used as an effective evaluative tool is included Appendix G.

2.11 Termination

I worked with a principal in high school who had the ability to fire people for whatever reason. He was a strong but fair administrator who had little problem terminating those he believed incompetent. I was a young, inexperienced administrator who told him that I could never fire anyone. He just smiled and replied that when I gained maturity I would be able to fire people when necessary. He was right, and although firing is never easy, it is essential in the operation of a successful program.

A colleague of mine on the collegiate level, who fired two of his coaches and was subsequently sued by them, was under considerable pressure from alumni, students, and members of the athletics department. I called one day to offer help with his situation. He gratefully accepted the several court cases I provided his attorney that said, in essence, the "right to hire is the right to fire." The attorney for the athletics director settled one case out of court and won the other.

It is helpful to understand the attitude of the court in situations involving the termination of coaches. One must be aware that juries and courts decide each case on its own merits and no one can give a definitive answer regarding termination lawsuits. There are, however, several criteria that do offer guidance for the sports administrator.

A former basketball manager accepted a position as a teacher and head basketball coach at a county school in North Carolina. His basketball team had a poor record and he was fired as basketball coach but was allowed to remain as a teacher at the school. He asked my advice about a lawsuit he was planning to file against the athletics director, principal, and school board. I sympathized with him but told him that, in my opinion, he could not win a lawsuit and would only receive negative publicity that would follow him when he sought another coaching job. He accepted my opinion and has had basketball jobs at three colleges, with each situation representing a promotion in his coaching career. My recommendation was based on considerable court precedent in various states.

Secondary School

In most situations, high school coaches are hired on contracts that are separate from their teaching contracts. A school system, for little or no reason, can terminate a coaching contract at the end of an academic year. Coaches who are fired often insist that they are teachers and, are therefore, protected by teacher tenure acts (Appenzeller 1985, 79). If the coach has tenure for teaching, he or she may continue to teach, but generally under a divisible contract cannot expect to coach. Very few states grant tenure for coaching. Therefore, a coach can lose his coaching job but can continue to teach if tenure has been granted. In order to handle the problem of keeping a person to teach but not coach, many school districts require a teacher/coach to sign an indivisible contract. Loss of either position results in a loss of both positions.

When Title IX was passed by Congress, women were given the opportunity to participate in interscholastic and intercollegiate sports, and women were hired to coach and assume administrative positions. I asked two physical education instructors if they would coach women's teams that were added to the program. Both turned me down, and rightly so, because they had joined the program to teach and had little interest in coaching. From that time on, out of necessity, all teachers and coaches hired came under an indivisible contract. This made sense because we needed coaches with the addition of women's sports and as a result grew from five to thirteen sports.

It is unfortunate but too often true that coaches without tenure, and this represents the majority, are not extended basic due process when fired. In *Smith v. Board of Education of Urbana School District*, a school board's decision to retain two physical education teachers to teach but not coach was upheld by the court:

> At most, the Fourteenth Amendment due process clause guarantees a state athletic coach the right to know why he is being dismissed and to convince school officials before they dismiss him that they are making a mistake and that their reasons for dismissing him are either not supported by facts or less compelling than they think. (*Smith v. Bd. of Educ.* 1983)

In *Sports and Law: Contemporary Issues*, I summarized the court's attitude when faced with lawsuits filed by secondary school coaches regarding employment:

> Employment issues involving coaches are among the most highly litigated areas of sport law ...
>
> State and federal courts over the years have been reluctant to usurp the discretionary powers of local school boards as they relate to personnel matters. As a result, local school boards have considerable freedom in matters that pertain to the employment, assignment, nonrenewal, suspension, transfer, and dismissal of coaches. Courts basically require only that school boards exert reasonableness in dealing with their personnel ...
>
> The typical coach signs a divisible contract which requires the coach to teach and assume responsibility to coach one or more

sports. The coaching assignment is separate and apart from teaching and can be terminated for little or no reason. If a coach acquires tenure for teaching, he may be able to keep the teaching position although the coaching assignment has been terminated. Some school districts throughout the nation favor indivisible contracts which mean that individuals are hired on one contract to teach and coach. Termination of either duty leads to loss of both positions.

It is interesting to note that coaches seeking redress in court, when they lose their coaching positions, can win their suit if they can prove that school districts have discriminated against them on the basis of gender or race. When coaches prove that their constitutional rights such as freedom of expression have been violated, the courts consistently rule in their favor. School administrators must uphold the rights of their athletics staff. (Appenzeller 1985, 79)

Two cases with different judicial decisions are important for the sports administrator when considering termination procedures for a staff member. A football coach of eight years who taught biology and physical education met with his administrator to discuss unauthorized purchases of football equipment and a major change in team colors. The coach allegedly failed to follow policy and procedure in ordering equipment. Other allegations included

• A lack of communication with his administrator,
• Use of an ineligible player in a practice game,
• Grabbing the face masks of players when he lost his temper,
• Profanity, and
• Conduct that resulted in penalties by the officials. (*Shimoyama v. Bd. of Educ. of Los Angeles* 1981)

The coach wrote a letter after his initial meeting with the administrator denouncing him and blaming him for low morale at the school and failure to support the athletics program. Copies of the critical letter were sent to the district superintendent, assistant coach, two faculty members who were active in the teacher's union, and the booster club president. As a result, the coach was fired. He filed suit, arguing that he was dismissed because he exercised his right of freedom of expression guaranteed by the First Amendment.

The trial court favored the administrator and school district and the appellate court affirmed the decision:

If attacks upon a superior such as we have here were given constitutional protection, it would require a hardy administrator to maintain a working relationship and to risk criticizing a subordinate's performance, knowing that the subordinate was free with impunity to retaliate by broadcasting accusations implying that the administrator was a conspirator, a liar and a hypocrite. (*Shi-moyama v. Bd. of Educ. of Los Angeles* 1981)

On the other hand, another case has a different and important decision that is noteworthy. A high school teacher and coach sued his school district, principal, superintendent, and assistant principal for "retaliating against him for exercising his First Amendment rights." Knapp received permission from the school board to discuss a grievance question because the board wanted input from teachers. No one in the administration told Knapp it was against school policy to talk with board members. Knapp discussed several issues and then filed a grievance based on unequal mileage for coaches and a lack of liability insurance for coaches who transported students to athletic events. Knapp's superintendent pointed to an existing regulation that required all communication to the board to go through him. This statement was in the superintendent's contract. When Knapp responded that such a policy violated his right of free speech the superintendent replied, "Your rights end where my nose begins." A jury awarded Knapp over $500,000 in damages, observing that the policy did, in fact, violate his right of free speech (*Knapp v. Whitaker* 1983).

Collegiate Level

On the collegiate level coaches can be fired for little or no reason. In most instances, however, the reason for termination is because of a losing record. The courts have been consistent in ruling that coaches who are fired must be paid for the years that remain on their contract. The issue is not the remaining years of their contract but the value of the perquisites. In most cases, the perquisites greatly exceed the base salary, and coaches who are fired refuse to give them up. In several recent cases, school officials have arrived at a settlement for the perquisites of coaches who have been fired.

It seems that administrators should clarify the question of perquisites when hiring a new coach. Unless contracts include provision for the termination of perquisites when a coach is fired, it will be an issue that will continue to plague school officials. However, with the number of legal cases involving employment issues, school officials (including athletics directors) will finally have guidelines in their role as decision makers. As the examples cited illustrate, the question of what action to take in terminating an employee becomes important for the sports administrator.

There are several things relating to the dismissal of employees that an athletics director should avoid. I called a colleague at a major Division I university about a coach who had recently resigned as an assistant at his institution and had applied for the head football coaching position at my college. I asked if he had been fired and my colleague of many years emphatically replied, "No, not at all." The first thing this candidate told the search committee was, "I am sure you all know I was fired!" I was shocked and disappointed that another athletics director would not tell me the truth. The reason for dismissal was understandable—one man was a strict and devoted churchman and the other a person with a more liberal lifestyle. Both were outstanding coaches who had differing philosophies of life. We hired the former assistant, who contributed much to the overall program and touched the lives of those with whom he came in contact. From that day on, however, I could not rely on my athletics director friend for a recommendation. If he had explained the reason for dismissal we would have understood and still considered the fired coach a viable candidate.

Another problem I have seen in my over forty years of administration is the person who wants staff members to leave but cannot find the opportunity or courage to make the move to terminate. When called for recommendations about individuals, they give a glowing, positive (often untruthful) recommendation in the hope that someone will hire this person and take them off their hands. I remember one situation so blatantly unfair that I asked the individual what would happen if the person was not hired by another institution. "Sooner or later," she replied, "I will have to fire him." My response was simple, "How will you be able to fire him when you wrote such a great recommendation? If he goes to court, your evaluation will be used against you." I do not recommend falsifying a recommendation to get a person out of your organization. Your credibility will be questioned.

Sooner or later all athletics directors face a situation that calls for them to fire someone. From my experience, it will never be a pleasant situation or one that you look forward to. John Halbrooks, writing in *Marriott Portfolio*, suggests several things that are important in such situations. Halbrooks emphasizes timing—not too hasty nor too long in coming. It is important to decide if the employee can be "salvaged" before firing (Halbrooks 1990, 14). One of my finest student athlete's entered the coaching profession after graduation from college. I predicted a bright career for him because he had character, intelligence, drive, and determination. He was named head football coach at a school that was just starting a football program. As coach he had dismal records of 0–9, 0–10, and 1–9, and the community wanted him fired. The athletics director, responsible for all coaches in the county system, was a veteran coach who was highly respected by his colleagues. He refused to be pressured into firing this young coach because he knew he had many obstacles against him with the new program. His support and faith paid off as this coach went on to win several state championships and was recognized as one of the top coaches in the state of North Carolina.

In my position as athletics director, it was important to consider the circumstances regarding a coach's lack of success. Did that coach have a poor assignment or a lack of resources or support? If so, I had to help correct the problem to give the coach a chance to succeed. I called in a coach because he recruited by writing letters to potential athletes. I felt this lack of aggressive recruiting was a reason for his failure to attract outstanding athletes, which led to his lack of success. We discussed recruiting strategies and together we set new goals and deadlines for reaching them; but I gave fair warning of what to expect if the goals were not reached. How lucky could I be? This coach became the winningest coach in the school's 150-year history. In another situation, I was advised to terminate a coach shortly after I first accepted the position of athletics director. I asked for time to evaluate the person's coaching ability before making such a decision. Again, timing was important because this coach was one of the most successful in history and received national honors.

Documentation with written records may prove to be important when termination is in order. Record only relevant information that will be helpful if you are challenged in court by the employee. Do not wait too long if you decide termination is the only option left to you. Don't lecture the person. Be factual in your criticism. Avoid vague terms like "poor performance" as a basis for your action. Be open and honest, but at all times compassionate.

I have witnessed situations in which the termination turned out to be the best thing that could happen to an individual. In several situations, people who were terminated returned to thank me for helping them change direction in a way that had a positive affect on their lives.

2.12 Staff Exit Interview

The athletics director can learn much from staff members who leave the program for whatever reason. The sports information director or assistants, head coaches and assistants, athletics trainers, academic counselors, and secretaries will usually respond well to an exit interview. The athletics director can use a formal questionnaire or have an informal discussion (or both) with the staff member.

Some of the questions that may open dialogue include

- How satisfied were you with the particular program with which you worked?
- How satisfied were you with the overall sports program?
- What were the strengths of both specific and overall programs?
- What were the weaknesses of the programs?
- Were you satisfied with the support the program received? with the support you received as an individual?
- What could be done to improve support?
- Did you feel that some programs were neglected while others received special status? Elaborate on this statement.
- Please rate on a scale from 1 to 5 the following:

(5) = very satisfied; (4) = satisfied; (3) = neutral; (2) = dissatisfied; (1) = very dissatisfied. If no contact with following please
put N/A.

Academic dean's office
Academic support staff
Admissions
Alumni office
Athletics office
Business office
Counseling services
Dean of students office
Development office
Financial aid office
Health services
Sports medicine and athletics training staff
Minority students office
International students office
Residence life

• In what way has the college changed since your first year?
• Are you satisfied with the changes since your first year?
• What would you change in the sports program?
• What would you do different if hired today?
• What are the strengths and weaknesses of the athletics program, in your opinion?
• From the list below, please circle all the words or phrases that you would say best describe your image of the athletics program.

Excellent	Traditional
Conservative	Impersonal
Intense	Prestigious
Isolated	Apathetic
Friendly	Creative
Competitive	Diverse
Stressful	Challenging
Not well-known	Exciting
Overbearing	Innovative
Upbeat	Close-knit
Flexible	Rigid
Demanding	Motivating
Accepting	Other _____
Caring	

• How satisfied were you with your experience at the college?

This is not an exhaustive list of questions, but with the addition of those relating to your program, they can provide valuable insight.

3
The Student-Athlete

I graduated from college in midyear and began coaching immediately. The school principal was the former coach who continued coaching the girl's basketball team and was relieved to give up the boy's team. On my first day at school, I passed the team members walking toward the home economics building. I asked if they were enrolled in a class but never expected their answer: "Coach, this is the day of a ballgame. We go lie down and rest all day in the home economics building." A small rural school, not a major university, and here were eight or nine students "resting" for the big game. I told the group to go back and attend regular classes for the remainder of the season—no more resting. The thing that saved me from dissension was the fact that the team's record up to that point was 2–12. We went on to win 14 of 15 and the county championship. That was 1948 and things have changed; or are they really different today?

In Tennessee, a tenured English teacher was harassed after a high school coach circulated a petition against her for failing the star player on the basketball team, rendering him ineligible for the rest of the season. The situation received notoriety in the community and in the local newspaper. Someone fired a shot at her car while she was driving to school one morning. Bumper stickers were sold at concession stands during games that read "I didn't shoot Anne McGhee I tried and missed" (*McGhee v. Miller* 1988). The teacher, pressured by the community, gave in and changed the grade to D+. The teacher, upset and depressed and fearing for her safety, sought psychiatric help, missing two-and-one-half days of teaching. The school board fired her for missing school. The teacher filed suit against the school board, and the Tennessee Supreme Court awarded her back pay and reinstated her. In a day when reports of scandals, cheating, drug use, illegal payments, and grade fixing in college sports have filled the media, this situation is another example of misguided values in sports. By allowing the star forward to play although he did not earn his grade in English, the principal and local school board made a statement about their priorities.

3.1 Athletics Recruiting

In another instance of misplaced priorities, Curtis Jones was "intellectually deficient and would require special education in a school for slow learners" (Appenzeller and Baron 1989 11). Jones was placed in a school for slow learners in the fourth grade, but transferred into regular junior and senior high school when his outstanding basketball potential was discovered. Jones allegedly was "academically carried for two years" and, although he could neither read or write, attended North Idaho Junior College (NIJC) with the expectation of transferring to the University of Michigan after he completed his eligibility. Curtis Jones testified that students at NIJC ridiculed him when they learned of his illiteracy causing a "complete nervous breakdown from which he has not recovered." Jones has been in and out of hospitals since 1970 and lives on welfare. Maria Ironside, writing in *Athletes' Rights, Bulletin*, puts the blame on an educational system that allowed Jones to be exploited.

If Curtis Jones had ever known one school administrator, one advisor or coach, or anyone with clearheadedness and courage to stand up and speak for his educational rights, he might have stood a chance for something better than what he got. He, and all of us, deserve better. (Appenzeller 1985 118)

Certainly we can cite similar instances of educational exploitation, but there are just as many instances, it appears, of cases where high-risk students were able to overcome deficiencies to achieve academic success.

As an athletics director, I wanted the sports program to achieve success because I believe a winning program can teach more values to the participants than a losing one. The answer is not just winning, but winning within the rules. When the new football coach was interviewed at a press conference announcing his hiring, he quoted Vince Lombardi and said, "Winning is not the most important thing, it's the only thing." Saying, "That's my philosophy and I plan to win." After the session I told him his philosophy was fine as long as it included winning within the rules.

With the move by college presidents to control athletics and promote academics in the 1990s, educators on the high school and collegiate level need to protect the sanctity of athletics by condemning such situations as those that took place with McGhee and Jones. It is time that we emphasize the student-athlete, not the athlete-student.

The presidents of NCAA institutions have begun to take an active role in their athletic programs. Much has been written about Proposition 48, which currently requires the student athlete to score 700 on the Scholastic Aptitude Test (SAT) or 18 on the American College Test (ACT). In addition, the student-athlete must have a grade point average of 2.0 in at least 11 high school core subjects in English, mathematics, social studies, and science to participate in sports as a freshman. The Presidents Commission of the NCAA recommended more stringent rules that would require a 2.5 grade point average in 13 core subjects. The SAT and ACT test scores would remain the same with an added variable; an SAT score of 800 would permit a 2.2 GPA, while a 900 and up allows for a 2.0 average. At its annual meeting, the NCAA approved these key measures that will go into effect on August 1, 1995 (*Chronicle of Higher Education* 1992).

In response to the attempt to raise the academic requirements for the student athlete, Larry Davis, a Wake Forest University basketball assistant coach, made an interesting comment when he said:

> One of my friends was talking about it one day and he said if it keeps going like it's going now, the national game of the week will be Odessa (Texas) Junior College versus Midland (Texas) Junior College, because that's where all the players will be. (*Greensboro News and Record*, 27 July 1991)

As athletics director, I was concerned that a student-athlete would be recruited without a chance of success in academics. My philosophy was simple, "recruit only those who you honestly feel can succeed at our institution." Occasionally we failed, but in most instances we succeeded in the recruitment process.

George A. Selleck, a specialist in the field of recruiting, conducted a study on recruiting with NAIA and NCAA institutions across the United States. He included in his study discussions with more than 250 student-athletes, parents, and high school coaches. As a result of the two-year study on recruiting, Selleck reports that "five specific needs" repeatedly emerged:

- The need for a more professional approach to recruiting. Instead of being played like a game with flabby parameters, recruiting should be treated as a no-nonsense business.
- The need to maximize recruiting dollars. If one of the Fortune 500 companies was going to spend the equivalent of an athletic scholarship, it would have to go through layers of approval first, yet colleges and universities often make this decision off-handedly.
- The need to eliminate irresponsible recruiting practices. Lots of high school athletes have their lives disrupted, if not occasionally harmed, by the pressure of what is done in the name of recruiting. Developing proper skills and techniques for recruiting increases a coach's confidence level and reduces the temptation to bend or break the rules.
- The need to strive more consistently for compatible matches between prospect's needs, interests, values, and objectives and those of the recruiting institutions. Considering that colleges and

universities spend thousands of dollars on athletics scholarships, it is critical for them to select students whose interests and abilities complement their athletic, academic, and social programs.

- The need for the expedient training of young coaches in recruiting skills. Most coaches learn to recruit by the seat of their pants, taking anywhere from three to five years to acquire the necessary knowledge and techniques. (Selleck 1983)

3.2 Athletics Advisory Council

One of the first things I did at Guilford College was to organize a captain's council made up of the captain of each sport, a representative of the athletics training staff, and cheerleaders. Later, I changed the name to the athletics advisory council when I realized that, on occasion, the captain was not the best representative of a particular sport. Each coach nominated a person and an alternate who best represented the team. This group of students and athletes is invaluable to the athletics administrator because they do so much to improve communication between the administrator and members of the various teams, athletic trainers, and cheerleaders. Some of the things they do include

- Liaison with the members of the team and the student body;
- Update the administrator on perceptions, rumors, and misinterpretations that often damage the credibility of the athletics program;
- Act as a sounding board for the athletics administrator for policies, procedures, rules, and regulations;
- Boost morale and overall esprit de corps among student-athletes and the student body; and
- Assist with the awards banquet.

The council met once a month, at a time mutually agreed upon, for one hour. Two regularly scheduled dinner meetings met longer. Don't make the mistake I made the first time we met. We had fifteen representatives and I assumed they all knew each other. I was surprised to find that the group knew only two names, the captain of the football team and the center on the men's basketball team.

One of my goals was to create a climate where everyone felt free to discuss the program honestly and openly. I promised to listen to their concerns and respond to all questions in an open manner. I think I surprised them and also opened the door for discussion when I passed out copies of the budget at the first meeting. Too many administrators keep their budgets hidden. As expected, I received many questions and comments about the inequities of the men's and women's basketball, lacrosse, soccer, and tennis budgets. In some instances, the women's budget was higher than the men's. All the questions had rational responses that gave insight into the financial planning and the reasons why we did certain things. As an aside, I regularly put a copy of the budget in the library for all to see.

The team representatives would frequently discuss different teams on campus and what could be done to improve perceptions. In one instance, they felt that one of the coaches was so unpopular with opposing teams that they were often mistreated when they played at an opponent's school. The coach refused to meet and greet teams, and often let them wander around without a schedule or information on the proper location of facilities and events. The team volunteered to designate one member as host for the visiting team for each home match. It certainly helped create a better relationship with the opposing schools.

In two situations, members reported that a professor told his classes that football was too expensive to operate and should be eliminated because budget cuts were being made in the area of academics. The professor insisted that the cost of equipment to outfit a player was ten times the actual cost. We sent a catalog with the exact cost of equipment per man and received an apology from the professor for spreading misinformation. An administrator reported that tuition was increased 10 percent to pay for a new sports complex. This administrator was totally misinformed and reluctantly apologized when he learned that the total cost of the facility had been raised through private funds.

Occasionally a team representative felt the need to meet one-on-one with me to discuss a problem. One said that every team but his went somewhere to practice and play during spring break. His coach told him that he did not have funds in the budget to travel during spring break. After I talked with the coach, he planned a trip. He had the money, but for personal reasons he did not want to go away during spring break. That year the team traveled to Florida, had a great trip, improved morale, and got the season off to a good start.

Near the end of my tenure, a serious situation developed involving drugs. A member of one of the spring sports teams was preparing to play in the conference tournament. He called to tell me that his name would be in the local paper that day charging him with selling drugs. He insisted that he was innocent and had no part in the alleged selling of drugs. What a dilemma! The fact that he was a strong tennis player and valuable to the team was not a consideration. The overriding factor was my desire to not accuse him of anything until I was sure he was guilty. I met with the following people within hours: the student, his coach, the president of the college, the dean of students, and the student's attorney.

There was a consensus that we should not prejudge him, holding him innocent until proved guilty. We all realized the public outcry and criticism that would follow if we did not suspend him from the team and school. I agreed to support him with the proviso that if he changed his plea to guilty, he would be dropped from the team and school. The following day I called an emergency meeting of the athletics advisory council to explain the situation and the action school officials had taken. I asked for their opinion, criticism, and comments. The response was unanimous:

- Thank you for telling us the facts because rumors are rampant and totally distorted.
- Thank you for the action that was taken; we would hope this would be the action if we were involved.
- We support you and the school officials.

Their support meant much to me, particularly when the student changed his plea to guilty a few days later and, as promised, we dropped him from the team and school. Today this young man, after serving time in a halfway house, has graduated from another college and is living a productive life. I still believe the action was right and the support of the athletics advisory council was important to me and the program.

Each year at the final meeting, I routinely asked each representative to list the good accomplished in the sports program; but more importantly, to tell me without reservation their negatives, needs, and disappointments. I waited for a response and receiving none, stated that I would not be offended, I really needed to know how to improve the program. Once again, a long silence and then the representative of the tennis team, known for his outspoken manner said, "Well, I guess I'm the one to tell it." I waited expectantly for the "axe to fall." Then he said, "Since I have been here, the water fountains on the tennis courts haven't worked." We all laughed and I remember saying, "We must be doing something right, if that is your only complaint."

At the annual banquet, members of the council planned the details and presided over the event, much to the delight of the athletes.

I highly recommend an athletics advisory council as a constructive way of getting to know the leaders of the teams, gaining helpful insight into existing problems, and developing esprit de corps.

3.3 Student Exit Interviews

The NCAA passed Proposition 19 which requires an exit interview with all senior student-athletes. The exit interview, coupled with various student-athlete's evaluations of specific coaches, gives the athletics director and the entire staff information that can be important to the welfare of the overall program. John Burns, assistant athletics director at Furman University, noted that the senior athletes attending the interview session "were enthusiastic about the opportunity and encouraged that the athletics department would open itself up to this kind of self-examination."

Discussion was meaningful, sometimes very personal, often emotional, and on occasion critical, as the athletes realized that this was their opportunity to make an even larger contribution to the university than what they might have made on the playing field. (*NCAA News*, 24 Apr. 1990)

A well-conceived questionnaire can reveal much about the program and serve as a starting point for group discussion. The athletics advisory council can assist in developing the exit interview.

I recommend also that a questionnaire be sent to former student-athletes on a random basis. This questionnaire will reveal the perception of past programs and present programs, and the response from various eras can be extremely helpful. When we conducted one survey the responses were positive and helped us understand the attitude of former athletes.

In a random questionnaire, respondents were asked to describe a course, coach, or professor that had an impact on their lives. It was an eye-opener, as 80 percent of the respondents, almost apologetically, talked about a very demanding, stern, and rather unpopular professor who taught an art history course. "I never realized the way she touched my life, how she created a love of art and an understanding of the ancient treasures as I traveled through the world." This typified the comments.

Part 2
Managing Operations

4
Operations

4.1 Preparing for the Upcoming Year

The offseason is typically the time to prepare for the upcoming year in sports. Offseason is an excellent time to review purchasing procedures, travel policies, ticket office operations, eligibility, grants-in-aid, medical and liability insurance coverage, scheduling, cheerleading, facility use and maintenance, fund-raising, marketing and promotions, handbook updates, publicity, and risk management strategies. There is a natural tendency on the part of many people, including one's own staff, to take for granted the multifaceted things that go on behind the scenes that ensure game day success and a smooth operation. Unless you have been a part of the offseason preparation prior to opening events, there is really no way you can understand the time, effort, and planning that takes place.

Dennis Haglan, currently athletics director at Catawba College in Salisbury, North Carolina, was event manager for sports as assistant athletics director at Wake Forest University. Prior to the fall season, Haglan would plan and prepare checklists for men's and women's soccer, men's and women's basketball, baseball, and football, as well as develop maintenance lists and improvement recommendations for programs and facilities. His maintenance list was thorough and essential for implementation, sport by sport. The maintenance list included the football stadium, guest and press parking, stadium club, concourse area, vomitories and stands, press box area, box and guest seating, photography room, and seating in the stadium. The checklist for football included 123 items and was used annually and updated when necessary. One page of this checklist, pertaining to the press box area, is shown below.

4.2 Maintenance Checklist

1. _____ Paint urinal wall in men's bathroom
2. _____ Clean toilet on far right in men's bathroom

3. _____ Clean toilet dividers of rust
4. _____ Clean window sill
5. _____ Clean rug

Press Box Area—Level #4

6. _____ Wash double doors leading into area
7. _____ Paint door hinges which are rusting—check other hinges on doors of all levels
8. _____ Replace several ceiling panels
9. _____ Paint all walls in Press Box area
10. _____ Repair water fountains
11. _____ Replace hand-written signs indicating telecopier charges, etc., with first class signs
12. _____ Clean closet area that contains computer accessories, wires, etc.
13. _____ Clean scoreboard operation room
14. _____ Repair and clean walls in scoreboard room
15. _____ Can we slide computer mechanism, etc., over about one foot to facilitate an additional seat on the same landing?
16. _____ Replace panels in scoreboard room
17. _____ Wash walls in operations booth
18. _____ Replace appropriate ceiling panels in operations booth
19. _____ Plywood on lower level of press row (front facing of upper level of press row in middle) needs to be varnished
20. _____ Repair leak in sink
21. _____ Clean refrigerated area as well as toastmaster area
22. _____ Clean floor behind counter area
23. _____ Clean initial entrance into men's room
24. _____ Clean towel dispenser of rust in men's room
25. _____ Wash walls in men's room

In addition to the maintenance checklist, Haglan would constantly make recommendations designed to upgrade the athletic facility. An interesting recommendation was included in his report to athletics director, Gene Hooks, regarding restrooms:

Potty parity: Virginia draws the line today at women waiting in long lines to use public facilities. A new state regulation requires new public buildings to provide more toilets for women than for men—twice as many in some places. Researchers timed lines and found women often take more than twice as long as men in restrooms. Reasons: clothing restrictions, attending to small children.

Haglan researched the use of restrooms at the football stadium and found that restrooms for males included sixty urinals and forty commodes for men while women had a total of only sixty commodes. As a result of his investigation, Haglan recommended the following:

Convert one restroom on each concourse from men to women. This would reduce the number of commodes and urinals available for men to 24 and 36 respectively, and bring the number of commodes for women up to approximately 90. This does not bring the ratio to 2 to 1, but it does raise it to 1.5 to 1.

4.3 Game Day Operations

Checklists were also prepared for game day operations that ensured a smooth and efficient operation of events in all sports. One page of the game day operations checklist for football is shown below.

1. _____ Check outside main gates for scalpers selling tickets.
2. _____ Check the restrooms for trash and overflows.
3. _____ Check the concession operations, complaints, etc.
4. _____ Check the positioning of security and police personnel.
5. _____ Walk outside of the concourse area checking all things that are on map beginning approximately two hours before game time.
6. _____ Check police headquarters before the game to make sure the cookies and coffee are there and check it after the game to see if the refreshments have been consumed.
7. _____ Be around the official's dressing room right before halftime to coordinate with the band and cheerleaders the drink pouring.
8. _____ Be responsible at the site of the fireworks. You will be our primary site coordinator.
9. _____ Check various parking lots per the paper handout, also check the traffic flow in and out of these areas periodically.
10. _____ Help monitor the field pregame, as well as during the game, to see that no one is unnecessarily on the sidelines.
11. _____ Periodically check the program sellers on your side as well as the ushers and the ticket takers.
12. _____ Take a small pad and pencil to make notes of items that need your attention. I would like a report on Monday.
13. _____ Make notes of anything that appears to be broken or needs repair before the next game—lights out, urinals overflowing or something in concession stands that might be broken.
14. _____ In the press box and stadium club areas in particular, check to see that there are trash cans available, restrooms, etc.

In addition to offseason meetings, Haglan had a pregame party that seemed to bond people together. All those involved in the operation of the sports program would participate in a family outing at the stadium. At the outing, which was popular with the families, specific responsibilities would be discussed and assignments reviewed. Besides being a fun night, it served to define each persons role and responsibility in the operation. While Haglan's program was devised for a Division I program, its principles and guidelines can be adapted to virtually any sports program.

In Appendix H, a copy of the basketball operational checklist is available. The checklist is thorough and detailed, and can serve as an excellent guide for any school's program.

5
Transportation

It was ironic that I had been invited to speak to athletics directors in Wichita, Kansas, regarding the legal aspects of transportation for sport activities. A month before I was scheduled to speak, two air crashes shocked the nation. Fourteen members of Wichita State University's football team and sixteen other passengers died when their chartered plane crashed into Mt. Trelease near Silver Plume, Colorado (*Brown v. Wichita* 1976). About one month later, seventy-five people on a Southern Airways DC-9 carrying the Marshall University football team and members of the booster club died when their chartered plane crashed in Huntington, West Virginia. In just two months, over 115 people were killed. Following the two crashes, the Federal Aviation Administration (FAA) immediately sent material regarding special safety guidelines for air charters to athletics directors.

During my third year of teaching, a bus at a neighboring school traveling on an unsafe vine-covered bridge collided with a truck, killing everyone on the bus. The state of North Carolina promptly inspected every bus route in its 100 counties.

Four girl scouts, two supervisors, and a bus driver were killed in California when the brakes on a chartered bus went out on a mountain road causing the bus to tumble down a steep incline. The crash led to renewed demands for the installation of seat belts on buses (*Greensboro News and Record*, 4 August 1991).

It is sad but true that safety becomes important after tragedies take place. Such events result in changes that should have been in effect prior to accidents. Today's athletes travel as never before, not only across the nation but around the world. Each mode of transportation has unique problems, and travel policies are essential. It is crucial that sport administrators examine various modes of travel and develop policies to promote safe travel.

Schools have a duty to provide safe vehicles and qualified drivers when transporting student-athletes. There are four categories of transportation: "(a) independent contract for transportation, (b) use of school vehicles, (c) use of employee vehicles, and (d) use of vehicles of non-employees" (van der Smissen 1990).

According to van der Smissen, "liability for travel to and from events can be avoided only when no transportation is provided, and that can occur by establishing the policy that there will be no transportation provided for anyone and designating that the site of convening will be at the location of the event."

5.1 Charter Vehicles

The ideal method of transportation may be chartering a commercial vehicle, by which the school transfers tort liability to the independent contractor. The contracting party, as a rule, does not assume responsibility for liability, although van der Smissen urges caution: "[E]mployers remain liable for injuries caused by negligence of independent contractors if the employer fails to use reasonable care to select a competent contractor, and where the contractor was in fact incompetent."

I expect that most athletics directors or the person designated to arrange charter services do not go beyond sending in a bid with the sport schedule and providing minimal information to the charter company. For years, John Morley, a risk management expert with Lawrence Risk Services in Schenectady, New York, has urged that the person responsible for arranging transportation go into specific details to ensure safe procedures. Morley has devised a valuable checklist that is timely and unique. It includes the contractor, vehicle, driver, passengers, and school. In my opinion, Morley's charter coach checklist represents a major contribution to sport administrators.

Charter coach checklist

A. The contractor

1. Has been in continuous operation for at least five years with coach charter service a significant part of the business.

2. Has full-time management and a regular full-time operations and maintenance staff.

3. Has a place of business that reflects an ability to carry out the contract in terms of organization, resources, and appearance.

4. Can provide at least three references from current customers who contract for the services you want, and can provide you with the contractor's Interstate Commerce Commission (ICC) authority number or the state authority number for its operation. Either or both should be checked with the appropriate authorities for validity.

5. Can demonstrate an ability to handle emergencies with plans and available resources at maximum distance from the place of business.

6. Has adequate insurance to cover your exposure and available to you as an additional insured, in writing from the contractor's carrier.

Note: You should confirm this coverage and receive written documentation of it from the insurance carrier, not the agent. It should not be on a "claims made" basis.

7. Will inform you in advance if the services of another carrier will be used to fulfill your contract and will assume full responsibility for the performance of the substitute carrier.

B. The vehicle

1. Shall be maintained in accordance with all applicable, current state and federal Department of Transportation motor carrier regulations.

2. Must be clean and attractive inside and out. There shall be no evidence of excessive wear and tear or unrepaired body and interior components.

3. Shall have all lighting and climate control systems fully operational, including individually operated reading lights available to each passenger and an illuminated aisle floor and entryway for walking safety.

4. Vehicle toilets must be clean, sanitary, and operational.

5. Public address system shall be adequate to communicate effectively with all passengers, and video equipment, if supplied, shall be in operable condition and available for use.

6. Adequate storage space outside the passenger compartment shall be available for all large, bulky, or other items not carried on by passengers. Such space shall be lockable and secure. Interior space shall be provided for carry-on items out of the way and secured in place to avoid loose items moving about in emergencies.

C. The driver

1. Shall be fully qualified under all current applicable state and federal Department of Transportation motor vehicle carrier regulations.

2. Shall be a regular employee of the contractor and carry documentation of that status, preferably in a photo I.D. format.

3. Shall be appropriately dressed and groomed and present a courteous, helpful, and businesslike demeanor at all times.

4. Shall not exhibit any evidence by appearance, speech, or action of diminished physical or mental capacity to perform the responsibilities assigned.

D. The passengers

1. Should be appropriately supervised by school staff at all times. While the driver has overall responsibility for the vehicle and the trip, he or she cannot supervise the passengers individually.

2. Should avoid behavior that will distract the driver. A moment of distraction on a crowded interstate in bad weather can be dangerous.

3. Should be courteous to one another and be prepared to occupy themselves quietly on the trip.

E. The school

1. Should be prepared to provide enough qualified supervision for the kind of trip and the passengers entrusted to its care.

2. Supervisors should be instructed to cooperate fully with the driver and meet all schedule requirements. Trips should be planned so that the driver is not put in the position of violating federal regulations which limit on-duty time to fifteen continuous hours and driving time to ten hours. After each such work period, a driver must have eight consecutive hours off duty. These rules are for your safety.

3. Should communicate with the contractor after each trip to review performance in terms of both positive and negative actions or impressions.

4. Should assign one staff member to arrange all such trips after the approval process is completed.

5.2 Transportation Contract

The following is a sample transportation contract.

This document will serve as the contract between (bus company) and the (school) athletic department. The purpose of this contract is to put in writing the conditions for the chartering of buses from (bus company) by (school) to transport athletic teams for the school year _____ .

Let it be known that (school) athletic department has investigated (bus company) and found them to be a full regular operating charter coach company. (Bus company) has a full-time management staff and full-time maintenance operations program. (Bus company) has the number of buses that will allow them to handle emergency plans and the resources available to replace any bus that may be broken down on a particular trip. With this document will be the insurance coverage (bus company) has in case of accident or personal injury.

All buses are maintained in accordance with state and federal Department of Transportation motor carrier regulations. They are attractive and clean inside and out. The buses have lighting and climate control systems that are fully operational and an illuminated aisle for the passengers. The buses have rest rooms that are clean, sanitary, and operational. There is adequate storage space for the student-athlete to store equipment under the bus and space for books and personal belongings above the seats on the bus. All (bus company) drivers are fully qualified under current applicable state and federal Department of

Transportation motor vehicle carrier regulations. All of their employees are under contract and carry the proper documentation to prove it. (School) is prepared to provide qualified supervision by the coach on each trip. The coach has been instructed to cooperate with the driver and meet all schedule requirements. Trips have been planned so that the driver is at no time put in the position of violating federal regulations which limit the on-duty time to fifteen continuous hours and driving time to ten hours. After each trip the coach will report any problems to the director of athletics, who will address the contractor.

(Bus company) will document each and every trip and a copy will be given to the coach at the time of trip departure. (School) will pay (bus company) on a monthly basis for trips accumulated to that date. Payment will begin with the billing and the contractor will be paid within 10 days of billing. Final billing will be _____.

5.3 Air Charters

Air travel has become routine, enabling schools to save time and reduce the number of classes student-athletes miss. Following the Wichita State and Marshall University air crashes, the FAA sent warning letters to colleges and universities alerting athletic officials to the potential dangers presented by some charter companies. The FAA cautioned that while there are countless legitimate charter companies, there are others or persons who have no legal operator's certificates. In a brochure *Look Before You Lease*, athletics administrators are warned to avoid a "dry lease" in which they may be misled about the operation of the aircraft and find that they:

> are provided with an aircraft on a lease basis although it is actually serviced and flown by the leasing company. Such an arrangement (depending on the terms of the lease) may make you the responsible operator of the aircraft, even though, in fact, you do not intend this and have nothing to do with the flight other than to indicate where and when you wish to fly. (FAA 1973)

The FAA warns those who schedule air charters, "that while a charter company's price might appear enticing because its fares are low, that very operator might not be certified and, in fact, will cause you to break the law and put the lives of your personnel in jeopardy."

Nineteen years after the FAA warned athletic directors of the danger of unsafe air charters it, once again, warned:

> major professional and collegiate sports leagues and associations that some teams are traveling on aircraft that are not held to the Federal Aviation Administration's highest safety standards. (NCAA 1992)

As a guide for administrators, the FAA recommends:

• Before you sign for a charter, ask to see the operator's FAA certificate.
• If you are not certain of the status of the company, call the FAA office in your local area for information. (Appenzeller 1975)

5.5 Activity Buses, Vans, and Cars

Many schools own and operate activity buses, vans, and cars to transport students who participate in co-curricular activities. State statutes vary regarding vehicles that transport students in co-curricular activities. United Educators, in its publication *Managing Athletic Liability: An Assessment Guide*, point out that:

Supervision of every aspect of transportation is essential, down to and including credentials of drivers, the type of licenses they possess, their competency with the vehicles they are driving under realistic load conditions, the purchasing of vehicles with proper adaptation for foreseeable loads and the number of passengers. (United Educators 1991)

The assessment guide, has seven important action steps that are applicable to those who manage transportation:

1. Draft a transportation policy and disseminate it to all personnel involved in athletic activities, clearly defining all responsibilities.

2. Ensure that procedures for obtaining authorization for all proposed transportation are clear and understood by all staff members and users.

3. Check to see that private carriers have appropriate permits and licenses and that certificates of insurance are obtained. Inquire as to whether the school is named an additionally insured.

4. Maintain individual records and files for each vehicle that includes (a) maintenance history and a list of accidents and repairs; and (b) an annual evaluation of the condition of the vehicle and its remaining expected life.

5. Establish a policy for use of personal vehicles in transporting athletes.

6. Establish an accident and injury reporting policy.

7. Establish an accident review board to determine the preventability or nonpreventability of accidents.

The sports administrator can use the items listed above to develop a sound transportation policy for student-athletes. The safety committee can be valuable in the process of developing a transportation plan, and discussion with the school's attorney and insurance carrier can determine the development of the plan. Staff meetings should be devoted to presenting the plan and answering any concerns regarding its implementation.

In addition to United Educators' action steps, I found the following suggestions regarding transportation to be helpful during my tenure as athletics director:

• Use only vehicles that are in safe driving condition.
• Try to secure adult drivers when possible. If this is not possible, consider student drivers who have excellent safety records and reputations for safe and careful driving.
• Go as a team and return as a team. Avoid letting individuals return on their own unless they comply with approved policy.
• If a staff member drives theircar on a regular basis for the athletics department, consult with the insurance carrier regarding liability.
• If involved in an accident, discuss the accident only with police or representatives of your insurance company.

States vary on requirements for employees driving school vehicles or personal cars and nonemployees, such as parents or other volunteers, driving student-athletes to events. The sports administrator needs to consult with the proper authorities in developing a sound policy when using any of the above persons to drive students.

The form listed below, attached to the glove compartment of every school vehicle, can be a tremendous help to any driver who encounters problems, and can help them answer questions if an accident occurs.

Notice—Emergency Procedures

In case of an accident or emergency:
Name of automobile insurance carrier
Address of insurance carrier
Policy No.:
Phone No.:
Always notify business office
A copy of the registration is in the glove box of the vehicle. The original is on file in the business office.
Emergency contacts:
Name
Office No.
Home No.
Name
Office No.
Home No.
College Security No.

The Cuyahoga Community College system in Cleveland, Ohio, has a travel form that can serve as a model for schools to use (see Appendix I).

6
Officials

Early in my career, I learned how coaches can trigger violence by their actions. In my first year of coaching basketball, I seldom got off the bench and the fans noticed this. Near the end of basketball season, in a hotly contested game, I called time-out to ask an official his interpretation of a controversial call. I was not angry or challenging the call, I was merely seeking information, and when the official responded I accepted his ruling and returned to the bench. I had absolutely no idea that the home crowd felt that I was upset, until the game ended. The team was in the dressing room when we heard frantic pounding on the locker room door. We were surprised to see the officials who were asking if they could escape through the restroom window to avoid the fans' attempts to assault them. I realized the effect I had on the supporters and tried thereafter to avoid what appeared to be harassment of officials.

My understanding of officials and their role in sports came when I joined the advisory board of the National Association of Sport Officials (NASO). As a nonofficial, I had a rare opportunity to experience first-hand the goals, integrity, and problems that confront the average official on all levels, from Little League to professional sports. I wish every coach and athletics director could share the experience I had and meet with officials like Jim Tunney (NFL football), Jim Bain (Big 8 and Big 10 basketball referee), and Joe Brinkman (American League baseball crew chief umpire).

Athletics directors have the responsibility to create the best possible climate between officials and participants, coaches, and spectators. In most instances, athletics directors on the secondary school and small college level are the game managers, while universities often designate a game manager. Game managers can prepare the way for successful relations with officials by meeting with the supervisor of officials prior to the start of a season. Rule interpretations, safety procedures, and other relevant information should be discussed which can facilitate things during the season. The athletics director or game manager, not the coach, has responsibility for the behind the scenes operation that ensures success. Several suggestions can assist the game manager with officials:

- Meet the officials prior to the game and provide them with a reserved parking spaces. Pay them before the game begins.
- Let the officials know where the athletic trainer, physician, and game manger will be located during the game.
- Provide locker room space for officials away from the home team, coach's locker room, or office. Nothing worries a coach more than seeing officials in close proximity to opposing head coaches.
- Talk with officials about the safety conditions of the particular playing field or gymnasium.
- Ensuring the safety and welfare of the student-athletes is top priority.
- In instances of disruption by spectators, have school officials help by using the public address system to talk to the crowd.
- Have a policy that officials needing treatment or taping use the athletic training room and not the coaches' locker room or office.
- If one coach wants to talk with an official, invite the opposing coach to join the discussion.
- It is important to remember that the athletics director of the host school has the responsibility for crowd control.
- When coaches want to issue a complaint have them go through the athletics director who, in turn, will contact the official's association, giving creditability to the complaint.
- Place security personnel behind the visitors bench to ensure player safety.

In the preseason meeting between the supervisor of officials and game managers, the question of procedures for injured athletes needs clarification. For several years, officials were advised to walk away from an injured athlete to avoid potential liability. A member of NASO's advisory board joined me in disagreeing with this recommendation and gave an example to support his opinion. In Florida, an officiating crew walked to the end of the field during a football game after a player was seriously injured. The crowd, observing the officials' action, became upset and voiced their displeasure at what appeared to be an uncaring act. In another situation, an official turned his back on an injured player and failed to protect the injured player from teammates who lifted him and dropped him to the ground exacerbating his injury. The player was rendered quadriplegic.

Atlantic Coast Conference (ACC) supervisors of football and basketball report that they have an understanding with coaches in both sports that a physician or athletic trainer can come on the field or court if they suspect a serious injury without being signaled on by an official. If the official is near the injured player, they recommend that he/she stand over the injured player reassuring him that help is on the way, and preventing teammates from touching the injured player. The official should not touch the injured player, preferring to protect until qualified medical personnel arrive on the scene. In basketball when a player is injured, the ACC supervisor recommends that the official near the injured player stand by while play continues, if it is away from the player, and to stop play whenever the player is in danger of additional injury.

Consider the action of an NCAA Division I-A institution's football coach who thought his players were getting soft and injury prone. He advised all concerned that a trainer or physician could not come on the field until he waved them on. He was determined to be the decision maker regarding medical issues. This was not a very safe thing to do. In another instance, a football coach highlighted a paragraph in his players handbook that warned athletes who did not return to practice when he deemed it necessary that, *punitive action would be taken*. In my opinion, a plaintiff's lawyer could use this statement in an injury case to great advantage.

The athletics director should be aware of such conduct and statements of policy and control action of this type. Once again if the student-athlete's safety is a priority, bad decisions like the ones above should be eliminated. The athletics director plays a key role with officials in all sports and can set a positive tone promoting safety and good sportsmanship.

7
Crowd Control

I was concerned for years over my responsibility as athletics director for the safety of those who participate and attend sporting events. Crowd control is a problem for athletics director no matter what part of the country or at what level. The athletics director can be held accountable for incidents that occur at events.

I received a telephone call from the athletics director for the entire city asking to use the stadium that day for a game between two intracity junior high school rivals. Because of previous incidents only the bus drivers, coaches, and administrators would know the site and no one else would be permitted to watch the game. In my travels, I found that several cities adopted similar procedures, and a western state played its basketball state finals in an empty gymnasium because of unruly crowd behavior and disruptions at previous tournament games.

Some people in sports advocated that we change "sudden death" playoffs to "sudden victory" and "crowd control" to "crowd accommodations." Neither term lasted long and while crowd accommodation is what it is all about, crowd control is more appropriate. In forty years, I think I have experienced just about every situation possible with game management and crowd control. The teams have been involved with fights of near-riot proportions, unruly spectators, belligerent participants, and attacks against game officials.

A potential problem stands out in my memory that fortunately was handled satisfactorily. A young basketball coach was devastated after a humiliating loss at the hands of a bitter rival. He was determined to even the score someday when the opposing team played in his tiny gymnasium, appropriately named the "Cracker Box." The rivalry intensified when the basketball team improved to a competitive level and was playing for the conference title. The coach came to me and asked not to exchange tickets for the big game against the rival that had humiliated him. He did not want anyone in the gymnasium but our students and fans. He was determined to gain every edge possible. Rather than accede to his wishes, I sent a limited number of tickets to the visiting school and a drawing was held during their chapel program to determine the lucky students who could attend the game. The coach became distraught when I tore down the derogatory signs the students had placed all over the walls and rafters.

Some years later he was a talent scout for a professional basketball team in the American Basketball Association (ABA). He reported that he attended a game in which thousands of spectators were unable to get in the sold-out gymnasium. Tempers flared, fights broke out inside and outside the arena and general confusion existed. He commented that the only person in the entire gymnasium that seemed to care and tried to resolve the crisis was the host athletics director. "I know now what you went through and I apologize for not understanding at the time," he said. He was right; crowd control is a universal problem that faces sports administrators at all levels, and in all countries. With this as reality, athletics directors need to develop and implement crowd control procedures to ensure the safety of all involved in athletic competition. There are several components to crowd control: preseason, pregame, during the game, and postgame. The following ideas seem to work for athletics administrators (Appenzeller 1970, 193–202).

A. Preseason

It is important for the athletics director or designated game manager to meet prior to the beginning of each season with representatives of the safety committee, campus security police, ticket takers, sellers, coaches, medical personnel, cheerleading sponsor, band director, student representative, and public address announcer. Anyone indirectly or directly involved in crowd control should attend the meeting because the more people that are involved the better. Put things in writing so everyone has an understanding of their role in the overall crowd control plan.

B. Pregame

1. Contact the visiting school's athletics director and schedule a meeting or discuss details over the telephone. Discuss any unusual situations regarding the arena or stadium.

2. Send a map of the campus to the visiting school's athletics director designating specific areas for parking, dressing rooms, bleacher areas, and other information.

3. Keep gates locked until time to open.

4. Provide well-lighted and supervised parking areas prior to, during, and following games.

5. Assign someone to meet the visiting team and make certain they know where things are located.

6. Have a security plan to protect the visiting team's and home team's valuables.

7. Reserve parking for visiting team officials, physicians, and game officials (referees).

8. Distribute checks to game officials, representatives of visiting teams, and others prior to the game.

9. Custodians should check the restrooms and other facilities.

10. Determine the number of police needed for each game.

C. During the game

1. Keep sidelines clear of unauthorized people. Provide armbands or badges for authorized personnel from each school. Utilize police to keep sidelines clear.

2. Rope off areas to restrict unauthorized people from the sidelines.

3. Have a medical response plan and be prepared to implement it in emergencies.

4. Have an emergency medical service or ambulance on site in the event of a medical emergency.

5. Designate someone to provide personnel with updated directions and information.

6. Print warnings in the game program or announce over the public address system that, "No one is allowed on the field or court during or after games and no one is to engage in body passing or other hazardous conduct. Violators will be asked and expected to leave."

D. Postgame

1. Keep police on duty until all spectators and the visiting team have gone.

2. Confer with visiting team officials to discuss any problems relating to the game.

3. Write down any suggestions regarding game day procedures.

7.5 General Suggestions

The host school athletics director can utilize several suggestions to facilitate a smooth game day operation:

- Check the terms of the current contract at least one week prior to the game.
- Check the availability of a game day physician and medical emergency vans.
- Meet the visiting team.
- Oversee the distribution of game programs.
- Check on ticket takers, sellers, press box attendants, scoreboard, officials dressing room, ambulance, and public address announcer.

• Check on opening ceremony.
• Designate someone to handle crowd control duties in the event you are absent.
• Stagger police scheduling so all do not arrive and leave at the same time.
• In the event of spectator ejection, provide a suitable location for those who are removed.
• Reserve seats for the bands.
• Assign a competent person to take charge of the scoreboard.
• Have properly trained scorers and timers for the game officials.
• Avoid scheduling high-risk halftime activities.

There are several groups that can assist the athletics director or game manager in crowd control procedures such as officials, cheerleaders, and public address announcers. These groups can be invaluable in game day operation.

A. Officials

Game officials are responsible for the conduct of players and coaches on the playing surfaces and enforce the rules of the game. Therefore, they must be able to officiate a contest without fear of retaliation or physical injury from spectators. It is good risk management strategy to escort them to and from the playing field with security or school staff members.

B. Cheerleaders

Cheerleaders should be encouraged to avoid cheers that provoke hostile action from opponents. Cheerleaders should cheer in a positive manner using cheers that boost their team, without antagonizing opponents. Cheerleaders should remain quiet when opposing players have a free throw, applaud when an injured player leaves the arena or playing field, and lead welcome cheers for visitors.

C. Announcers

The announcer is a key person and carries a great deal of responsibility for setting the tone for positive crowd behavior. What is said and how it is said can greatly affect the behavior of the crowd. The game should be reported without showing favoritism to teams or players. Proper language should be used at all times. Show enthusiasm without losing control. Only those authorized to use the microphone should be permitted to announce or report the game. An official's decision should not be criticized directly or indirectly.

Planning and implementing crowd control procedures is time consuming, but in the long run it is time well spent.

7.6 Special Situations

Athletics programs have been challenged by boycotts, take-over of facilities, bomb threats, and other disruptive behavior. Athletics directors, unaware of the legal aspects of disruption, are vulnerable to the tactics of student activists. Students often take advantage of the administrator's lack of legal knowledge to obtain concessions "that have little relation to either law or education (*Washington Post* 1969). In most cases involving disruptive behavior, students assert that they have freedom of expression guaranteed by the First Amendment of the United States Constitution. The courts consistently hold, however, that institutions have the right to set reasonable rules to govern their campuses and students have an obligation to follow these rules. Students may lose their constitutional rights when disruption is accompanied by force. United States Supreme Court Justice Arthur Goldberg held that school officials can take disciplinary action when disruptive behavior takes place. Goldberg said:

> We do not subscribe to the notion that a citizen surrenders his civil rights upon enrollment as a student in a school. As a corollary to this, enrollment does not give him the right to immunity nor special consideration, and certainly does not give him the right to violate the constitutional rights of others. (*Buttney v. Smiley* 1968)

I realized during the days of activism against the Vietnam War that a group of militant students could disrupt an athletics event. We had no plan or policy to meet such a crisis. I could envision protesting students occupying the basketball court during a game and I could foresee tension and fighting among the protestors and students. I also knew that college officials did not want police to intervene. I asked for guidance and received good advice. One administrator, other than the athletics director, would be present at each home basketball and football game where problems might arise. If demonstrators took over the facilities, the administrator would acknowledge that a problem existed and invite the students to meet off the court or field to discuss the grievance. However, if the protestors refused to leave, the administrator would summon the police to escort them out. I felt secure because an approved policy was in place.

During Desert Storm, a group of protestors disrupted the singing of the national anthem prior to the start of a basketball game between Minnesota and Northwestern Universities in Minneapolis. The protestors objected to the players wearing United States flags on their uniforms and displayed a banner that read "Athletes are not flagpoles." The "protestors lay down on the court and made moaning, crying sounds. They left after the anthem was over." (Appenzeller and Baron 1991). Setting policy before disruptive behavior occurs is sound risk management strategy.

National Anthem

We played the national anthem prior to our basketball and football games. It was a tradition in our program. On one occasion, a group of students refused to stand during the playing of the national anthem, preferring to sit quietly in the packed gymnasium with heads bowed. An irate alumnus raced toward me after the game and ordered me to terminate a member of the group's football scholarship. When I told him that his only financial assistance was a federal Pell Grant, he shouted, "Let the government take it away then." I attended a meeting of the state high school athletic advisory board several months later. Two basketball officials, who were also members of the board, reported that a principal grabbed several students and literally threw them out of the high school gymnasium because they refused to stand during the national anthem. They commented on the principal's action: "We loved it." I referred the board members to a New York court case in which three students refused to stand or repeat the pledge of allegiance to the flag (NOLPE Notes 1970). The students argued that the words of the pledge did not apply to them and repeating them would violate their conscience. They claimed that the Constitution of the United States protected their freedom to abstain from repeating the pledge.

The Justice responded to critics who believe that school officials should remove dissenters from the stadium, classroom, and athletic field by ruling that:

> students had a right to silent protest by remaining seated and that the right included the privilege of expressing themselves in their own way as long as they didn't disrupt the school or infringe on the rights of others. School officials will have to prove disruption or infringements of other's rights before discipline can take place. (NOLPE Notes 1970)

Students or spectators have the right to dissent if they sit quietly during the pledge of allegiance or national anthem.

Bomb Threats

Two telephoned bomb threats delayed a basketball game between New Mexico University and Texas-El Paso. The standing room crowd of 18,000 had to be evacuated from University Arena (Appenzeller and Baron 1991). As athletics director, what would you do if you received a telephone threat minutes before the start of your biggest game of the year?

Frank Russo, an event management authority, states that, "A code system to communicate critical information should be developed and all security personnel should be required to memorize and use it." A code system should be developed for a bomb threat as well as fire, medical emergencies, accidents, and disruptive activities. Russo suggests the development of a manual for all security personnel that is written in plain and simple language. The manual should provide guidelines that describe what is expected of security personnel when emergencies such as bomb threats arise. Solicit input and written approval of emergency procedures in the manual from "the state and local fire marshal, police civil preparedness departments, and contractual medical and ambulance services" (Lewis and Appenzeller 1985).

The emergency evacuation plan should be outlined in detail with specific directions for making a search with instructions on how to deal with a bomb if it is discovered. Employees should stay calm and never use panic words such as "bomb," "fire," or "explosion." Many facilities use a phase coding system to report a particular type of problem to personnel because the purpose of the coding system is to prevent "the greatest of all threats, panic." Russo explains the coding system:

Phase 1A indicates smoke, water, or small crowd disturbance or lighting failure. Descriptive information should be provided on the location, size, seriousness, and nature of the problem. Security should clear the immediate area until the problem has been controlled.

Phase 1B indicates a bomb threat has been received and all staff should immediately conduct a search for an explosive device. Notification should be given when the search is completed.

Phase 2B indicates that a suspicious package or device has been located. The fire department and police bomb squad should be dispatched to investigate and decide whether or not a full or limited evacuation is necessary. Ambulances should be called for standby.

Phase 3B indicates the need for an immediate emergency evacuation. Appropriate alarm must be sounded and pre-recorded messages activated. Ambulances should be called for standby and the security/usher staff should begin to calmly but firmly evacuate patrons. Security should also be sure no patrons reenter the building regardless of the reason (Lewis and Appenzeller 1985).

The athletics director or facility manager should establish the chain of command and determine who has the responsibility to call for an evacuation. In most instances, that decision is the responsibility of the "ranking on-site member of the police bomb squad." It is essential to develop a telephone bomb report form for the person who receives the bomb threat call. The phone operator needs training by the bomb squad of the police department to keep the person talking to try and learn the location of the bomb. The information should be recorded and reported as soon as possible to the event manager, athletics director, or police department. Most people who actually place a bomb in a building "want" to be caught or the bomb found before it goes off. The

University of California at Berkeley has a thorough detailed procedure plan for bomb threats and a checklist for the phone operator. It includes the following items:

Bomb Threat

Questions to Ask
1. When is bomb going to explode?
2. Where is it right now?
3. What does it look like?
4. What kind of bomb is it?
5. What will cause it to explode?
6. Did you place the bomb?
7. Why?
8. What is your address?
9. What is your name?

Exact Wording of Threat

Caller's Voice

__ Calm	__ Nasal
__ Angry	__ Stutter
__ Excited	__ Lisp
__ Slow	__ Raspy
__ Rapid	__ Deep
__ Soft	__ Ragged
__ Loud	__ Clearing throat
__ Laughter	__ Deep breathing
__ Crying	__ Cracking voice
__ Normal	__ Disguised
__ Distinct	__ Accent
__ Slurred	__ Familiar
__ Threat language	__ Message read by threat maker
__ Well spoken (educated)	__ Incoherent
__ Foul	__ Taped
__ Irrational	

Remarks:

Background Sounds

__ Office Machinery   __ Factory machinery
__ Street noises   __ Animal noises
__ Crockery   __ Clear
__ Voices   __ Static
__ PA system   __ Local
__ Music   __ Long distance
__ House   __ Booth
__ Motor   __ Other

Report call immediately to:

Phone number

Date   /   /

Name

Position

(University of California at Berkeley 1989).

The athletics director or event manager should post the procedures in strategic areas and institute a series of practice drills so that personnel can develop a routine for emergencies. Russo notes that a facility and its patrons are always vulnerable to emergencies such as bomb threats, and concludes:

The best defense is a plan carefully evolved to fit the facility and the organization. Being able to evacuate a facility in an emergency with a minimum of injury or loss of life is one of the greatest challenges and responsibilities. (Lewis and Appenzeller 1985)

Planning and implementing crowd control procedures is time consuming, but in the long run it is time well spent.

8
Drug Education

A well-respected sports administrator at an NCAA Division I institution commented that his drug testing and drug education programs were working extremely well, serving as a deterrent to the use of drugs by the athletes at his institution. He was sincere in his perception of the situation that existed at his institution until one of his outstanding athletes died unexpectedly and tragically from a drug overdose. National attention was focused on this university and the negative publicity turned the program into chaos.

This colleague was not alone. For years I believed that the athletics program was free from drugs. I was unaware of any problems and, I must confess, very naive. I should have suspected something when I observed a 175-pound freshman graduating four years later at 220 pounds or a 165-pound baseball player leaving school at 250 pounds. I gave too much credit to the weight training program, attributing the growth in muscle to student-athletes who trained daily with unusual dedication.

In 1986, I witnessed the banning of twenty-five intercollegiate athletes, including Oklahoma's Brian Bosworth, an All-American linebacker, from postseason play for using anabolic steroids. Canadian sprinter, Ben Johnson, received international attention when he forfeited his gold medal in the 100 meters at the Seoul, Korea, Olympics for using steroids.

The NCAA budgeted an estimated $3.2 million for drug testing in 1990. It is estimated that it would cost approximately $100 million to drug test every high school athlete; a figure prohibitive in a day when sports budgets are being drastically cut, eliminated, or subjected to individual fees for participation.

After I became aware of the seriousness of the problem I met with the sports medicine coordinator who agreed to two things: (1) a willingness to be a confidential counselor to the student-athletes to discuss the use of anabolic steroids and other drugs, and (2) a desire to research and investigate every aspect of drug testing and education. He spent considerable time visiting universities and testing centers throughout the nations that were leaders in the field of drug education and testing. He became convinced that educational programs regarding drugs will not succeed unless a drug testing component in included to the program. We held a series of forums regarding drug testing on campus to allow interested parties the opportunity to discuss the implementation of a drug testing program for the athletics department. The opposition to a formal drug testing program was so overwhelming that it was shelved. Although drug testing received little support, the confidential counseling proved helpful.

Private and public schools face different guidelines when they consider a drug testing program. The courts have ruled in several instances, but clarity is needed regarding the legality of testing. In the event an institution plans to develop and implement a drug testing program, it should discuss the proposed drug testing policies thoroughly with school counsel and school officials.

Dr. Jerald Hawkins, the sports medicine coordinator, moved to Lander College in Greenwood, South Carolina, where he holds a similar position. Hawkins developed a handout for students that answers questions regarding the use of drugs, such as (1) Is it safe? (2) Is it legal? (3) Is it effective?

8.1 Drugs and Other Ingesta: Effects on Athletic Performance
by Dr. Jerald Hawkins

Many substances are taken by athletes with the belief that they are ergogenic (work-enhancing) and will improve performance, while other substances are consumed with the belief that they are harmless and will have no adverse effect on performance. Before an athlete is permitted to use any substance (vitamins, steroids, alcohol, etc.), three important questions must be considered:

1. Is it safe?
2. Is it legal?
3. Is it effective?

Unless all three of these questions can be answered affirmatively, use of the substance should be discouraged. The following are some of the more common drugs and ingesta used by athletes:

Amphetamines

Amphetamines are synthetic drugs that stimulate the central nervous system. Often found in cold medications and "diet pills," amphetamines are generally used by athletes to produce a feeling of stimulation or "being up" to attempt to delay fatigue or to increase aggression.

The physiological effects of amphetamines include

• An artificially induced heart rate increase,
• Peripheral vasoconstriction,
• Blood pressure increase, and
• Masking of the normal fatigue response.

Is it safe? Because of its paradoxical effects on the cardiovascular system and its masking of fatigue, this is a very dangerous drug when used during exercise of any type.

Is it legal? Amphetamines are basically prescription medications, and are among drugs banned by the International Olympic Committee (IOC) and other governing bodies.

Is it effective? Research has failed to demonstrate any significant performance enhancement with amphetamine intake.

Androgenic anabolic steroids

Anabolic steroids are drug compounds containing male hormones, primarily testosterone. They are often used by athletes with the belief that they will produce gains in muscle size.

The physiological effects of anabolic steroids include

• Stimulation of male sex characteristics.
• Liver dysfunction.
• Choestatic jaundice.
• Liver tumors (possibly cancerous).
• Possible improvement in protein metabolism.
• Male-specific effects including
  — Reduced spermatogenesis,
  — Testicular atrophy, and
  — Prostate damage.
• Female-specific effects including
  — Menstrual alterations, and
  — Unwanted male sex characteristics.
• Adolescent-specific effects including
  — Premature epiphyseal closure,
  — Muscle/tendon strength imbalance, and
  —Degenerative orthopedic disease.

Is it safe? Anabolic steroids are considered to be among the most dangerous drugs used by athletes in an attempt to gain a "competitive edge."

Is it legal? Anabolic steroids are banned by the IOC, NCAA, and other sports governing bodies.

Is it effective? It is true that steroids are probably effective in producing gains in muscle size and strength in some people under certain conditions. However, research has failed to conclusively determine the specific relationship between steroids and muscle hypertrophy. One known side effect of steroid use is water retention, and it is speculated that some increase in muscle girth may be the result of intramuscular water content.

Somatotropin (human growth hormone)

Somatotropin is a growth hormone usually extracted from the pituitary glands of cadavers or primates. It is used in the United States for children with pituitary-related growth deficiencies, but it has recently become popular with athletes who hope that it will increase their body size and strength.

The physiological effects of somatotropin include

* Enhanced general body growth, though it has not been established if this occurs in anyone other than those with growth hormone deficiency.
* Acromegaly—An irregular growth of feet, jaw bones, hands, etc., producing a Frankenstein-like appearance.
* Medical history indicates that persons who experience gigantism (abnormal growth) and acromegaly have a significantly shorter life span than their "normal" counterparts.
* Other specific effects are currently under scientific study.

Is it safe? Current information available on the side effects of somatotropin raises serious questions regarding the safety of its use.

Is it legal? Because growth hormone is an endogenous substance (found naturally in the body), standards for acceptance levels have been difficult to establish. However, the IOC and similar bodies have placed human growth hormone on its list of banned substances. Also, it is illegal in most states to use human growth hormone for any human purpose other than the medical treatment of growth hormone deficiency.

Is it effective? Somatotropin has been shown to be effective in treating children with growth hormone deficiencies. However, research has not established its effectiveness in healthy adults.

Dextrose (sugar) tablets

Dextrose tablets (and other sugar forms) are used by athletes in an attempt to provide "quick energy" prior to or during competition. The effects of "sugar pills" are no different from those of dietary sugar.

Is it safe? Dextrose is as safe as any other sugar form.

Is it legal? Yes.

Is it effective? No. There is no "quick energy" substance, and dextrose tablets offer no advantage over sugar consumed as a part of the athlete's daily diet.

Oxygen

Oxygen is commonly used by athletes in an attempt to recover more quickly from strenuous exercise or to enhance performance during strenuous exercise. The primary physiological effect of oxygen intake is a temporary increase in oxyhemoglobin saturation.

Is it safe? There appear to be no negative side effects associated with oxygen ingestion.

Is it legal? Yes.

Is it effective? Research has failed to show any significant increase in work capacity or decrease in recovery time associated with oxygen ingestion. The one exception is the use of oxygen by athletes working in an environment of oxygen deprivation (high altitudes). For oxygen to have a favorable physiological effect, it would need to be consumed while exercising.

The concept of "recreational drug use" provides a sad commentary on the current state of our society. However, it must be recognized that athletes, like their nonathlete counterparts, often abuse drugs with the misconception that such behavior will have little if any negative effect on their athletic performance. While the abuse of drugs is recognized as an unsafe (and often illegal) practice, the athlete must also understand the potential negative effects that such abuse may have an his/her athletic performance.

Alcohol

Alcohol is the most commonly abused drug in the United States and is often used by athletes with the belief that it will not adversely affect their performance.

Alcohol can cause

- Impairment of the liver's glycogen production capacity.
- Depression of the brain's respiratory center, limiting CO_2 removal.
- Inhibition of the release of antidiuretic hormone, causing excessive fluid loss via urination. This can cause the loss of cellular potassium into the extracellular space.
- Appearance of nystagmus (bouncing of the eyeballs when the head is turned, causing difficulty in focusing). This condition has been shown to exist for several hours after alcohol consumption.
- A decrease in the body's magnesium level resulting in possible adverse effects on carbohydrate metabolism. It is also believed to have an adverse effect on muscle relaxation capacity.
- Inhibition of the body's ability to absorb certain essential nutrients.
- May adversely affect strength, endurance, speed, and power.

Tobacco

Tobacco is used recreationally by many athletes. While tobacco's worst effects relate directly to smoking, it should be noted that the effects of smokeless tobacco are currently under investigation, and

currently available information indicates that it is not a safe, harmless practice, and may lead to death via oral or throat cancer.
Tobacco can cause

• A decrease in airway conductance (up to 50% after only ten inhalations);
• A reduction in the oxygen-carrying capacity of the blood via carboxyhemoglobin (carbon monoxide/hemoglobin) bonding;
• Acceleration of the clotting process; and
• Chronic pulmonary obstruction.

Marijuana

In many segments of our population, the recreational use of "pot" is more common than that of alcohol. Unfortunately, this is also true of the athletic community.

Marijuana can cause
• Depression of pulmonary function;
• Chronic pulmonary obstruction;
• Irregular blood pressure responses during changes in body position;
• Tachycardia;
• EKG changes;
• Reduction in the oxygen-carrying capacity of the blood via carboxyhemoglobin (carbon monoxide/hemoglobin) bonding; and
• Inhibition of the normal sweating responses resulting in increased body temperature.

Cocaine and "Crack"

One of the most disturbing trends in today's athletic community is the use of cocaine and "crack." Not only is this an addictive and potentially deadly practice, the effects on the body can adversely affect the athlete's ability to perform.
Cocaine and crack can cause

• Tachycardia;
• Vasoconstriction;
• Elevated blood pressure;
• Chronic rhinitis (greater vulnerability to upper respiratory infection);
• Possible coronary artery spasms and myocardial infarction;
• Cellulose granulomas in the lungs; and
• Vascular blockage caused by the inert substances used to cut cocaine when injected.

For sports administrators who want to develop a drug testing program, I recommend the policy used by Lander College. It is efficient, cost effective, and legally sound (see Appendix J).

The American Council on Education (ACE) developed guidelines for institutions that initiate drug testing programs. ACE urges schools to provide students with "clear written procedures governing the program and only when they intend to abide strictly by those procedures." ACE recommends that institutions that drug test accompany the testing program with a drug education program that includes a rehabilitation program for students who have used drugs. The ACE guidelines are as follows:

Resource Documents for Colleges and Universities

Student Athlete Drug Testing Programs

Introduction

Colleges and universities are properly interested in the use of drugs by student athletes. Performance-affecting drugs undermine the integrity of athletic competition, which is grounded on the principle that athletic achievement is the result of individual and team ability, training, and motivation. Tolerance of drug abuse by student athletes encourages others to use drugs to equalize the competition. Drug use may also pose a risk of injury or even long-term harm to self and others. Additionally, drug use by student athletes damages the institution in the eyes of the public.

Given these causes for concern, many colleges and universities have undertaken, or are considering, routine testing to detect and deter use of drugs by college athletes. While many college and university officials are drawn to the notion of drug testing by the concern over the harms caused by drug use, they should also consider the interests of student athletes—many of whom, of course, do not use drugs—in minimizing intrusive and embarrassing testing. Some feel that such tests constitute an invasion of students' privacy and, in effect, require students to prove their "innocence." There are, in addition, the risks of mistaken test results and intentional or unintentional misuse or unauthorized release of confidential testing information.

Accordingly, colleges and universities should undertake drug testing programs only after giving thought and care to the development of clear, written procedures governing the program, and only when they intend to abide strictly by those procedures. The alternative can be protracted and costly litigation. It is possible that some courts will strike down testing programs that are not so closely related to important institutional interests as to justify the effects of the program on the student athletes. Consistent with the goal of avoiding unnecessary intrusion into students' private lives, testing should be scheduled so as to detect drug use likely to affect athletic performance, not merely any use of drugs at any time by an athlete.

Any institution with a drug testing program should also provide a formal drug education program with emphasis on the hazards of drugs in regard to their use generally as well as in athletics specifically. Coaches, trainers, student trainers, and student managers should also be involved in the educational program. Likewise, assistance should be provided in rehabilitating student athletes who have engaged in the use of performance-affecting drugs.

No institution should institute a drug testing program without first conferring with its legal counsel. Institutions and their counsel may wish to consider the following guidelines in devising or reviewing programs:

Guidelines

1. The purpose of programs testing intercollegiate athletes for use of drugs should be to detect and deter use of performance-affecting drugs that undermine the integrity of athletic competition and to promote the physical and/or psychological well-being of athletes. Tests should focus upon drugs whose abuse can reasonably be anticipated to affect performance, health, or safety in athletic competition. It is undesirable to employ drug testing programs to detect more general use of drugs.

Each program should be set forth fully and completely in writing. Each element of the testing program should be covered, including the responsibilities of all persons administering the program, the persons entitled to receive confidential information, and the procedures to be followed to preserve the confidentiality of the information.

2. The drug testing program should incorporate procedures to protect the accurate identification of each individual's test results and provide for additional verification of initial positive test results through reliable test procedures.

3. The drug testing program should provide students for whom test results are positive with notice and the right to a hearing prior to any adverse action based on the test. The hearing procedures should afford the student the opportunity to present information in his or her defense and to challenge evidence and testimony against him or her before neutral hearing officers. Procedures should incorporate a right of review and appeal prior to the imposition of severe sanctions, such as loss of eligibility or rescission of an athletic scholarship. University counsel familiar with the requirements of due process in student disciplinary cases should be consulted about the procedures that should be established and followed in cases involving positive drug tests.

4. The drug testing program should include procedures protecting the privacy of all student athletes. Information disclosed by testing must be restricted to personnel responsible for administering the pro-

gram. No other release of the information is to be authorized without the athlete's written consent or appropriate legal process.

5. The drug testing program should include written rules governing each step of the program, including: means of selecting student athletes for testing; scheduling and collection of samples; testing of samples; determination that a test result is positive; means of verification of positive results; communication with student athletes and third parties about positive test results; counselling to be provided; sanctions to be imposed for violations of the drug use policy; applicable hearing/due process procedures; and schedule of penalties imposed for particular violations or cumulative violations.

6. Each student athlete subject to drug testing should receive a copy of the rules, together with written materials explaining how the program is to operate. There must be clear and unambigous disclosure of all elements of the program, including such risks as there may be of disclosure of information to third parties. Participants should sign acknowledgements that they have received the pertinent materials, had the opportunity to ask questions, and decided to participate in the program. The drug testing program should require students to give their written consent to the program prior to their participation in any intercollegiate athletic program.

7. Any college with a testing program should provide full and complete information about the program to all intercollegiate athletic recruits early in any recruitment process (and certainly before any recruit makes a decision upon any offer from the college) and to all student athletes prior to their enrollment.

8. The information provided to students should at a minimum include the written program itself; a full description of the purposes of the drug testing program; the procedures for collecting samples; procedures upon determination that a test result is positive, including both verification of the result and the hearing procedures; and sanctions to be imposed for the first and subsequent violations of the drug use policy as determined by the testing program. The information should be clear, complete and accurate, and acknowledge the risk that information from the testing program may be accessible to third parties.

9. The drug testing program should include procedures for training (and regularly monitoring or retraining) college personnel in all aspects of their responsibilities related to the program, including: testing techniques; the need to adhere to the governing rules and procedures; legal rights and responsibilities implicated by the program; the overriding need for confidentiality of information about drug testing results; and who is to be consulted in the event of any questions or controversies that may arise.

10. Any college with a student athlete drug testing program should also have a policy forbidding any college personnel from providing performance-affecting drugs or encouraging or otherwise inducing stu-

dent athletes to use drugs, except as specific drugs may be prescribed by qualified medical personnel for treatment of individual students. The college should also establish and publicize its procedures for handling complaints that staff or faculty has encouraged or induced use of performance-affecting drugs. Such complaints should be processed by institution personnel independent of the athletic department and who have full authority to investigate such allegations.

9
Sports Medicine Services

Dr. James Nicholas, an orthopedic surgeon, received national attention as Joe Namath's surgeon when Namath was drafted by the New York Jets in the National Football League. Dr. Nicholas commented that Namath would have been turned down for professional football if sports medicine had been a reality in 1964 (Appenzeller 1980, 221). Nicholas noted that, "sports medicine is one of the fastest growing areas of interest among orthopedic surgeons and team physicians." Today, sports medicine is one of medicine's newest subspecialties.

9.1 Who is Responsible?

The sports administrator wears many hats, but none, in my opinion, is more important or of a higher priority than sports medicine. The sports administrator has responsibility for the sports medicine budget, personnel, insurance, record keeping, certification, general medical policies, preparticipation physical examinations, physician contracts, and related matters. In addition, the sports administrator must review the sports medicine team and evaluate the program on a regular basis.

9.2 Organization

Dr. Jerald Hawkins, Sports Medicine Coordinator at Lander College and an authority in the field of sports medicine, writes that successful sports medicine programs are well organized. He notes that organizational success doesn't just happen and without a chart or organizational model

the sports medicine program will not function as effectively as possible. At best it will become a group of individuals each performing the duties that he/she deems appropriate, inevitably resulting in duplication in some services and a complete absence of others. (Lewis and Appenzeller 1985 82)

Hawkins suggests the following organizational model

Sample Organizational Model

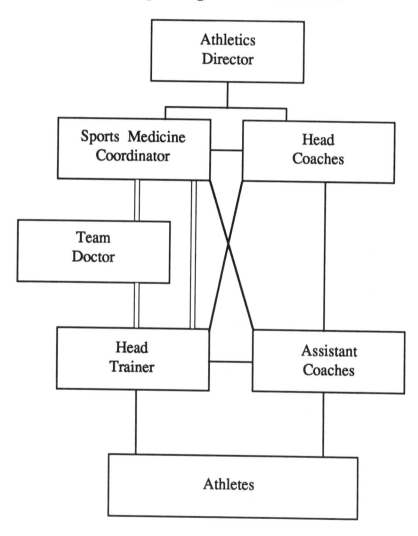

9.3 Problem Areas

Major problems for the sports administrator in administering the sports medicine program include inadequate knowledge of sports medicine, lack of standards, poor communication, and lack of a system within the school. Another very real problem is the fact that two-thirds of all sports-related injuries occur at practice when personnel are less prepared to handle medical emergencies. At most contests (at least for collision sports such as football and ice hockey), physicians, proper equipment, and ambulances are usually present to care for the injured participant.

9.4 The Sports Medicine Team

The sports administrator has the duty to develop the best sports medicine team according to available resources. Several years ago an athletics director at a major Division I-A school reported that because it cost $200 per student-athlete for a preparticipation physical examination, he decided to forego the examinations strictly because his budget could not afford it. Many institutions utilize their health services for examinations of nonrevenue sports using team physicians from revenue sports such as football and basketball. The sports administrator should develop a system that provides for preparticipation physical examinations. See Appendix K for a student medical history form, a parental medical form, an emergency medical contact form, and a physicians postillness consent form. In addition, see a postinjury agreement for intercollegiate athletics.

9.5 Athletics Trainer

As a coach on both the high school and college level, I had to assume the duties of head trainer over the years because there was simply no certified athletics trainer. Although the number of schools employing certified trainers is increasing, many states lack trainers. In one far western state, the only certified trainers are the few employed for college programs and in professional sports. Efforts should continue to employ certified athletics trainers. The comment I hear most often when a trainer is hired is, "What did we ever do without a trainer."

When the school added several sports to the program, by necessity, part-time coaches with little or no sports medicine background were hired. These coaches became concerned that a serious injury would occur and they would not know what to do. They feared for the safety of their student-athletes and liability to themselves. After 143 years, a certified athletics trainer was finally hired for the athletics program. Today the college sponsors thirteen sports, has two certified trainers, a National Athletic Trainer's Association (NATA) certified graduate assistant, and twenty-five student trainers. The athletes, coaches, and athletics director appreciate the institution's commitment to the student-athletes.

9.6 Teacher Athletics Trainers

I realize that a number of schools still continue to use coaches as trainers. Such a situation places the coach in a precarious position—first because the coach may lack the knowledge necessary to recognize and treat sports injuries, and second because of a possible conflict of interest. For whatever reason, the coach may be critized for returning an injured student-athlete to practice or games too soon.

The state of North Carolina has addressed this problem and has pioneered in implementing a teacher athletics trainer (TAT) program. North Carolina's legislature passed a bill that provides emergency life saving services in sports medicine for its students. The goal of the legislature was to employ a teacher athletics trainer (TAT) for every school in North Carolina that offers a sports program. The primary goal is "a reduction in the rate of injuries and reinjuries, and total prevention of deaths and catastrophic injuries in sports activities" (Shahady and Petrizzi 1988, 153). In addition the legislature, in cooperation with the state's sport medicine department, set goals that included prevention of injuries, a provision for emergency medical treatment, rehabilitation of sports injuries, paramedical lifesaving, and cardiopulmonary resuscitation (CPR). A minimun of four basic courses are required for TATs: standard first aid, basic athletic training, advanced athletic training, and CPR. All TATs are encouraged to pursue NATA certification, which represents the highest level of expertise available to athletic trainers.

9.7 Coach

The athletics director, sports medicine coordinator, or athletic trainer may set guidelines and policies, obtain adequate insurance coverage, provide transportation, and develop a communications system for the sports medicine program, but the coach's role is still paramount. Alan Haines, a certified athletic trainer, writing in the *Cramer First Aider*, admits that while the administrator is in charge of the details of the sports medicine program, "in reality, it all boils down to the coach."

Everyone involved in coaching is involved with emergency care and first aid. Each coach should evaluate his or her program to decide how it should be handled. By virtue of the position held, the coach is expected to exercise a certain standard of care in all actions involving the welfare of the athletes. This obviously includes first aid and emergency care. The coach cannot plead ignorance of safety factors and first aid techniques. (Haines 1984)

Many athletics directors realize the truth in Haines's statement and acknowledge that it is impossible to have an athletic trainer or physician available at all practices and games. For this reason, coaches and other staff members are encouraged to become certified in emergency first aid and CPR. Such certification is not a national standard at this time, but may become one in the future.

9.8 The Team Physician

In most instances, the team physician is usually the only member of the sports medicine team who is a nonemployee of the school or organization. Athletics directors should look for an individual who has a genuine interest in young people and has a love of sports. Thomas Newton, a family physician, writes that

A physician whose basic training included all forms of illnesses is an ideal choice for the role of team physician, particularly if he/she continues to keep up with sports medicine issues through continuing education opportunities. (Shahady and Petrizzi 1988, 158)

Dr. Jerald Hawkins, writing in *Successful Sports Management*, suggests that the team physician

Compile and maintain a medical history of each program participant;
• Conduct preparticipation physical examinations;
• Attend all games or contests and as many practices as feasible;
• Supervise and provide instruction to sports medicine personnel;
• Be available to see injured program participants during regular office hours and provide treatment or referral as deemed appropriate;
• Be "on call" for the emergency care of injured participants at times other than during office hours;
• Make decisions relative to the return to action of injured participants; and
• Work closely with the other members of the "sports medicine team" in establishing policy and coordinating program activities. (Lewis and Appenzeller 1985, 81)

When a school utilizes the services of a physician outside the umbrella of the school (this is characteristic of most sports programs), it is a good administrative strategy to use a physicians agreement. The agreement between the institution and the physician is extremely important for both because it defines responsibilities and thereby protects both parties. A sample is found in Appendix L.

9.9 Policies and Procedures

There is a need for the athletics director to develop policies and procedures for the sports medicine team and make certain everyone understands them. In some instances, coaches overrule athletics trainer's decisions causing tension and a lack of trust. This still exists in many schools. It is less likely to happen today, but unfortunately coaches do overrule athletic trainers.

Mary Broos, North Carolina trainer of the year, comments that "any coach who overrules an NATA certified athletic trainer is placing himself/herself in a position of extreme jeopardy with regard to a potential lawsuit." Dr. Jerald Hawkins agrees:

> In my opinion, a coach who knowingly chooses to override a trainer's decision should understand that the coach must accept legal responsibility for the consequences of his action. Also, this should be conveyed to the coach and administrator in writing with a copy maintained on file in the trainer's office. (Appenzeller and Baron 1989, 11)

The sports administrator, in cooperation with the athletics trainer, should develop a policy manual/handbook for the coaches and sports medicine staff. The athletics trainer or sports administrator should discuss medical policies at a preseason staff meeting. The athletics trainer should conduct sessions with student trainers so that everyone knows the modus operandi and protocol regarding injuries to student-athletes.

Some of the items that should be included in the handbook are personal conduct, training room policies, daily duties, daily practice schedule duties, game day procedures, injury management guidelines, classification of individual treatment card, treatment selection policy, athletic training regulations for student athletes, record keeping procedures, and modalities and guidelines.

9.10 Sports Emergencies

Without an athletic trainer

When a school lacks an athletic trainer or TAT, the sports administrator should have a plan prepared before the season begins that includes the following strategies:

1. Keep a chart on file with the telephone numbers of the players' family physicians or the nearest physician available to the school.

2. Have the numbers of the local hospital and ambulance service available.

3. Appoint a staff member to administer first aid in an emergency. This person should be certified in emergency first aid and CPR.

4. Designate a staff member to transport the injured person to a physician or hospital.

5. Have exact change (coins) needed for an emergency call taped in the on-field first aid kit.

6. Consider purchasing walkie-talkies or cellular telephones for use on fields that are a distance from the training room.

With an athletic trainer

The following written guidelines can be adapted to particular programs when an athletic trainer is part of the sports medicine staff. The guidelines are those used at Guilford College and may serve as a model. They were developed by Mary Broos, Dickson Schaefer, athletic trainers, and Dr. David Martin, orthopaedic surgeon and team physician.

Sports Emergencies

The sports medicine staff consists of the head athletic trainer, the assistant athletic trainer, student athletic trainers, and the team physician. These individuals provide health care to athletes participating in the intercollegiate sports program. During the course of practice sessions and games, medical problems or injuries may occur which necessitate emergency care or transport. The following guidelines and action plans outline those steps to be taken in the event of emergency.

General Guidelines

1. The most senior athletic training staff member present will be the team leader.

2. Rescue service will be provided by an EMS unit for all home football games.

3. Communication steps to be taken to access EMS units:

   a) Handheld radios to security (Channel 1). Security will telephone EMS and meet them at the campus entrance to escort them to the site of the emergency.

   b) During practices, a handheld radio will provide communication between the practice area and the staff trainers. Channel 2 is to be used by sports medicine and intramural athletics. Channel 1 is only to be used to contact security. Two radios are available. These will be used by the staff trainer in charge and by the trainer (or student trainer) at the most distant or appropriate athletic venue (practice or game).

   c) The press box telephone is the second line of telephone communication available at home football games.

   d) A cellular telephone will be available on the sideline at all home football games.

   e) The telephone at the physical education center desk will be the backup to the handheld radio at home basketball and volleyball games.

4. Venue access for EMS vehicles
   a) Football/lacrosse field: Fieldhouse end of the field, gate will be open (see map).
   b) Fieldhouse competition courts: Down gravel road to the right of the building to the back entrance of the fieldhouse. (see map).
   c) Fields: Drive off road near restroom building to field.
   d) Baseball field: EMS unit will be directed to the fieldhouse/baseball field parking lot. Injured athletes will need to be transported from fields to the gate at the left field foul pole (see map).
   e) Departure: Security can unlock the gate behind building for EMS unit to exit from campus to avoid speed bumps (see map).

Action Plans for Specific Occurrences

Head/neck injury

1. Senior staff person stabilizes head/neck and is team leader.
2. Cervical collar will be kept in the football/lacrosse splint box and be available for all practices/games.
3. Backboard will be on the field for football games and will be kept in the training room at all other times.
4. An injured athlete will not be placed on a backboard by staff unless the athlete is prone, in which event he will be rolled onto the backboard.
5. Helmet and shoulder pads will be left on and the facemask removed.
Lacrosse helmets will be left on.
6. One student trainer or athlete will be sent to direct the EMS unit to the field and the injured athlete.
7. In the event of an injury, in the absence of the staff trainer or team physician, the student trainer in charge will stabilize the head and neck and maintain basic life support.
8. A staff trainer will be called to the area and the EMS activated by appropriate methods as listed in the communication section (#3).

Medical Emergency

1. Senior staff person (or the training staff member in charge at the time) will administer first aid and be the team leader.
2. The second responder will assist in first aid as needed and access the EMS through communication lines as outlined above.
3. The team leader will designate an individual to handle transport consideration. This will include meeting the EMS unit and ensuring that field access is available and well marked.

Heat Injury

1. Senior staff person (or the training staff member in charge at the time) will administer first aid and be the team leader.

2. The second responder will access the EMS through communication lines as outlined above.

3. Water/cooling is available at the following sites:

   a) Football/lacrosse field: at 50-yard line on press box side of field, there is a water hose (in ground box).

   b) Fieldhouse: Men's locker room shower or women's volleyball/ tennis locker room shower. These are located adjacent to the training room and the trainer in charge is responsible for access.

   c) Fields: Water is taken from the locker room to the field. Building showers are available in an emergency. The trainer in charge is responsible for checking on and ensuring the availability of water/cooling.

   d) Baseball field: Men's locker room adjacent to the training room or in the home team's dugout.

9.11 Record Keeping

Too many sports medicine programs rely on oral communications between physicians and athletic trainers, and athletic trainers and coaches. This often leads to a lack of communication and misinterpretation. It is important policy to have physicians put recommendations in writing. Documentation and accurate record keeping are essential to the success of the sports medicine program. Appendix M has a specific accident/injury report that features a multiple-copy form that enables all parties (athletic trainer, student-athlete, physician) to verify the action prescribed. In addition Appendix M has sample injury treatment and injury care recommendation forms.

9.12 Insurance

An increasing number of schools use parental insurance for primary coverage of their student-athletes. The schools provide secondary coverage after the parents primary coverage. *A word of caution!* Schools usually send printed material to parents explaining the insurance coverage provided for their sons and daughters who participate in athletics. This is good administrative procedure particularly if exclusions are noted. Most parents and athletes, however, assume that any and all medical bills for injuries sustained in athletics will automatically be paid by the school. It is important, therefore, that both the parents and the athlete know prior to the start of a season *what will not be covered*

A large number of schools make a statement in their insurance letters to parents that could later come back to haunt them. They explain that parental insurance is primary and go on to say that the institution will pay any remaining balance. The question is, "Will you really pay the entire bill, no matter how large it is?" The immediate response is, "Oh no, just up to the limits of our policy." My advice is to say just that—"up to the limits of our policy." It seems minor, but it could be a major factor in avoiding poor public relations or potential litigation.

Health Maintenance Organizations and Preferred Provider Organizations

An increasing number of companies utilize HMOs (Health Maintenance Organizations) and PPOs (Preferred Provider Organizations) for their employees. When parents are required to furnish primary insurance for coverage of their son or daughter in athletics, HMOs and PPOs become important. For example, Mary Doe sustains a serious knee injury during a women's lacrosse game. She is rushed to the emergency room of a local hospital where surgery is recommended. In all probability, the student-athlete's emergency room visit will be paid for by her parents insurance (HMO/PPO) company. Now the problem arises! The institution must contact Mary's parents' insurance company for permission to have surgery at a local hospital and for approval of the physician who will perform the surgery. If unauthorized surgery is performed, the company could deny the claim, and from past experience, so could the institution's carrier. Unpaid medical bills present a public relations problem as well as a financial burden on the athletics department. For this reason, athletics trainers should identify those student-athletes whose parents are covered by HMO or PPO policies. When a student-athlete is injured and the card reveals HMO or PPO, the athletic trainer must contact the company immediately for authorization of further treatment.

In several situations, the athletics trainer was responsible for handling insurance claims and in particular for sending medical bills to parents for claim purposes. One trainer, refused to fill out any insurance forms or check HMOs and PPOs. As a result, all medical bills became primary for the school. As a result, the athletics department was forced to pay thousands of dollars needlessly. The sports administrator should check to see that set policies are being carried out.

Preexisting Conditions

Preexisting conditions must be addressed by the sports medicine staff or, once again, public relations and financial damage can occur. Many insurance companies refuse to pay claims when the athlete's injury was due to a preexisting condition. To prevent this, parents and athletes alike should be required to list any preexisting conditions that may preclude payment for an injury to the same part of the body. This information is crucial, and notification to both the athlete and parents that payment may not be made is important. Some sports administrators pay extra premiums on their medical policy to take care of preexisting conditions. The extra payment could be beneficial to the athletics program and the athletes that participate in the program. A sample insurance form for parents, asking for information regarding HMOs, PPOs, and preexisting conditions is included in Appendix N.

9.13 Human Immunodeficiency Virus (HIV)

When "Magic" Johnson, the Los Angeles Lakers basketball star, revealed that he had the AIDS virus, the dreaded disease received immediate attention worldwide. Since Johnson's announcement on national television, much has been written and spoken about the disease that, in 1989, had infected over 1.5 million Americans. It has been estimated that one-half of those infected with HIV will develop AIDS within the next nine years (Welch, Sitler, and Horodyski 1989, 27–28).

In an article, "Should Athletic Trainers Be Concerned About HIV? Guidelines For Athletic Trainers," the authors write that athletic trainers need an awareness of the disease and its transmission. They include guidelines and recommendations for the athletic trainer.

Guidelines

"Health care workers should wear rubber gloves when exposed to patients' body fluids. Rubber gloves should also be worn whenever one is exposed to mucous membranes, nonintact skin, or other materials contaminated with blood or body fluids. Hands or skin should be washed immediately and thoroughly if contaminated with blood or body fluids. Hands should also be washed after removing gloves. One should take precautions to prevent injuries caused by needles, scalpels, or any other sharp instruments. To prevent needlestick injuries, needles should not be recapped, removed from disposable syringes, or purposely bent or broken by hand. This is important, as almost all cases of transmission of the HIV virus to healthcare workers have been the result of needlesticks. The use of mouthpieces, resuscitation bags, or other ventilation devices should be available for emergency resuscitation. Athletic trainers with open lesions should exercise caution when treating an injured athlete." (Welch, Sitler, and Horodyski 1989, 28)

Recommendations

"Considering the health implications and pervasiveness of AIDS, appropriate steps should be taken to rectify deficiencies in the clinical and educational settings in order that risks associated with the disease can be minimized. The use of a 10% solution of bleach is recommended for the cleaning of training room tables and other surfaces. The use of rubber gloves is recommended for all athletic trainers when handling blood or body fluids. Although it would appear that the majority of the NATA programs reviewed include information on AIDS, curriculum guidelines should be established by the NATA. Established guidelines would ensure that the topic of AIDS is included in all NATA educational programs. It is recommended that policies and guidelines be formalized in writing. Written instructions would ensure a uniform standard of conduct, as well as ensure that consistent information is disseminated." (Welch, Sitler, and Horodyski 1989)

Greg L. Landry, M.D., author of *AIDS in Sport*, lists universal precautions for coaches when dealing with HIV. He suggests the following:

• Using barrier precautions

Wear rubber gloves whenever touching open skin, blood, body fluids, or mucous membranes. Change gloves after contact with each athlete. You may wear a mask or protective eyewear if the care you are giving is likely to produce droplets of blood or body fluids. These barriers will prevent exposure of the mucous membranes of the mouth, nose, or eyes to the blood or body fluid. (Landry 1989)

9.14 Legal Aspects of Sports Medicine

Because no one associated with sports is immune to the threat of litigation, the sports administrator and the sports medicine team should consider the following recommendations to prevent situations that can lead to injuries and subsequent litigation:

• Require a thorough physical examination before the athlete engages in the sport.

• Assign someone to make certain all equipment fits properly.

• Assign someone to inspect equipment for defects and facilities for hazards. Keep an accurate record of the inspections.

• Obtain medical insurance coverage for the athlete and liability insurance for coaches and other personnel.

• Adopt a medical plan for emergency treatment for all athletes involved in physical contact or strenuous exercise.

• Assign activities within the athlete's range of ability and commensurate with his/her size, skill, and physical condition.

• Prepare the athlete gradually for all physical activities, and progress from simple to complex tasks in strenuous and dangerous activities.

• Warn the athlete of all possible dangers inherent in the activities in which he/she is involved.

• Follow the activities as designed. If a coach deviates from the prescribed activities, the decision to do so should be based on sound reasoning. Extra safety precautions should be taken.

• Adopt a policy regarding injuries. Do not attempt to be a medical specialist in judging the physical condition of an athlete under your care.

- Require a physician's medical permission before permitting seriously injured or ill athletes to return to normal activity.
- Avoid moving an injured athlete until it is safe to do so. Whenever an injured athlete is moved, make certain he/she is taken away from potentially dangerous playing areas.
- Conduct periodic medicolegal in-service training programs for all personnel. (Mueller and Ryan 1991, 45)

10
Financial Aspects

10.1 Role of the Sports Administrator

Sports administrators have a responsibility to oversee the financial operation of the sports program by preparing a realistic budget and making certain that expenditures do not exceed the amount allocated. This is true for the small high school, as well as the large university. On the high school and small college level, athletics directors usually handle finance; while assistant athletics directors or business managers for athletics assume responsibility on the major college and university level.

John Swofford, athletics director at the University of North Carolina at Chapel Hill, instituted a concept he calls "responsibility budgeting." He defines it as a "budgeting and control process that identifies a specific individual who is responsible for a particular financial area of an organization and involves that individual in both preparation and control of the budget for that particular area" (Kinder 1987, 94).

In many schools, individuals who prepare and control the budget for a particular area are typically the coach, athletics trainers, sports information director, facility manager, and marketing director. Swofford calls these individuals cost center managers and the particular area they manage the cost center. He comments that the school's chief financial officer and the athletics director have overall responsibility for the financial well being of the sports program, but acknowledges that there are advantages in designating individuals as cost center managers.

When we can pinpoint personal responsibility for each and every category of the department, the ability to responsibly control expenditures increases dramatically....

In terms of financial controls, if you have one individual who is held accountable for his or her specific area, your ability to control increases. (Kinder 1987, 94)

In my opinion, Swofford is on target because coaches and other staff members take pride in being able to manage their particular area of the sports program. I remember telling several staff members that while I encouraged them to be team players and support the entire sports program, I wanted them to be jealous of their particular program. "If you get overzealous," I would say, "I'll certainly tell you."

It is amazing what responsibility can lead to among a staff. For several years we lacked a contingency fund for postseason play, mainly because we never expected at that particular time to qualify for postseason competition. When the basketball team unexpectedly won the right to participate in the national tournament, the football coach volunteered to fund the trip because he had monies left in his budget. The following year the basketball coach returned the favor when football needed additional funds. Both coaches were proud to help the other and pleased that good fiscal management enabled them to do so.

An outstanding athletics director inherited a program in which most sports were overrunning their budgets. He took drastic action informing the coaches that unaccounted overruns in their sports would result in payment of the deficit by the head coach. At the same time, he promised that any money left in the budget at the end of the year would be carried over into their new budgets. The athletic program experienced a complete turnaround and budgets were balanced. I understand responsibility can be a major battle in successful budgets.

10.2 Staff Orientation

Before individual cost center managers begin the budgeting process, an orientation meeting should be held to prepare the staff for the upcoming budget preparation. Harold Vander Zaag, a noted sports administrator, suggests posing the following questions at a prebudget orientation:

- How is the program financed? What are the major sources of revenue?
- What are the major areas of expenditure?
- What are the possible sources for increased financial support?
- How are funds allocated within the program?
- When are budget requests submitted?
- Who authorizes expenditures?
- What is the system of accountability?

Vander Zaag notes that the sports administrator has three major areas of responsibility when developing and overseeing the budgetary process: planning on an annual or five-year plan, acquisition or generation of funds, and control that emphasizes budget accountability.

10.3 Planning Process

It is important in the planning process to determine the goals for the athletics program. When our program moved from a scholarship program to an NCAA Division III need-based program, the financial goals changed dramatically. Improvement of current facilities became priority items and the budget reflected this change. Irrigating and up-grading fields and enlargement of athletic training facilities became goals to be met. Budgeting should agree with the goals of the institution.

10.4 Projecting Income

The first thing most athletics directors do in the budgetary process is to develop projected income for the upcoming year. This list should be realistic and lean toward conservativism. In projecting income, I estimated that 10,000 spectators would attend a benefit game for our proposed fieldhouse. Interest and enthusiasm were at an all-time high and the attendance figure seemed reasonable. A week-long rain and a torrential storm the night of the game devastated attendance and dra-matically affected projected income. Sports administrators rely on the following sources of income to meet budgetary costs: Season tickets, donations, sponsorships, booster club funds, radio and TV rights, ticket sales, buy-out games, program advertisements, fund-raising, and guarantees

Speaking of guarantees, the college had a history in the 1940s of opening the football season against a major college for one reason only—money! In 1945, the football team traveled to Maryland to in-augurate Paul "Bear" Bryant's debut as a college coach. Maryland gave Bryant his first college win 60–6, and the guarantee supported our football program that year. In the 1960s, I received a telegram from "Bear" Bryant offering a sizeable guarantee to play his Alabama team in Tuscaloosa. Needless to say, the offer was quickly turned down and did not contribute to his eventual record of 315 victories (Appenzeller 1987, 68).

Other sources of income include parking fees, game programs, concessions, souvenirs, and cash at the gate.

10.5 Concessions

It is appropriate to discuss concessions because many schools operate concessions differently. Some schools lease out concessions to private contractors for a percentage of the profit, while others operate conces-sions "in-house," opting for larger profits. Frank Russo, an event man-agement expert, operated the Hartford Civic Center in Hartford, Con-necticut, in 1982. Russo recalls that concession revenue that year totalled $2,100,000 or 36 percent of the operating budget. Concession revenue led to a profitable year for the civic center. For those consid-ering the feasibility of "in-house" or leased concessions the following advantages of each are:

• In-house operations

— Management has complete control of concessions.
— Management controls pricing.
— The quality of the product can be controlled.
— There is a greater potential for generating revenue.

• Lease arrangement

— Volume purchasing enables the vendor to provide quality products at reduced prices.
— Sales will be expanded beyond anything that could be generated with an in-house system due to supervisory experience, efficiency, expertise, and capacity.
— Capital outlays for equipment are avoided.
— Management, staff, purchasing, maintenance, inventory, storage, and vendor relations are eliminated. (Lewis and Appenzeller 1985, 130–131)

10.6 Projected Expenditures

Basic items for consideration as projected expenditures include the following:

- Lodging and meals
- Officials
- Guarantees
- Rentals
- Preseason expenses
- Professional improvement
- Personnel costs
- Dues and memberships
- Transportation
- Postage
- Accounting
- Equipment
- Laundry
- Medical (ambulances, preparticipation physicals, etc.)
- Recruiting and scouting
- Photography
- Insurance
- Postseason play
- Taxes
- Telephone
- Reconditioning
- Office supplies

When preparing the projected income Robert Purdy, author of *The Successful High School Athletic Program*, suggests that high school booster clubs contribute to the overall sports program, not just one or two sports. The tendency has been to give added financial support to the major or preferential sports in a particular program. Purdy makes important suggestions regarding financial assistance from booster clubs that can prevent potential problems.

1. The actual allocation of the money as to respective teams and projects shall be the decision of the principal and the athletics director and not the Boosters Club executive board.

2. All sports should benefit from this money. This may be done by applying the funds to assist in transportation for all teams, an equipment fund affecting all teams, or similar projects. Since every sport is important, each one should receive monies.

3. No coach should be permitted to request funds for his particular sport from the Boosters Club. (Purdy 1973, 62)

10.7 Booster Club Funding

A suggested ratio for the distribution of funds by the boosters club is as follows:

• Football	28%
• Cheerleaders	4%
• Cross-country	4%
• Basketball	18%
• Swimming	10%
• Wrestling	10%
• Track	10%
• Baseball	8%
• Golf	4%
• Tennis	4%

From experience, I share Purdy's ideas. For years, coaches who expressed a need for funding would ask permission to present their request to an executive board meeting of the booster cub. It became obvious that the same coaches were requesting supplemental funds each year and the executive board never turned anyone down. The members of the board appreciated the coaches and sincerely wanted to meet their needs. This process was changed and produced better results. The procedure now is to have coaches present their funding request to the athletics director in writing. In turn, the athletics director meets with a special subcommittee to discuss the proposals. The subcommittee considers each proposal and the availability of funds and makes recommendations to the full board. The subcommittee also makes certain that all sports are given consideration. The policy has worked well. Purdy would approve this new procedure because he believes:

Each coach feels his sport is most important and that his needs must be met. If this practice is permitted, bedlam will prevail. The Booster Club will not know which coach has the most pressing request. (Purdy 1973)

10.8 Staff Involvement

In December or early January, after the staff orientation budget meeting, each cost center manager should receive work sheets to complete and return within two weeks. The athletics director or individual responsible for preparation of the budget meets with the cost center managers to discuss their budget proposals. In many instances this meeting involves compromise on various items. A second meeting is held after the individual meetings to discuss a final budget for the particular sports area.

A meeting is held with the chief financial officer and copies of the proposed budget are distributed to the analytical studies team who has the responsibility of reviewing every budget on campus. The budget is finally approved in February and is sent to the business office for computerization. It is then sent to the cost center managers. Monthly reports are sent to the athletics director and each cost center for appraisal. When discrepancies are present, the athletic director and individual cost center managers meet to discuss the items. In some instances, adjustments are made in the budgets.

10.9 Financial Reporting

There is a need for accurate accounting of each cost center and financial reporting that includes the following elements:

- An up-to-date record of every purchase. This includes a receipt for every cash payment.
- A daily ledger of expenditures and balances.
- Monthly statements. Most institutions send departments or programs monthly statements of their accounts. These should be checked against departmental records and any discrepancies should be worked out. Each coach and sport coordinator should also be given a monthly account of the financial status of their sport.
- An annual comparative report between the budget and actual expenditures. Needless to say, this is the bottom line in the financial aspect of control.
- An end-of-year audit. This should be conducted by an external source. (Vander Zaag 1984, 196–7)

There are three areas that are very important to the athletics director in the budgeting process that need special consideration These are requisition and purchase orders, bidding on equipment, and zero-base budgeting.

10.10 Requisition and Purchase Orders

I remember receiving a bill for several hundred dollars from a sporting goods manufacturing company for dozens of athletic socks. There was no code number on the bill identifying the person who ordered the equipment. It was impossible to identify the coach who ordered the equipment. From that time on, procedure changed. Companies who furnished equipment and supplies were notified that no order could be made without a purchase order authorized by the athletics director or an individual in the business office. A code identifying the sport was also required.

Each cost center manager, according to policy, fills out a requisition form with the details of a proposed order. After approval by the athletics director, the order is recorded on computer and sent to the business office for a purchase order. In an emergency, coaches and other cost center managers can call the athletics director for a purchase order and the order can be telephoned in to expedite the shipment. A system of requisitions and purchase orders is a must for the efficient operation of the budget.

10.11 Bids

For years the staff had the freedom to order equipment from whomever they felt had the product they wanted at the best price. Through the years, equipment and supplies were purchased at different locations, spreading the funds around. The staff members developed friendships and mutual trust with local dealers, and for the most part, the system worked.

When the local YMCA leased facilities at the college, school officials believed that club sports, physical education, YMCA, and athletics program could advantageously combine their equipment and supplies and put them out on bid. Most companies would be ready to cut costs to get a large order and considerable savings were anticipated. The bid system, however, was very unpopular with many of the coaches who felt that they could shop around and get equipment at a price lower than those on the bid. In actuality, they argued at times they were paying more from their budget to save money for others. There were two problems that became evident. First was the argument that a coach could often find a much lower price than that listed on the bid. The other was the temptation to purchase a different brand of equipment than the coach ordered.

I remember well an alumnus of a local college who owned a sporting goods store and loved the athletics program and college. He gave the athletics department the lowest prices he could through the years. When he was told that he had to compete with 10 companies for a baseball order, he told me he would definitely get the order although he knew several companies would try to underbid him. He won the bid, but the baseball team lost out. When the shipment arrived, we realized the alumnus had won the bid because the business manager who took the lowest bid did not realize he was getting junior high school baseball caps instead of the usual professional caps and similar high school equipment. After the first rain, a new "professional" set of caps were ordered as well as uniforms.

The athletics director and ice hockey coach of a major university reported that the business manager let a salesperson convince him that a certain protective helmet would save considerable money. As a result, inferior helmets were ordered that put the safety of the hockey players in jeopardy.

Larry Horine, writing in *Administration of Physical Education and Sport Programs*, raises the question: "To Bid or Not To Bid?" The disadvantages of bids include:

• Quality may suffer.
• The bid system sometimes adds to equipment costs if the item is rather inexpensive but the purchase system is complex, requiring a great deal of paperwork.
• The system is slow.
• The system may discourage local dealers from bidding.
• The system may encourage vendors to compete to see who can cut the most corners and still meet technical requirements.
• Frequently, when the product delivered doesn't meet the specifications, the goods are not returned because they are needed immediately.

The advantages of the bid system include:

• It may stimulate honest competition among reputable vendors, resulting in lower prices.
• It may result in on-time delivery of products that meet the needs of the consumers.
• It may stimulate the competitors to include warranties and reliable service.
• Bidding spreads the purchases among vendors.
• It will ensure that purchasing is not based on friendships or relationships.
• It will lessen the possibility of mistaken judgments on the technical quality of equipment or merchandise. (Horine 1991, 167)

For whatever method is chosen, two suggestions that work may help:

• Put an item veto in the bid that enables a coach to withdraw a particular item. For example: when a coach finds an item that can save considerable monies, an item veto is granted.
• The purchaser should consult the coach before changing a specific brand and both agree to the change. This will serve as protection for the coach who wants a definite type of equipment.

When I received my first budget at Guilford College it was slightly over $5,000. This budget included football, basketball, baseball, track, tennis, and golf. It also had an administrative line for the athletics director and his administrative duties. It was obvious to everyone that the budget would be exceeded by the third month. I was told the usual procedure dictated my meeting with student government to "beg" for additional funds. Because the school was in "Big Four" country, surrounded by six institutions within a radius of fifteen miles and all with athletics programs, raising income to equal the budget expenditures was virtually impossible. There was a dilemma that had to be resolved. I met that with the president, explaining the inadequacy of the budget and the fact that the athletics program could not generate large income-producing revenues. I asked for athletics to be an educational expense similar to the library, cafeteria, faculty, choir, and other programs. None of these programs were required to balance their budgets. From that day on, the president and administrative officers allowed the athletics program to be a part of the total educational program and we were given a budget to operate on without involvement of student government or game receipts. The program was not required to raise funds to meet the budget expenses. This was a step in the right direction.

10.12 Zero-Base Budgeting

Later a problem developed due to a lack of funds. The total athletics budget was given from 2 to 5 percent of the previous years' total to meet inflation. The larger budgets received the same percentage increase as the small budgets, and consequently the small budgets failed to get a significant increase. I can't forget the soccer coach's comment that the new increase meant that he could purchase one more soccer ball for the upcoming year.

To remedy the situation, the athletics director was empowered to take the percentage increase, and, instead of giving across the board increases for each sport, decide on the distribution as needs arose. The larger budgets then received no increase so that the minuscule budgets of several sports could begin to catch up. This was not a satisfactory solution.

I suggested a zero-based budgeting process in which each cost center would actually start from zero in building its budget. After a careful look at the cost centers inventory, cost center managers would review the needs of their programs. Football, with fewer away games and new uniforms purchased the year before, cut its budget significantly. Some sports drastically reduced their budgets, while others requested additional funds. For several years, the school decided to go back to the previous budget and simply add a figure to cover inflation. This approach frustrated the cost center managers who spent an inordinate amount of time on the zero-base budget. Today the zero-base budgeting process has been in effect for several years. The athletics director, with staff approval, meets with each individual to discuss the overall situation, reducing some budgets and adding to others in need. By mutual agreement, individual budgets are established. The athletics director believes zero-base budgeting should be instituted every three or four years. Zero-base budgeting can be adjusted to meet program needs even if it is required procedure every three or four years.

One final suggestion that improved communication between the athletics department and the campus community (administrators, faculty, and students). I put the complete, detailed budget in the library for everyone to see. Very few people took time to read it, but it dispelled any misconceptions about the contents of the budget. For any who had questions regarding the budget, the athletics director was willing and eager to respond. It proved to the general community that the athletics program had no secrets and was open for all to see.

11

Fund-Raising and Promotion

A difference that distinguishes modern sports administrators from those in the past is today's emphasis on fund-raising and promotion of sports events. High school baseball teams in the 1950s frequently wore uniforms donated by local businesses that advertised Darlene's Deli, Sue's Sweet Shop, Ray's Restaurant, or Scott's Fertilizer. It was the only way many schools obtained uniforms. When the economy improved traditional baseball uniforms appeared, devoid of advertisements. With the increase in sports offered at the high school and college levels, funding has become a major problem. As a result of limited resources, corporate sponsorships have become common on both levels. Traditional sporting events have become the Kelly Tire Blue-Gray Game, the Jeep-Eagle Aloha Bowl, the USF & G Sugar Bowl, Poulan's Weed Eater Independence Bowl, and the McDonald's East-West High School All-Star Game.

Today the survival of sports programs are linked with fund-raising and promotional efforts. During the five years I administered a sports program and coached in junior college, the football team never wore its Carolina blue and white school colors. Instead, three major universities donated uniforms they were discarding. The team wore gold and black, navy and white, and royal blue, red, and white during my tenure, causing townspeople to speculate each year on the college we would represent. After I accepted the position of athletics director and head football coach at Guilford College, I thought I had finally reached the "big time." Uniforms were in school colors without advertisements! I learned, however, that the budget lacked capital outlay and if I wanted anything but basic essentials, I had to raise the funds. For the next 31 years, I solicited funds for scholarships, goalposts, bleachers, scoreboards, uniforms, trophy cases, locker rooms, classrooms, athletic fields, banquets, and a new field house. I would like to attribute my fund-raising efforts to the fact that I was a visionary, ahead of my time. That would be incorrect, because athletics directors in those days maintained the status quo and were not required to raise funds. I did it to help the program survive. I learned important lessons from fund-raising—tactics that worked, as well as those that failed. Several suggestions may prove helpful to the athletics director who raises funds.

11.1 Stay Within the System

There was always a temptation on my part and on the part of the coaches to call upon supportive alumni and friends for funds. The problem with bypassing the development staff is that these people are usually cultivating the same prospective donors for major gifts. Our requesting funds could jeopardize their efforts, resulting in tension and animosity. Therefore, I would meet regularly with the development staff to get clearance and approval to solicit selected prospective donors. Coaches, in turn, did the same for me. Everyone knew what was going on, and this awareness led to a spirit of cooperation.

When I returned from a fund-raising visit I recorded comments, both negative and positive, with details of the visit for use by future fund-raisers. This practice helped the future fund-raiser avoid problems.

11.2 Be Program Specific

Successful fund-raising, depends on identifying a specific need. People are often reluctant to contribute to a general fund, preferring to meet a specific need. After the football team played a game in late November in the mountains of West Virginia on a blustery, rainy day, I had few turn downs when I helped the coaches raise the funds for sideline parkas. Program specific fund raising is essential.

11.3 Be Realistic

There is a tendency to underestimate and overestimate the amount of funds to request. I planned to ask a businessman to donate $2,000 to the proposed field house campaign. I reduced the amount, however, when I saw the number of plaques of appreciation on his wall from his alma mater. I thought his school would be the recipient of his funds. I learned a valuable lesson when he asked, "How about $3,000?" I found that you can ask for too little when it is just as easy to ask for a larger amount.

In North Carolina, two institutions were located in the same area of the state. Both had capital campaigns at the same time and reportedly one president asked potential donors to contribute $50, while the other started at $1,000. Reports have it that the school that asked for the $50 failed and closed its doors, while the other met its goal and is a strong institution today. Be careful not to underestimate your donor's generosity and ability to contribute.

After saying that, let me caution you not to be unrealistic in your request. Know your donor and don't be tempted to ask for an unreasonable gift. A member of the development staff ignored my apprehension and insisted that I ask for a gift of $50,000 for the proposed field house. The amount was unrealistic and, as I expected, caused the person to leave the program. He was embarrassed and, quite frankly, humiliated at the request. He has yet to return to the program.

Officials of a civic club contacted the football coach about a possible gift. The coach asked for a movie camera to film games. I convinced the coach that we had a greater need, and together we requested enough funds to build a much needed press box. The club is proud of the facility that bears its name and proud of the opportunity it had to meet the need. Once again, know the financial situation of potential donors and be realistic in your request.

11.4 Prospect List

Professionals in the field of fund-raising report that fund-raising involves the principle of three. During forty years of raising money for sports programs, I found the principle to be valid. In planning the prospect list, remember that one-third of the money raised comes from approximately 10 people, one-third from the next 100, and one-third from all the rest. Identify your prospects and set a priority for the first 10 and then the next 100. This is sound strategy.

11.5 The Importance of Two Words

The words "thank you" are an important key in fund-raising, as I soon discovered. Two things stand out in my efforts to raise money. A local merchant annually bought a full page advertisement in the football program. We thanked him on several occasions, sent tickets for the employees, and made his gift special. He surprised me when he told me that his company had decided to transfer an annual percentage of its profits to the school. He had terminated an annual gift (which was substantial) to another school because the neighboring school never acknowledged the gift or ever said, "Thank you." He pointed out that our school thanked him several times for what he felt was a very small donation. His company's gift has been important to the institution and the athletics program.

An alumna, in like manner, transfered a baseball scholarship from a large state school to our institution for the same reason—failure to say, "thank you." You cannot say "thank you" too much!

In the 1960s the president received a postcard seeking information about the college. The president recognized the person's name and prepared a thorough response. He sent a detailed package that gave the person valuable information about the institution. Because of the thoroughness and promptness of the response, the institution became the recipient of funds to build a science building, a 1,000-seat auditorium and music building, endowed scholarships for students, endowed professorships, and faculty houses. Being alert and following up on an innocuous request resulted in gifts in the millions.

11.6 Don't Reinvent the Wheel

Don Canham, former University of Michigan athletics director, was one of the finest fund-raisers for college sports in the United States. Canham writes:

> One of the biggest mistakes that novice fund-raisers make is to search for something new and different, when, in actuality, it would be far better to adopt some program that has been successful at other institutions or other organizations. There are a multitude of events and projects that have been used successfully by others that can be adopted and used effectively regardless of the size and scope of the original undertaking. The challenge is not to originate activities but to be creative in the implementation of those things that have produced results elsewhere. (Lewis and Appenzeller 1985, 139)

In 1977, I decided to try one more way to upgrade the golf program or drop it from the intercollegiate athletics program. I asked an outstanding coach on the staff if he would consider coaching golf in addition to basketball. He had won the NAIA Basketball Championship in 1973 and was a person who could build a program. He agreed on one condition—enough funds to add fall golf. He shocked me when he candidly said that it was impossible to win a national championship in golf without a fall as well as a spring season. Talk about the "eternal optimist" or the "impossible dream!" The golf program during the past years had fallen to an all-time low and thoughts of a national championship were absurd. The school could not support a full season, but they agreed to let us try to raise funds. Area schools promoted golf by sponsoring a celebrity golf outing. We used their idea, but adapted the outing to fit the school. A two-day golf outing created interest in the program and raised sufficient funds to support a fall and a spring golf season. The rest is history. From 1977 until 1990, the golf team finished in the Top 10 at the NAIA Golf Tournament seven times. In 1985, 1986, and 1987, the team was runner-up for the title, and won the championship in 1990. The team produced thirteen All-American's, two medalists, and two World University Champions in that period. This was accomplished by copying and adapting golf outings that were successful by others.

Canham recommends seven guidelines for the fund-raiser:

- Be program specific.
- Establish a prospect list.
- Meet Internal Revenue Service (IRS) standards for deductions.
- Set up an accounting system that ensures checks and balances.
- Use projects that others have used successfully.
- Acknowledge every donation.
- Utilize written contracts. (Lewis and Appenzeller 1985, 139–40)

11.7 Promotion

John Moore, a sports marketing consultant, writes that "there are more ways to promote ticket sales for revenue sports than there are promoters" (Lewis and Appenzeller 1985, 147). Moore notes that the sports administrator needs to plan promotional events at least four to six months prior to the event. He suggests a promotional budget, a realistic time schedule, objectives for the promotion, and established "dates for the completion of various items."

The common source of assistance for promotions is business and industry. Many schools such as Duke University utilize sponsorships, shopping center visits by members of various teams, and promotional events at particular contests. Duke University's athletics program has been successful in promoting special days such as "helmet day, jersey day, parents day, or celebrity day" (Lewis and Appenzeller 1985, 153). Many athletics programs set up autograph days so that the community can visit their campus to meet athletes and coaches. One of the most successful promotions utilized by Greensboro's ice hockey and Class A baseball teams has been the appearance of the "San Diego Chicken." The Greensboro Gaters, a professional basketball team, featured the Chicago Lovabulls to attract crowds to its games. Whatever the promotion is, advertising and adequate publicity are essential.

Once again, it is not necessary to use original promotions. Use creativity in using other's successful promotions. With business and industry being called upon to assist athletics programs, several suggestions can be helpful.

Richard J. Ensor, commissioner of the Metro Atlantic Conference, writes about the importance of the "affinity factor" that matches a particular sports event with a corporate identity" (Ensor 1990). Ensor refers to Capital Sports, Inc., a sports marketing firm that lists evaluative criteria to determine the proper fit between sports event and a sponsor that includes

1. Do the demographics of the event match those that the corporation seeks to market?

2. Does the sport season or timing of an event match the time requirements of the sponsor?

3. Is the sporting event held in the geographic market that the sponsor is trying to reach?

4. Does the facility that the event is held in match the image and marketing needs of the sponsor?

5. Are there hidden costs that the sponsor will have to absorb beyond the initial sponsorship fee?

6. Is the administration of the sports event of the same caliber as the sponsoring corporation, and will they be able to help the sponsor achieve corporate goals?

7. Is the sponsor getting involved because the event is a sound marketing tool or because it is "fun?"

In return for sponsorships, the athletics director needs to provide opportunities for the sponsor such as tickets, yearbook ads, program ads, press guide ads, scoreboard ads, use of on-air talent, sponsorship announcements to wholesale traders, special stadium nights, arena signs, press releases, and participation of the sponsor in half-time and pregame shows.

Individuals seeking sponsorship by corporations of their sporting event or product should be mindful of the corporate viewpoint toward sponsorship while developing their proposals. Continued emphasis will be placed by corporations on evaluating the sponsorship in terms of meshing the corporate product with the sport event and of the extended value received by the corporation because of the sponsorship. Sport marketers will have to become more adept at meeting these corporate criteria in order to remain successful. (Ensor Nov. 1987, 2–6)

Part 3
Managing Risk

12
Risk Management Strategies

Sports-related litigation has become a multibillion dollar industry involving millions of participants. The sports administrator faces legal issues in the 1990s that did not exist in the past. Pressure is on sports administrators as courts hold them responsible for situations involving tort, criminal, employment, contract, and constitutional law.

A friend of mine in high school suffered a fatal blow to the head when he made a hard tackle during a football game. The alleged cause of his death was a helmet that did not fit. When I was teaching and coaching in high school, two teenage boys died tragically in preventable sports-related accidents. In all three instances, no one thought of suing because it was not the thing to do in the 1950s and early 1960s.

In my opinion, two cases opened the door for sports-related lawsuits. A fourteen-year-old boy ignored his physical education teacher's warning to stay off the springboard when the instructor left the class to attend to an injured student (*Miller v. Cloidt* 1964). The boy jumped on the springboard, landed off the mat, and was rendered a quadriplegic. A New Jersey jury awarded the boy $1,216,000 in damages, an unprecented amount in 1964. The second case that received national attention occurred in California when a high school quarterback was seriously injured in a pregame scrimmage (*Welch v. Dunsmuir* 1958). The boy could move his hands and fingers when his coach first checked him, but was rendered quadriplegic after his teammates moved him to the sidelines. A medical expert testified that moving the boy from the field exacerbated the injury, causing paralysis. A jury awarded the boy $385,000. The size of these awards gave impetus to a spiraling number of sports-related lawsuits.

12.1 Common Problems Regarding Risks

When I retired after forty years as athletics director to accept an endowed professorship in sports management, I joined the Center for

Sports Law and Risk Management as a special consultant. I conduct risk reviews across the United States for elementary and secondary schools, colleges and universities, professional sports venues, and municipalities. These clients have similar problems. Negligence is negligence. Here are some examples I've seen over the years:

- Exit doors locked in sports arenas while events are in progress.
- A lack of policy dealing with potential catastrophic events such as fire, tornado, earthquake, or bomb threats.
- An absence of proper signs in swimming pools, weight rooms, playing fields, racquetball courts, bleachers, and other areas.
- A lack of informed consent agreements for participants in many schools.
- A lack of emergency medical response plans for participants and spectators at sports events.
- Accident and injury reports worded in such a way that they cause problems in litigation.
- People with disabilities denied access to facilities in violation of federal law.
- A lack of an expulsion policy for unruly spectators. Ushers, not security personnel, often mistreat spectators.
- Open drains and irrigation heads on playing fields.
- Participants playing on overlapping fields in sports such as softball, soccer, and football, baseball, and track.
- Areas where water and electricity mix that lack ground fault interrupters (GFIs).
- Inspection of facilities and equipment is often overlooked and not documented.
- Schools often lease facilities without requiring a certificate of insurance from the lessee. In many cases, the lessee is not required to indemnify the lessor in a facility use agreement.
- Insurance contracts often contain exclusions regarding sporting events, resulting in the facility or program having inadequate coverage.
- Glass doors and windows located under or near goals.
- Lack of due process procedures.

These are just a few situations observed during risk reviews that can plague a sports administrator. A risk management program is necessary as well as essential in today's litigious society. The number of sports-related lawsuits against administrators, coaches, and schools has increased dramatically. As a result, "managing risks associated with athletics activities must be a top priority" (United Educators 1991). Experts in the field of sports law agree that:

A comprehensive risk management program can help evidence that those in the care of the college or university have received necessary care and attention. Furthermore, a well-structured management policy executed and enforced by a committee of senior administrators is the key to both preventing injuries and minimizing liability. (United Educators 1991)

12.2 Developing A Risk Management Plan

There are risks inherent in sports activities. Even the safest program will never avoid accidents and injuries. The courts recognize this and do not require those who teach physical education and recreation or coach sports to become ensurers of the participants' safety or hold them responsible for every injury that occurs. The fact that an accident takes place does not necessarily mean that the teacher, coach, or administrator is liable. The law does require, however, that school personnel provide a reasonably safe program. The following material is designed to help identify and eliminate potential risks in sports programs before injuries and lawsuits arise. It is not legal advice, but risk management strategy. Sports administrators are advised to consult with school attorneys to determine the applicability to individual state law.

12.3 Safety Committee

While attending a high school football game in a nearby town, I saw three boys come crashing to the ground when the wooden bleachers collapsed. The boys were taken to a local hospital with one reportedly sustaining crippling injuries. A week later, I was sitting on the bleachers in a college stadium when the footboard collapsed, sending a student hurtling to the ground. I have visited several school districts to determine who was responsible for the inspection of bleachers, facilities, and equipment. Some thought it was the responsibility of the school principal, others pointed to the athletics director or coach, and others believed the maintenance department had an obligation to keep the facilities safe. No one seems to know where responsibility lies. This is an important reason to have a safety committee. They provide accountability to ensure that risks are addressed. Each secondary school, college, and university should organize a safety committee to implement a safety review and policies for physical education classes, sports clubs, and intramural, interscholastic, and intercollegiate sports programs.

The safety committee should meet on a periodic basis to review the following:

• Potential trouble spots, hazards, and risks in the various programs;
• Accident/injury reports to ascertain if a specific pattern of injuries or accidents is associated with a particular activity or location;

- Results of equipment and facility inspections to ensure that they are properly initiated, completed, and documented, and that problems are eliminated or remedied;
- Implementation of accident/injury reporting procedures;
- Development of safety policies for all sports activities;
- Various city, county, and state statutes and ordinances.

The committee should include campus representatives. Representation will vary with each school, but generally the following persons or their representatives should be on such a committee:

- Director of athletics,
- Director of physical education,
- Director of intramural or sports clubs,
- Director of maintenance,
- Representative from the security department,
- Athletics trainers,
- Student representatives, and
- Representative of disabled people.

If the institution has a risk manager or safety officer, that individual would be a valuable asset to the committee. It is important to document when meetings are held, as well as the topics discussed and actions taken. Documentation can demonstrate that the institution is actively working to promote safe programs.

The safety committee can set the stage for the development of the risk management plan by having each member of the committee complete the "Athletic Liability Self-Assessment Audit" by United Educators found in Appendix O. This audit will reveal many important facts about a particular sports program and is a good place for the safety committee to start its work.

12.4 Warnings and Consents

If someone had told me prior to 1980 that I had to warn a football team that there were inherent risks that could lead to catastrophic injury and possible death, I would have questioned his sanity. I wanted the members of my football team to play with "reckless abandon," and such warnings had no place in my coaching philosophy.

All this was changed when Chris Thompson, a student with exceptional athletic ability, settled for $3.5 million for a football injury that left him a quadriplegic. Thompson sued the Seattle School District and his coach for failure to warn him of the dangers inherent in football. As a result of this case, warnings regarding potential catastrophic sports injuries have become a requirement by most institutions (Appenzeller 1985, 17). Approximately 80 percent of injured sports participants allege failure to warn as a complaint when a person is injured. Previously unheard of "warnings to participate" are now common procedure.

12.5 Agreement to Participate in Athletics

Courts generally do not favor waivers. Waivers, however, can hold up in court if worded carefully and properly. In *Garrison v. Combined Fitness Centre*, the plaintiff sued the health club and the manufacturer of the bench press when he injured himself lifting weights. He claimed that although he signed a membership contract that included an exculpatory clause, he did not realize that "he would be relieving the defendant from liability for injury." The court upheld the waiver. I recommend the term *agreement to participate* as a warning to the participant and insurer in a consent agreement. The individual in this instance acknowledges that sports involve risk, with the potential dangers specifically spelled out. The participant agrees to follow the coach's instructions regarding playing techniques, training, and team rules, and holds blameless the school district or university and its personnel in the event of an injury. Minors are not legally competent to contractually waive their rights to redress in the event of negligent injury. Parents or guardians, however, can sign the agreement to participate. For a sample copy of a typical agreement to participate for intercollegiate athletics, see Appendix P.

Prior to participation in a specific sport, all students, parents, or guardians should be required to sign an agreement to participate. The sports administrator is the logical one to read the agreement to participate prior to a team's first workout. The administrator can make certain that the members of the team understand the agreement and can answer questions relating to it. It is important that a record be kept of the date and time the warnings were read, who was present, and who read the agreement to participate. Documentation is the key.

Good risk management planning advises that no equipment be issued until the following items are completed:

- An agreement to participate
- Insurance coverage is in place,
- Preparticipation physical examinations and updated medical histories, and
- Confirmation of eligibility.

The sports administrator can facilitate things by sending a letter to parents or guardians setting guidelines for physical examinations, stating insurance requirements, and establishing the rules for participation in sports. One of the techniques I used to monitor the completion of matters regarding participation in sports was to have a loose-leaf notebook for each team. The book contained an alphabetized roster for each sport with the above items checked. For example, the football book included the eligibility roster for that season, insurance forms, scholarship agreements, contracts with other institutions, and completed inspection forms for the facilities and equipment used by football (see Appendix Q).

Regarding eligibility forms, coaches should check rosters with the college registrar, who does the actual certification, as well as with the athletics director and faculty athletics representative. Prior to competition, athletes in a particular sport cannot receive equipment until they have insurance, a satisfactory physical examination, and a signed agreement to participate. At a glance, the administrator can immediately see who lacks the necessary requirements to participate. From my experience, it always seems to be the individual who has not met the requirements listed above who is injured, rendering the school and its personnel vulnerable.

It is essential that sports administrators require each participant to complete the items listed above. Coaches and students will be unhappy if the student-athlete cannot receive equipment to begin practice immediately, but if administrators adhere to the policy, it will soon become accepted and offer both participant and coach protection in the event of serious injury.

Agreement to Participate for Physical Education, Intramurals, Recreation, and Club Sports

Administrators of sports programs other than interscholastic and intercollegiate can use a modified, less threatening agreement to participate. It may be administratively impossible to require each participant to sign an individual agreement due to the number of participants in these programs. Warnings, however, can be posted in locker rooms, on bulletin boards, or in student handbooks to promote a positive safety image for the respective program and properly alert participants to inherent risks in the various activities.

12.6 Warning Signs

A colleague who conducts risk reviews visited our campus. After walking through the field house, he asked who was responsible for its operation. He pointed to a sign near the entrance to the racquetball courts that warned participants not to use black-soled shoes, but did not mention using protective goggles to ensure eye safety. Certainly eye protection is more important than black-soled shoes. A new sign was up the following day.

Facilities such as weight training rooms, swimming pools, and gymnastic areas often lack warning signs. It is essential to place signs regarding the use of spotters in proximity to the heavy weights in weight rooms. In swimming pools, signs should be placed near diving areas to promote safe diving. In other areas, signs should detail regulations for safe use of the pool.

Ronald Baron, executive director for the Center for Sports Law and Risk Management, believes in the value of signs:

A school can effectively warn participants with signage. Signs should contain large print and be conspicuously placed. Signage with large print can be attractive and informative. If used properly, warning signs can promote a positive safety image, while simultaneously warning students on the safe use of the facility or equipment. (Baron and Appenzeller 1990)

An example of inadequate signs occurred in a YMCA that complied with federal law by placing a metal ramp in its pool to provide access for people with disabilities. The bottom of the ramp had razor-sharp runners that posed a serious threat to anyone who swam under it. There were no warning signs near the ramp to alert swimmers to the potential danger of swimming under the ramp. A swimmer who seriously cut his arm was rushed to a nearby medical center. When questioned about the severe cuts on his arms, he commented that someone told him he was the tenth person to be cut by the ramp's sharp runners. It is hard to imagine anyone letting ten people receive injuries without correcting the dangerous situation. At the same time, however, commenting that a person was the tenth one injured without correcting the problem opened the door to a potential lawsuit. Proper warning signs were later installed when the accident was reported to the director of the facility. The condition should have been corrected after the first injury, however, not the tenth.

I received a call from an athletics director who said her administrator told her to keep the swimming pool open even when lifeguards were not on duty. She was told that the school's insurance carrier had assured them that all that was necessary was a posted sign that read, "Swim at your own risk." Could such a sign exonerate you if a lawsuit were filed? I told her they would be very susceptible to a liability claim and for that reason she should never leave the pool open without proper supervision. I suggested she contact her insurance carrier to request a letter from them supporting the use of signs. She later called to tell me that the insurance carrier refused to put anything in writing concerning signs in lieu of lifeguards. As a result, school officials who hoped to save money by limiting the use of lifeguards, instituted a policy that the pool remain closed unless qualified personnel were on hand to supervise aquatic activities.

Signs can be an asset to, but not a replacement for, sound risk management. During a risk review of municipal swimming pools, I found that all signs were in English when 95 percent of the people using the pool spoke Spanish. Administrators should be sensitive to such situations. (see Appendix R)

12.7 Game Programs and Public Address

Game programs and public address announcements can warn spectators about potential hazards. When the sport of ice hockey was introduced in the South and on the West Coast, facility managers wisely put warnings about flying pucks in game programs. They also used the public address system to alert spectators, who were unfamiliar with the sport, of the potential dangers in certain sections of the arena. This is good risk management strategy and should be used to advantage.

12.8 Accident and Injury Reporting

There are probably as many accident and injury forms as there are sports programs. Most forms appear to be standard and acceptable. There are two things, however, that should raise a red flag regarding forms. If the form has a statement that reads,"How could this accident have been prevented?," I recommend its deletion because a plaintiff's lawyer would like to read what caused the accident. The sports administrator needs to know what to do to prevent future injuries, but it should be in a session with the involved party, not on a report form.

An accident/injury report should also answer the question: "Did the person refuse treatment?" Not long ago, a woman slipped at the edge of an ice arena after a hockey game and fell to the concrete floor. She screamed at the ushers and officials of the arena, threatening a lawsuit. A paramedic attempted to administer emergency first aid but the woman refused treatment. It is important for future claims to make certain it was recorded that the injured party refused medical assistance.

Baron, a sports law authority, cautions administrators to document injuries carefully and accurately because it is impossible to determine when a claim might be filed against a staff member, administrator, or institution. He recommends filing reports if the injury results in the following:

• Lost class, practice, or game time, or
• Medical treatment or referral to a physician or hospital.

Furthermore, Baron states, "Document any injury reported to a member of the physical education, recreation, or sports staff by the participant or third party.... Injury reports are admissable in court and can document in court that a staff may not be responsible for the participant's injuries" (Baron and Appenzeller 1990).

Baron urges caution when he writes:

It is important to stress to staff members that they should prepare reports promptly but carefully when describing the participant's injury. Caution them not to diagnose injuries on the report, but use general terms such as bleeding over the right eye, or injury to the left leg in describing the injury. (Baron and Appenzeller 1990)

Instruct the staff never to issue a blank accident/injury report for the injured party to complete and return. This procedure could be dangerous because the injured party might complete the report in a way that is most advantageous to that party and it might not reflect the true facts. It is also important that you check with your attorney on the applicable statutes of limitations in your state for minors and adults to institute a lawsuit. Keep the accident/injury report on file for the number of years required by state statutes. See Appendix S for a sample accident/injury report for intercollegiate athletics and spectators.

Baron offers several key recommendations for proper procedure in the event of serious injuries:

1. Ensure that the injured party receives appropriate care before conducting any of the investigative procedures listed below. The welfare of the injured person is paramount.

2. Instruct the physical education instructor or coach to take a photograph of the scene of the accident before conditions change. These photographs can demonstrate in court that the condition of the school's equipment or facilities were safe at the time of the incident. It is a good idea to have camera available in the physical education and athletics departments at all times.

3. Obtain statements from all witnesses, including instructors, coaches, teammates, referees, and others who observed the accident or injury. The importance of these statements is to document what a witness may say at trial and to help evaluate a potential or actual claim. When taking a statement, record a second telephone number or address where the witness can be reached, in addition to his or her current address. This is vital, because at the time of the trial, which may be several years after the incident occurred, the witness may have moved and be difficult to locate. A sample witness statement form is given in Appendix T.

4. Identify the serial number of all protective equipment used by the injured party.

5. Isolate the injured person's equipment. Never reissue it to another participant or release it from the school's possession.

6. Compile all comments, warnings, and consent forms, in addition to relevant medical history documents, either signed by the student or disseminated to the student.

7. Compile all relevant equipment, facility, and playing surface inspection forms.

8. Locate and preserve records of purchase, maintenance, and reconditioning of relevant equipment used at the time of injury.

12.9 Postinjury Follow-up

Sports administrators should develop a policy with members of their staff that ensures immediate follow-up with the injured party and family. It is important to know that proper care and response have been carried out. The Lawrence Risk Insurance Company produced a video for teachers, coaches, and administrators in sports that points out the need for supervision, instruction, and the wise use of equipment and facilities. The video stresses the need for immediate follow-up as a way to limit litigation. From experience the company realizes that parents are reluctant to sue when genuine concern and attention are shown for an injured son or daughter. On the other hand, a lack of concern and indifference can lead to a costly lawsuit. Most teachers, coaches, and administrators show concern and compassion for injured students, but others fail to follow-up and often pay a price in court.

12.10 Contracts and Written Agreements

One of the key things I have learned in athletics administration is to put everything in writing. Charles Lynch, an attorney in High Point, North Carolina, specializing in contract law, writes in *Successful Sport Management*

> The importance of reducing oral agreements or understandings to writing cannot be overemphasized. If a dispute arises, each party will have a different opinion about the details of an oral agreement. At a minimum, a letter to confirm an agreement with a space at the bottom for acknowledgment by the other party might avoid any future misunderstandings. Of course, the letter should be well-written, to the point, and state in clear and concise terms the writer's understanding of the oral agreement. (Appenzeller 1985, 309)

For example, I once asked a graduate sports information director to solicit advertisement for the football program and, as an incentive, agreed to pay him a percentage of the revenue raised. The agreement was made informally with the approval of college officials. When the time came to pay, however, the request was denied by the one official that really counted, the business manager. He insisted that college policy prohibited extra compensation to a college employee. Up until that time, I had operated on the basis of a handshake or verbal agreement, but from that moment on, I operated like a business and put everything in writing.

A few years later, I met with five administrators to discuss and approve athletics policy. Following the meeting, I sent a copy of what we agreed upon to each administrator with a request that they send back anything with which they disagreed. I stated that the policy would be in effect if I did not hear from them. In the fall of that year, one administrator attempted to implement a new regulation that was very detrimental to the sports program and contrary to the agreement. I sent him a copy of the approved athletics policy and received an apology. A potential conflict was avoided. It helped to have the agreement in writing.

Carl Scheer, the general manager of the National Basketball Association's (NBA) Denver Nuggets, broadcast Guilford College basketball games in the 1960s as a hobby. When Scheer became general manager of the American Basketball Association's (ABA) Carolina Cougars, he offered the college $1500 to play preliminary games in the Greensboro Coliseum to increase attendance at Cougar games. The arrangement would give the program more exposure and revenue than we could receive in our very small gymnasium. Everything was fine until I asked Scheer to send a contract. He became very angry and questioned why friends needed a contract. I reminded him that as an attorney he knew friendship had nothing to do with good business practice. He left the meeting so angry and frustrated I felt the arrangement would not take place. However, I received a signed contract with a note of apology that said, "I respect your action. You were not asking for a contract for yourself but as protection for your college."

Ironically, when Scheer returned to North Carolina as general manager of the NBA's Charlotte Hornets, he worked without a formal contract. After the Hornets broke attendance records for a new franchise, Scheer tried to negotiate a written contract which was refused by Hornets' owner George Shinn. As a result, a disappointed Scheer returned to the Nuggets.

After fourteen months as president of the Denver Nuggets, there was serious discussion over Scheer's future with the NBA team, although he reportedly had signed a five-year contract estimated at $2 million. Scheer commented on his situation, saying, "I assume there will be discussions to terminate my contract. I haven't said I'm quitting and nobody with the Nuggets has said you're fired. But if they don't want me around, I have a contract and I expect them to honor that" (*Greensboro News and Record* 13 June 1991).

The Associated Press reported that Carl Scheer ended his association with the Denver Nuggets when lawyers for both parties reached a settlement. Without question, Scheer's signed contract enabled him to negotiate the settlement in a manner favorable to himself. It seems both Herb Appenzeller and Carl Scheer learned the importance of written agreements.

Student-athletes must ask college coaches who recruit them to put offers of financial aid in writing. *The Daily News* of Morehead City, North Carolina, reported that six athletes filed suit against North Carolina Central University for allegedly "luring them to school with deceptive promises" (*The Daily News* 15 June 1991). University attorneys, however, argued that some athletes failed to file their federal financial aid forms on time. The university had planned to supplement athletics department funds with these monies. University attorneys pointed out that "oral promises made by coaches or athletics administrators can't be enforced in court and that the university had no obligation to ante up money that was promised but not delivered." Another reason to put everything in writing!

Charles Lynch, in *Successful Sport Management*, has a final word for sports administrators suggesting that "the sports manager must approach his job as the chief executive officer of a business. Sports has become big business and affairs must be conducted according to prudent business practices" (Appenzeller 1985, 309).

12.11 Documentation

Documentation of equipment and facility inspections can be the key to a successful defense in the event of litigation. Inspection reports can be introduced in court to provide demonstrative evidence that an institution's sports equipment or facilities were not defective and not the cause of a participant's injury. Personnel who conduct these various inspections should be instructed to log the results of the inspections on a checklist with appropriate recommendations. Be sure to note if and when corrective action is taken. The inspector should also sign and date the checklist. Several facility and equipment checklists are included as examples for proper documentation of various sports equipment and facility inspections. (See Appendix U for sample inspection lists of facilities. Document when hazards are remedied by using the Maintenance Response Form in Appendix V.)

A common problem for most schools is the use of facilities and equipment without permission, such as joggers on a running track or pickup games of softball, baseball, or soccer. It is difficult to keep these people off fields or out of gymnasiums. When legitimate groups leased facilities on our campus they received a special permit that denoted the group and approximate time they would use the facility. Security received a copy of the permit and was aware of their presence. Unauthorized groups without a permit were required to leave the facility.

United Educators Insurance Risk Retention Group, Inc., offers these excellent risk management action steps for facilities:

- Maintain an inventory of athletics facilities used in intercollegiate, intramural, club, recreational, and instructional activities.
- Conduct formal routine reviews of the conditions of all athletics facilities, designating one person to be responsible for maintaining safety in each facility.
- Hold supervisors accountable for observing and maintaining facility safety.

- Include a formal review of safety considerations in the planning stages of designing a new, or rehabilitating an old, facility.
- Institute staffing plans for all facilities for all scheduled and informal activities.
- Institute special crowd control procedures for all activities where spectators could be harmed or could interfere with the activity. (United Educators 1991)

United Educators offers risk management action steps regarding equipment, such as gymnastic and weight machines:

- Maintain an inventory of equipment used in intercollegiate, intramural, club, recreational, and instructional sports that identifies all significant equipment by age and manufacturer.
- Conduct formal routine reviews of the condition of all equipment, including such things as weight machines in dormitory basements.
- Designate specific responsibility for the maintenance and safety of all equipment.
- Require that all users participate in an orientation and a safety check before first use of equipment.
- Purchase athletics equipment with prominent safety considerations in all specifications.
- Develop a clear policy on the use of college athletics facilities by outsiders. (United Educators 1991)

12.12 Risk Management Strategies for Coaches in the 1990s

I made a presentation to the North Carolina High School Coaches Association's annual clinic in which I suggested fifteen risk management strategies for coaches in the 1990s. They included the following:

1. Always put the welfare of the individual first. If you err, err on the side of conservatism.
2. Do not issue equipment until the following items are completed:
   A. A preparticipation physical examination,
   B. Confirmation of insurance coverage,
   C. Confirmation of eligibility, and
   D. An agreement to participate.
3. Inform athletes of the inherent risks of the sport and the ways they can protect themselves.
4. Develop a medical response plan according to the resources available. Conduct a practice drill occasionally to determine everyone's responsibilities.
5. Following serious injury to an athlete, rely on qualified medical personnel to decide on reentry into a game or practice session.

6. Develop a policy for athletes with disabilities (one eye, one kidney, one testicle).

7. Inspect equipment and facilities when appropriate.

8. Post signs regarding safety and behavioral expectations in locker rooms and gymnasiums.

9. Check your insurance coverage, including travel and liability.

10. Always supervise high-risk activities.

11. Avoid terminology such as suicide drills, death run, and hamburger drill. These terms could come back to haunt you in court.

12. In the event of injury, always follow-up with a call or visit to check on the athlete's condition. However, **never, never admit fault**.

13. In the event of a serious accident or injury that could lead to potential litigation, alert the athletics director or principal. Follow up with a call to the insurance company and then the attorney.

14. Isolate and keep under lock and key equipment involved in a serious injury (helmet, protective pad, etc.).

15. Be aware that you can be sued but don't panic; be prepared and coach with confidence. (Appenzeller 1990)

12.13 Do Not Admit Fault

I find that teachers and coaches have a tendency to blame themselves when students in their care are injured. This is not good risk management strategy. In North Carolina, a base runner collided with a catcher who was rendered quadriplegic. The well-meaning baseball coach of the base runner told his team and the public that he caused the accident because he thought his players knew the "slide rule" adopted in North Carolina in 1979. The coaching association passed a rule that runners coming into a base had to slide rather than run over an opponent. The plaintiff and his parents reportedly used the coach's statement as the basis for a negligence suit against the school district.

Investigators for the North Carolina High School Athletic Association noted that some witnesses said that the catcher moved down the third baseline giving the runner little option in trying to reach home plate. It is obvious that a gray area existed and the facts of the accident were in dispute. It has been reported that the injured boy received an out-of-court settlement of $500,000. Sound risk management strategy recommends that the individual involved be sympathetic and concerned for the injured party, but never admit fault.

13

Equipment and Facilities

An important responsibility of the sports administrator is to provide and maintain safe equipment and facilities. I remember well the concern of several coaches at a major university who sent equipment needs to the business manager. Their lists included specific brands they felt were required for safety. In many instances, the business manager, who did not understand sports equipment, would listen to a sporting goods salesperson and order less expensive, but also less protective, equipment. The men's ice hockey coach ordered top-of-the-line helmets because of the violent nature of the sport. A salesperson, however, assured the business manager that another brand was really as good and not as expensive. The coach's question was simple: "If one of our players suffers a serious head injury, who will be liable?" I think the business manager assumed more accountability than he really wanted.

An example of the effect improper equipment can have on sports occurred one season when I was totally unaware of a problem until it was almost too late. As athletics director and head football coach, I ordered all football equipment. I was very satisfied with the helmet the team used. It was the best we could buy and, fortunately, we had never had a serious head injury. That particular year seven of the varsity players received head injuries that kept them on the sidelines for various periods of time.

At the end of the season, each player kept his equipment in his locker in preparation for upcoming spring drills. When the regular salesman came by with the factory representative, I told them I planned to change helmets because of the high head injury rate we had during the season. The factory representative immediately asked if I had the helmets belonging to the injured men. I produced the helmets. The representative commented (much to the embarrassment of the salesman), "These helmets look like all the others, but they are for junior high school use." The salesman stammered and said that obviously a mix-up had occurred and the company would replace every helmet with the ones we had originally ordered. It is essential that the equipment purchased meet safety specifications. See Appendix W for a sample letter regarding donations of protective equipment.

The safety committee can be a powerful force in developing inspection lists for both equipment and facilities. The safety committee can also eliminate confusion over who will be the designated inspector. There should be a well-conceived plan for periodic inspections of equipment and facilities for hazards and other dangerous conditions prior to their use. Failure to inspect led to a huge damage award in New York. A school district failed to implement a program of preventive maintenance or inspection of its facilities and a loose nut and bolt on a ladder led to the death of an employee and a $1,400,000 award to his family (*Woodring v. Bd. of Educ. of Manhasset* 1981).

The following section discusses the areas that, in my experience, most frequently present problems for the sports program.

13.1 Indoor Facilities

A student in Alabama was cut around the eye by shattered glass from an unprotected light bulb in the ceiling of the gymnasium. The student filed a lawsuit claiming that injuries to his eye and face were permanent (*Beasley v. Morton* 1990). The sports administrator should alert staff that all clocks, lights, and windows should be properly shielded. In addition, keep unused equipment stored in a safe area and make certain that basketball goals are at a safe distance from walls and unprotected glass doors or windows located behind the goals.

The old gymnasium at Guilford College had panes of regular glass located several feet behind the basketball backboard. I used to stand in the lobby and watch basketball games through the glass panes until Bob Kauffman, a 6' 8", 240-pound all-America with tremendous speed, started running toward the glass panels with his hands outstretched. He used the window to stop himself. We replaced the window with a solid brick wall. What a case Kauffman, a first-round NBA draft choice with the Seattle Supersonics and three-time NBA All-Star, would have had against the institution if his professional career had been ended by our negligence. I breathed easier when the hazardous condition was corrected.

Ronald Baron cautions the sports administrator to:

> Provide and maintain safe equipment and facilities. Periodically inspect for hazards or other dangerous conditions prior to use. Upon the discovery of hazards, immediately remedy the hazard, remove the defective equipment, or avoid the use of the unsafe facility until the problem is corrected. (Baron and Appenzeller 1990)

13.2 Ground Fault Interrupters

A coach decided to enlarge an existing whirlpool so that more than one athlete could use it at a time. The coach sought the opinion of the industrial arts teacher and was assured that it would work and was safe. Three boys got into the whirlpool after baseball practice. Upon hearing their calls for help, a coach quickly disconnected it. Two of the boys recovered, but one died from electrocution. A Kentucky court held that the absence of a ground fault interrupter (GFI) was the cause of the accident (*Massey v. Persson* 1987).

The death of an amusement park guard and another man could have been prevented, a federal safety official said, if a safety device, readily available in hardware stores for about $10.00, had been installed (*Greensboro News and Record* 13 June 1991). On the day following the tragic death of the two men due to the lack of a safety device, there was a report that a "circuit breaker probably saved the life of a Burlington, North Carolina, electrical worker who was severely shocked while working on power lines. The circuit breaker diverted some of the electricity and saved the worker's life (*Greensboro News and Record* 14 June 1991).

A representative of the Occupational Safety and Health Administration (OSHA) commented that the safety device was not required when the park was built. This is a common argument heard when the Center for Sports Law and Risk Management conducts risk reviews in facilities that were built prior to a particular law. For example, the director of a very large sports complex pointed out that people with disabilities had no access to a rest room in his facility because it had been built prior to the 1973 Rehabilitation Act. Of course this is no excuse. Many facilities were built well before the act, but they must comply with federal law. Compliance with federal law is a must, no matter when a facility was built.

Sports administrators need to understand the function and need for a GFI. During a risk review at a large midwestern university, we found a lack of GFIs in a training room. The trainer had six whirlpool machines which student-athletes were using for rehabilitation purposes. None were connected with a GFI. The trainer explained that his athletics director did not want to spend the money (approximately $35 per GFI) it would cost to provide safety for the users. We find that many areas where water and electricity mix, such as athletics training rooms and locker rooms, do not have GFIs. Electricians can install these safety devices quickly and inexpensively. An awareness of this problem is essential.

13.3 Laundries and Dryers

Most schools on the high school and collegiate level have laundries complete with dryers. Most administrators assign a staff member and several student assistants to operate the machines and then pay little attention to their operation. This often overlooked area can create hazardous conditions.

A ninth-grader in Louisiana was a student manager assigned to the freshman basketball team. He was in a hurry to get the uniforms washed. In the process he tried to stop the extractor when it failed to stop spinning. None of the coaches had explained the use of the extractor, although the varsity manager had tried to explain the process to him. He climbed on the machine in an effort to get his foot on the lever. The next thing he remembered was standing beside the machine, his left leg in excruciating pain (Appenzeller and Baron 1990).

As a result of the injury, the freshman manager was hospitalized for thirty-seven days, and his leg was amputated. The manufacturer of the extractor testified that, "When the machine was built, it allowed the user to open the lid while the basket was still spinning, contrary to applicable safety standards." The manufacturer settled with the boy, and the school district was found liable for one-half of the damages because the manufacturer settled during the trial. The fifteen-year-old boy received damages of $1 million (Appenzeller and Baron 1990).

Bill Beale, an attorney and president of Belco Laundry of Charlotte, North Carolina, recommends the following safety tips and hints for the use of athletics laundries.

- Never use any product that does not have the Underwriters Laboratory (UL) Seal on the rear of the machine. The entire product should be UL approved, not just a valve or motor. (Recently seventeen people were electrocuted by non-UL hairdryers.)
- Never use or store any flammable products in the dryer room. Never dry any mops or rags that have touched solvents. Mops dipped in flammable solvents for floor cleaning cause most fires. Make sure the salesperson gives you written assurance that the solvent purchased will not burn.
- Never alter or change any parts or "hot wire" a machine to make it run temporarily. Units are made to government specifications for safe use, and reliable sales companies have national Teletech service for immediate help. They will also ship any part needed by air freight.
- Keep spare parts in a kit just as you do with your automobile.
- For fast and safe drying, keep the lint screens clean. If cleaned before use, it will save ten minutes in drying time because lint buildup on temperature sensors causes temperature controls to be useless.
- Keep all panels and protective guards in place at all times.
- Keep inspection and maintenance sheets up to date. Notify maintenance when service is needed.

Never leave machines running unattended for more than thirty minutes. Stay until all the items are finished and out of the dryer. Dirty uniforms can be left to soak in water overnight.

- Avoid heat, rough action, and hurry-up methods such as high-speed extraction for fast washing and drying.
- Avoid separate extractors—courts hold that they are dangerous and uniform manufacturers claim they tear and damage equipment.
- Avoid commercial laundries if they are not UL approved.
- Many states have laws that require schools to purchase only those electrical products that are UL approved. However, states do not tell salesmen and manufacturers that they cannot sell non-UL approved products to schools. In some ways, it is like drinking laws that permit a store to sell whiskey but penalize drunkenness.
- Follow the rules and your athletics laundry will give you good service. (Appenzeller and Baron 1990)

13.4 Locker Rooms

A Minnesota court held a school district negligent for failing "to inspect and maintain the equipment, building, and grounds for the protection of the students" *Kingsley v. Ind. Sch. Dist. no. 12*, 1977). A piece of metal protruding from a locker "tore the skin and tissue from a girl's finger." All that remained of her finger was muscle and bone. Ronald Baron, a sports law specialist, notes that, "the locker room should be free of sharp projections and dangerous objects. Surfaces should be kept clean and dry to reduce the danger of slipping and the spread of foot infection. Proper ventilation is important. Lockers should be secured to prevent tipping" (Baron and Appenzeller 1990).

13.5 Gymnastics Equipment

For years, students attending a summer music camp on the campus became upset with me for not leaving a trampoline on the gymnasium floor. They insisted they came from a state in which the sport of trampolining was important and they knew the art of spotting. However, I would not allow the trampoline on the court for anyone to use. If a crippling injury occurred, I explained to them, the institution could not successfully defend a lawsuit in court. I insisted that a member of the music staff, with expertise in the sport, be present to supervise this activity. The conflict was resolved and the activity carefully monitored by trained personnel. Today, the majority of schools on both the secondary and collegiate level have eliminated the trampoline from the program. Insurance became impossible to obtain, and while the number of trampoline-related injuries was small, catastrophic-type injuries were present. Too often equipment such as balance beams, parallel bars, mats, and vaulting equipment are left out when class is not in session. The sports administrator should make certain that all gymnastic equipment is kept in a locked area until qualified personnel are available to supervise.

13.6 Weight Room

Lifting weights has become popular among the general population. Students on all levels use weights in both supervised and unsupervised programs, presenting a need for safe equipment and conditions. The sports administrator should be aware of each teams' policies regarding weight training. In Michigan, a high school principal and athletics director were sued for allegedly breaching their duty of care to a student who was seriously injured when heavy weights fell on him. The boy claimed that the sports administrator failed to observe that weightlifting in the summer violated conference rules and failed to supervise the program. The Michigan court made an interesting comment when it said that sports administrators, because of their specialized training, were responsible for enforcing rules and supervising activities and eliminating unsafe practices engaged in by coaches under their direction (*Vargo v. Svitchan* 1981).

13.7 Spectator Seating

I remember an embarrassing incident that happened in the gymnasium when I invited a benefactor of the athletics program to a basketball game. I emphasized the need for a new facility because the 40-year-old, 900-seat gymnasium could not meet present needs. During the game, I looked from the balcony to see if the benefactor was in his seat, when suddenly the footboard and seatboard holding him collapsed. As I reached him, he looked at me and said, "I know you need a new gymnasium, but this is going too far." We were lucky he was not injured; instead of a lawsuit, he sent a check for $200,000 to start a new facility. I had requested a thorough inspection of the bleachers before the season and thought they had been approved for use. There are many cases in which spectator seating is found to be the cause of injury because the seating was not inspected for defective boards and worn out nuts and bolts. When spectator seating is defective, plaintiffs often succeed in litigation.

A tragic ending to a basketball game occurred when a parent left her infant baby on the bleachers so she could go to the basketball court to talk with her other son. The "clean-up" crew closed the bleachers electronically, without looking for objects or people, crushing the infant to death. It is imperative, therefore, to place a sign on the bleachers warning members of the "clean-up" crew to always check for objects before closing bleachers.

Another safety feature of seating involves guard rails on bleacher sections. Most state and federal regulations require guard rails for bleachers over five rows high, and officials recommend that sports administrators comply with seating requirements or face penalties.

13.8 Outdoor Playing Surfaces

A Tennessee newspaper reported a softball umpire sued a city worker and the Metro Nashville government for $25,000. The umpire claimed she suffered physical pain, incurred medical expenses, and lost wages when a softball struck a deep furrow near a base and caromed to hit her in the nose. She claimed the field was not in proper shape and the grounds attendant did little to protect participants. The supervisor of the grounds crew apologized for the condition of the field, attributing it to a new man who did not know how to properly drag a field.

The sports administrator should delegate a person to check playing fields for holes, glass, rocks, uncovered drains, sockets that protrude above ground, and other hazards. Check wire backstops on baseball and softball fields to make certain that holes do not exist that threaten the safety of spectators.

Four baseball players ran into an outfield fence because our field lacked a warning track. I put a warning track on the list of priorities, but unfortunately the $5,000 price tag delayed its construction. To protect the participants, I used an idea from an athletics director who advised us to cut the grass very low, ten feet from the outfield fence and paint a white or yellow line around the ten-foot area. We tried it as a good temporary solution. Since then a warning track has been installed to help alert participants that the fence is near.

13.9 Overlapping Fields

Participants in recreation and physical education activities often collide with each other when contiguous fields overlap. It doesn't matter what the sport, overlapping fields can cause problems, injuries, and subsequent lawsuits. A women's softball team reportedly attempted to play a game at a college in Boston when there was a track and field meet the same day. The hammer throw area overlapped the softball field and hammers fell frequently during the women's game. When the team ended an inning and the players ran toward the dugout, a hammer landed where the shortstop had been standing. The coach, using sound judgment, immediately called off the game and took her team home. Once during a risk review, I saw a men's and women's track team dodging baseballs. The baseball team used the astroturf field in the football stadium whenever the baseball field was wet, thus posing hazardous conditions to the members of the track teams. During fall track practice, the members of both the men's and women's track teams dodged footballs rather than baseballs. It seems that the members of the track teams should have been warned that, "track and field can be dangerous to your health." Overlapping fields are a definite hazard and participation by teams from two sports utilizing the same field should be eliminated.

13.10 Track and Field

Several years ago, I was preparing to speak on liability to a group of sports administrators. Before I could start, an athletics director told the group about an incident that happened to him. He said he had heard me speak at a conference in Minnesota, during which I suggested that when they returned home, they check their facilities for safety, particularly the location of their track in relation to field events. He definitely planned to do it, but like many of us, he became preoccupied with business. During a track meet at his stadium, spectators were watching running events while a discus thrower was spinning as he prepared to throw the discus from the rain-wettened circle. The discus area was located behind the stands. The thrower slipped and hurled the discus into the stands, striking a young spectator in the back of the head. The boy fell from the top row of the bleachers and was seriously injured. The sports administrator changed the discus area the following day and later settled out of court for $100,000 in damages. "Listen to this man," he said, "and don't wait too long to check your equipment and facilities."

On my return trip from that conference, I received quite a shock. While I was out of town, the recently hired part-time track coach changed the pole vault area, locating it five feet from a picket fence. If any pole vaulters slipped, they could be impaled on the fence. We had a meet scheduled that very afternoon. We had two choices: cancel the pole vault event or immediately correct the dangerous situation. We elected to pad the fence with layers of foam rubber. The next day we moved the landing pit to a safe place on the track. It's important to make certain that there is ample space between each field event and the running track so that the various areas are safe for both spectators and participants.

Another concern is safety for events such as the javelin, shot put, discus, and hammer throw. Frederick Mueller reports that:

> There have been six track accidents that involved participants being struck by a thrown discus, shot, or hammer. One injury resulted in death and two in permanent disability. In 1986 a newspaper reporter was killed by an errant hammer thrown during a college track meet. *Proper precautions* should be taken. Accidents like this should never happen. (Mueller and Ryan 1991, 35)

As a result of being appointed to the National Amateur Athletic Union (AAU) Track and Field committee some years ago, I went to their championship meet in Miami, Florida. I attended the shot put finals, aware that a fifteen-year-old in North Carolina had died when he was struck in the head by a shot put while measuring a throw. I thought that this could not happen in national competition, but within minutes I saw an official turn his head while measuring a throw, barely avoiding a direct hit that could have killed him. In *From the Gym To The Jury*, a textbook dealing with sports injury and liability, I recommended a simple precaution that could eliminate such injuries and possible death.

Every coach of track and field should assign one person to supervise the discus, shot put, javelin, and hammer throw event. This special official would not mark the flight of the various objects, record the throw, or judge a foul. The only responsibility would be the most important one: he/she should see that no throws are made when officials are measuring or someone is in the danger zone. This person would be responsible for the safety of everyone in the area of the throw. This is such a little innovation, but one that can save countless accidents. This person may become one of the most important figures at a track meet. (Appenzeller 1970, 143)

13.11 Distribution and Fitting of Protective Equipment

Protective equipment distributed by an institution should fit the participant and be free from cracks, tears, or other defects. To ensure compliance, the following procedures are recommended:

• All equipment should be inspected prior to distribution.
• Equipment managers or others who distribute protective equipment should be given specific instructions on the safe and proper method of fitting equipment.
• When equipment is distributed, your staff should document in writing the serial number of the piece of equipment issued to the student and check that it is in good condition. Proper documentation includes the serial number, the student's name, the date issued, and the signature of the staff member who distributed the equipment.
• Students should be cautioned not to modify any equipment. This warning can be read to the students when the equipment is issued and documented by noting when warnings were read and who read them.
Note: If a student modifies equipment and an injury occurs, the school can effectively demonstrate that it complied with its responsibilities.
• Headgear for sports such as lacrosse, wrestling, and football should be inspected to ensure that National Operating Commission on Standards for Athletic Equipment (NOCSAE) warnings are visible and proper.
• NOCSAE warnings should be posted in the locker room and placed on individual pieces of equipment.

- Ensure that the reconditioner of headgear and other protective equipment is NOCSAE approved.
- Follow the manufacturer's suggested guidelines for proper installation, maintenance, inspection, and repair of equipment.
- Do not pass down worn or defective equipment to students on physical education or intramural teams. Students at all levels should have the benefit of quality equipment.
- Provide a secure area to store equipment when it is not in use.
- Equipment should be checked occasionally by the coach to be sure it continues to be safe and usable. (Baron and Appenzeller 1990)

13.12 Use of Facilities and Equipment by Outside Groups

For years our institution leased facilities to various groups including a summer music festival and tennis, soccer, lacrosse, basketball, and cheerleading camps. The leasing of facilities has public relations value as well as financial returns, but it also extends the institution's responsibility to provide reasonably safe facilities and equipment. Ron Baron recommends that:

> any equipment distributed to outside groups or facilities should be inspected and maintained in a safe condition.... All activities by outside groups should be properly supervised by adults representing the group. The number of supervising adults depends on the type of activity, age, and number of participants. However, the specific number should be spelled out in an agreement prior to the use of the facility. A facility should not be made available until the requisite number of adults is, in fact, present. (Baron and Appenzeller 1990)

Many schools do not use a facility-use agreement when outside groups lease their facilities. The facility and its managers can be named in a lawsuit and possibly held liable for injuries that result from the use of unsafe facilities and defective equipment. To protect a school and staff from liability as a result of negligence or carelessness by an outside group using its facilities and equipment, a facility use indemnification agreement can be used to transfer the risk of loss. The agreement should contain the following items:

- A list of general rules a group should follow when using a school's facilities or equipment.
- A clause requiring the outside group to name the school as an additional named insured on their general liability policy for the dates of the outside group's use of the school's facility. A certificate of insurance naming the school as an additional insured

should be delivered to the school at least one week prior to use. In addition, the outside group or their insurance company should be required to notify the school at least seventy-two hours prior to use of any cancellation of the outside group's insurance prior to the leasing or use of the school's facilities or equipment.

- A clause requiring the outside group to hold blameless and indemnify the school for any and all claims or lawsuits that may result from their use of the school premises.
- A statement that the school district has absolute right of cancellation without penalty or liability if the facility is unavailable. (Baron and Appenzeller 1990)

A sample facility use and indemnification agreement is given in (Appendix X).

13.13 Due Process

I received an emotional telephone call at 1:30 A.M. from the women's basketball coach following a loss to a rival team. She explained that several members of the team reported that the loss was due to the misconduct of three starters who were violating rules. She told me she had scheduled an early morning meeting with the three students during which she planned to suspend them indefinitely from the team. I could not go back to sleep because something seemed wrong. Suddenly it became clear: the coach was taking the word of other student-athletes to suspend the three starters without affording them due process. I called her to discuss due process procedures prior to her meeting with the students. When she met with the students, who had allegedly violated good conduct rules, she extended procedural due process by observing the following:

- An individual must have proper notice that he or she is about to be deprived of life, liberty, or property.
- An individual must be given the opportunity to be heard.
- An individual must be afforded a fair trial or hearing with the right to appeal an adverse decision.

In her situation the students admitted fault and accepted the temporary suspension. If they had not admitted guilt and were not satisfied with the punishment, they had the following appeals procedure:

- Appeal to the athletics director.
- Appeal to the athletics committee, or
- Appeal to the president, whose decision is final.

During a risk review at an NCAA Division I institution, I was praising the athletics director and his staff for their outstanding handbook. I felt it was thorough, clear, and detailed, setting out policies and procedures for the members of the athletics department. I asked where due process was located, remarking that, "I am sure it is included, I just can't find it." The athletics director appeared puzzled and answered, "What do you mean by due process?" I thought he was kidding me, but I responded that on many occasions coaches dropped athletes from teams without giving them due process. "Oh, that's what it is," he responded. "Well, we don't need it because I will always back any coach who suspends someone from the team for any reason."

Rather than making an issue of due process before the administrator's staff, I explained that administrators and coaches usually have valid reasons for suspending people who break rules, but if they denied procedural due process, they usually lost if they were taken to court to defend their action. I explained this is the very reason we need due process; protection from arbitrary and capricious action on the part of the coach. And yet, here was the chief executive officer of the sports program automatically upholding any action, right or wrong, the coaches took. "Well," he said, "maybe I'll look into due process, but I will still back my coaches."

Due process has received national publicity and attention through the dispute between the National Collegiate Athletics Association (NCAA) and Jerry Tarkanian, head basketball coach at the University of Nevada at Las Vegas (UNLV). Tarkanian insisted, in a long court battle, that he was denied due process by the NCAA. In 1991, Tarkanian and Dale Brown, head basketball coach at Louisiana State University (LSU), testified before the House Subcommittee on Commerce, Consumer Protection and Competitiveness that the NCAA allegedly violates due process when it investigates its member schools (Sullivan 1991).

Legislatures in Nebraska, Nevada, and Florida passed legislation requiring that the NCAA follow due process procedures when it investigates colleges and universities in their states. Several other states have similar legislation pending (Appenzeller and Baron 1991).

For years due process has been extolled by people in sports as the right of an individual to receive fair play. The Bill of Rights states that each person has the opportunity of due process. The Fifth Amendment of the United States Constitution applies to the federal government only and states that "no person ... shall be deprived of life, liberty, or property without due process." On the other hand, the Fourteenth Amendment of the United States Constitution applies to the states and provides "nor shall any state deprive any person of life, liberty, or property without due proces of law" (Appenzeller 1975, 219). While courts traditionally support the authority of school officials to promulgate rules, they insist on rules that are fair and reasonable. Public schools, whether they are on the elementary, secondary, or college and university level, are governed by the Fourteenth Amendment regarding the obligation to afford due process.

Students in private institutions have no constitutional protection under the Fourteenth Amendment, but rely on a contract theory in which a private institution agrees that it will not act in an arbitrary or capricious manner toward students in disciplinary cases (*Dixon v. Alabama* 1961).

I recommend that athletics directors meet with all teams at the opening of school to explain due process procedures to student-athletes, coaches, and staff. Due process is an important part of risk management and needs attention. To oversimplify due process, the following conditions should exist:

- An individual must have proper notice that he or she is about to be deprived of life, liberty, or property.
- An individual must be given the opportunity to be heard, and an individual must be afforded a fair trial or hearing.
- An appeal process must be established.

13.14 Title IX

Prior to the passage of the Education Amendments Act of 1972 (Public Law 92–318), women's sports occupied a secondary role in many athletics programs on the secondary and collegiate levels. An outgrowth of the act was Title IX, which received immediate attention because it attempted to use federal funds to require equal opportunity for women in sports. The law was direct and stated:

No person in the United States shall be excluded from participation in, be denied the benefit of, or be subjected to discrimination under any education program or activity receiving federal assistance. (American Council on Education 1975)

In 1975, Casper Weinberger, Secretary of Health, Education, and Welfare (HEW), warned school officials that while Title IX regulations did not require equal expenditures, it did mandate equal opportunity for women in sport:

I have just one message: We can wait no longer. Equal education opportunity for women is the law of the land and it will be enforced. (Appenzeller and Appenzeller 1980, 72)

Title IX advocates realistically predicted that complex guidelines could take months, even years, to answer and, in all probability, will require court action to solve. In 1978, Joseph Califano replaced Weinberger as HEW secretary and took a hard-line approach to enforcement, promising to vigorously enforce Title IX because it was the "law of the land." By 1980, however, over 600 cases claiming noncompliance had been filed with the Office of Civil Rights (OCR), and yet not one institution had been denied one dollar in federal assistance.

In 1975, I attended a meeting of the National Collegiate Directors of Athletics (NACDA). The most controversial issue at the convention was the implementation of Title IX regulations. Emotions ran high as an attorney for the Department of Education discussed the required institutional self-evaluation. She commented that there are two things no one should see being made—laws and sausage! One athletics director became totally frustrated and irrational, running to the floor microphone to yell, "If I were your president, I would fire each one of you on your return to campus and replace you with a lawyer." Much anger and confusion was generated by Title IX. Following the convention, I completed the self-evaluation forms because the Department of Education notified each institution that noncompliance could lead to loss of federal assistance. I did not gloss over the weaknesses, but detailed areas of noncompliance openly and honestly. For fourteen years I had requested funds to build locker rooms, rest rooms, and shower rooms in the gymnasium for the women. The gymnasium was built in 1940 with only a single rest room on the main floor for women. The men had several locker rooms, rest rooms, and shower rooms. Physical education was required for all students for four years and women students had to dress for class in residence halls. When OCR notified the administration about a potential loss of federal assistance for noncompliance, I received an emergency call from the president. He implored me to keep the institution out of court. I informed him that I tried very hard, but to no avail, to correct the inequities that existed between male and female athletes, and could not help. As a result, a special emergency meeting was scheduled on Sunday morning to start work the next day on lockers, showers, and rest rooms for women. The Department of Education, OCR, and Title IX got the message across.

Linda Carpenter, a Brooklyn College professor who for twelve years has conducted research on women in sports wrote:

The impact of Title IX on physical education and athletics programs has been massive ... today, barriers to the participation of girls and women in sports has been markedly reduced. Competitive athletics for girls and women have been expanded and now include well-developed national championships. (Appenzeller 1985)

Just when Title IX was helping women participate at an all-time high, however, the movement was sidetracked by litigation involving a private, coeducational college in Pennsylvania. Grove City College received federal assistance in only one area, Basic Educational Opportunity Grants (BEOG) for approximately six percent of its 2,200 students. College officials contended that they did not discriminate in violation of Title IX and would not fill out compliance forms. As a result, federal assistance funds were terminated. The *Grove City* case went all the way to the United States Supreme Court which held, in essence, that a program within an institution that did not receive federal assistance was not bound by Title IX regulations. Because athletics programs (with the possible exception of service academies such as the United States Military Academy) did not receive federal aid, compliance with Title IX regulations was not required. Shock waves went through the United States and Title IX became a victim of that decision. As a result of *Grove City*, 674 gender discrimination cases were dropped and Title IX was put on hold (*Grove City v. Bell* 1984). The Civil Rights Restoration Act of 1989, however, was passed and Title IX was revitalized, and F. Michael Villalobos, a professor at Loyola School of Law in New Orleans, predicted that:

> With the passage of the Civil Rights Restoration Act of 1989, Title IX's regulations undoubtedly will be revived and be used to offer guidelines to sports administrators. It appears that women's sports once again will be given added impetus. (Villalobos 1990)

Six months after the passage of the Restoration Act, sixteen gender discrimination complaints were filed against twelve college and university athletics departments. Linda Carpenter and Vivian Acosta, authors of a twelve-year study on gender discrimination, filed suit against Brooklyn College, where they are professors of physical education and former coaches, contending that the institution violates Title IX regulations in "13 program areas cited in the law" (*New York Times* 12 Dec. 1990).

After a fourteen month inquiry, the Education Department's Office for Civil Rights decided that Brooklyn College "discriminated against its female athletes and coaches." The decision came a few weeks after college presidents were warned by the Education Department not to violate Title IX laws "when they make decisions about eliminating sports teams" (*The Chronicle of Higher Education* 1992).

It is clear that the Restoration Act has revived Title IX guidelines. As a sports administrator, it is important that your athletics programs comply with the regulations. An example of one of the regulations under Equivalence in Other Athletics Benefits and Opportunities includes the following:

> The regulation requires that recipients that operate or sponsor interscholastic, intercollegiate, club or intramural athletics, provide equal athletics opportunities for members of both sexes. In determining whether an institution is providing equal opportunity in intercollegiate athletics, the regulations require the department to consider, among other things, the following factors:
>
> 1. whether the selection of sports and levels of competition accommodate the interests and abilities of both sexes;
> 2. provision and maintenance of equipment and supplies;
> 3. scheduling of games and practice times;
> 4. travel and per diem allowances;

5. opportunity to receive coaching and academic tutoring;
6. assignment and compensation of coaches and tutors;
7. provision of locker rooms, practice, and competitive facilities;
8. provision of medical and training facilities and services. (NCAA 1991)

I was interviewed for the athletics director's position at an NCAA Division 1AA institution. This was a year before Education Amendments of 1972 were passed. Two things stand out from that interview. The chairman of the search committee started the session off by telling me that the students at the university contributed $1 million in fees to the athletics program and therefore should have the right to decide how the program was operated. He asked my opinion on that statement and my philosophy. I said, "I regretted that they paid my expenses for the interview since they obviously did not need an athletics director if the students were capable of directing the program. I was sure the interview was over and I was prepared to leave the meeting. The chairman shocked me when he said: "I love you, Herb. I am glad you responded that way. I'm tired of students trying to interfere with the operation of the program." I asked to qualify my position and stated that I did seek the advice and counsel of students through the Academic Advisory Council, but felt that, as a professional, I had to make the final decision.

The second question came from a female coach who noted that women on the campus contributed exactly one-half, or $500,000, per year in fees toward the athletics budget. "How do you feel about a situation," she asked, "where a men's team travels to its game on charter flights, and eats steak and lobster after a game, while the women travel in vans to distant tournaments and eat at fast food restaurants? Is that fair?"

She was right on target. One year later Title IX emerged to attempt to bring equity to athletics programs. Because of Title IX and the regulation of equity in travel and per diem allowances, her problem had a fair solution.

In 1991, however, inequality still exists, in part because of the *Grove City* decision, but more so because of administrators who tolerate discrimination. During a risk review in 1990, at an ice hockey arena which was part of a university's athletics program, I questioned the director about purchasing, maintaining and disposing of men's ice hockey helmets. The question was routine; the answer anything but routine. He replied that he purchased the best protective helmets he could buy and had a system of maintenance that included recertification of helmets. The unexpected came when he said that the worn helmets were given to the women's ice hockey team when the men could no longer use them safely. Under Title IX regulations, the part under Equipment and Supplies reads as follows:

Equipment and Supplies. Compliance is assessed by examining the equivalence of the:
a. quality
b. amount
c. suitability
d. maintenance and replacement, and
e. availability of equipment and supplies. (44 Fed. Regulations 416:29)

The guidelines go on to interpret its requirements:

Three categories of benefits are evaluated: uniforms and other apparel, sport-specific equipment, and general equipment and supplies. Institutions are not required to expend equal amounts of money for each team and program, to buy exactly the same equipment and supplies for men and women, or to replace equipment and supplies for both sexes simultaneously. The primary emphasis in this program component is on equivalent purchase, maintenance, replacement, and access policies and practices.

The interpretation of the regulation on equipment and supplies points out the factors that deal with quality, suitability, amount, availability, replacement, and maintenance. It also addresses the "amount of time, times of day, and days of the week equipment and supplies are available."

It notes that:

Equipment and supplies are inspected on site. Investigators also obtain information regarding the current budget and previous year's expenditures for equipment and supplies, as well as the adequacy of the amounts budgeted and spent.

The guidelines are not as rigid as one might think since:

Differences in the nature of particular sports and differences in team size are recognized as nondiscriminatory factors that may explain budget or expenditure differentials.

Other examples of nondiscriminatory factors that cause disparities are given in the Title IX *Manual*. Several things can help the sports administrator in complying with Title IX regulations:

• Obtain a copy of the Title IX manual.
• Obtain a copy of the NCAA's *Guide to Title IX and Intercollegiate Athletics*.
• Contact your school's legal counsel or affirmative action officer for advice on compliance.

13.15 The Student (Athlete) With Disabilities

Denial of participation in sports for people with disabilities is one of the most violated areas in many sports programs because administrators are often confused regarding participation by persons with disabilities. Part of the confusion comes from the American Medical Association's (AMA) 1976 recommendations for disqualification from sports for students with certain disabilities. Although they are only recommendations, they are often interpreted as mandates that disqualify students who lack a paired organ such as an eye, kidney, or testicle, or who have uncontrolled diabetes, an enlarged liver or spleen, or jaundice, among other conditions. Cairbre McCann, writing in *Prevention of Athletic Injuries: The Role of the Sports Medicine Team*, remarks that the latest commentary on the disabled athlete comes from the American Academy of Pediatrics Committee on Sports Medicine, "which recommends that if the convulsive disorder is well controlled, *there should be no limitations of involvement in sports, even in those with contact and collision or impact likelihood*" (Mueller and Ryan 1991) (emphasis added).

Supporting the American Academy of Pediatrics recommendation is federal legislation that prohibits discrimination toward people with disabilities. These laws include

• The Education for All Handicapped Children Act (Public Law 94–142);
• Section 504 of the Rehabilitation Act (Public Law 93–112);
• The Amateur Sports Act (Public Law 95–606); and
• The Americans with Disabilities Act.

Dr. Julian Stein, authority on the disabled in sports, writes in *Sports and Law: Contemporary Issues* that:

The Education for All Handicapped Children Act guarantees a free, appropriate public education for every child with a disability. In addition to physical education, extracurricular activities, including interscholastic sport, must be available to all students with disabilities up to and including 21 years of age. Some states have extended the age limit to 25.

Further than this, the Rehabilitation Act prohibits discrimination against any individual with a disability in any program sponsored by a recipient of federal funds.

The Amateur Sports Act placed responsibility for all United States participation in international sports competition on one organization. The act includes participation in sports for individuals with disabilities and gives the United States Olympic Committee the responsibility for coordinating the activities. (Appenzeller 1985, 124)

Two examples illustrate the effect of federal legislation regarding sports participation for people with disabilities. In *Poole v. South Plainfield Board of Education* (1980), a high school student born with one kidney was prohibited from wrestling during his senior year in high school. After graduation, the former student sued for damages under

Section 504 of the Rehabilitation Act, with a New Jersey court holding that the school's decision to prohibit participation in the wrestling program violated Section 504 of the Rehabilitation Act. The plaintiff was awarded damages.

An outstanding athlete was denied participation in intercollegiate football because he had vision in only one eye (*Wright v. Columbia University* 1981). Columbia University's physician, in consultation with university counsel, recommended that Joseph Wright not be allowed to play intercollegiate football. Wright sued the university and the court permitted him to try out for the football team on the basis of federal law.

A preparticipation physical revealed that one of the candidates for a linebacker position on our football team had only one kidney. This was the 1960s, prior to Section 504 of the Rehabilitation Act, and things were not as complicated as they are today. After consultation with the team physician, the student elected to become the student trainer. He was happy, we felt safe, and he later entered the teaching and coaching profession. At the same time, we had a young man who, as an infant, was the victim of polio. He refused to accept the decision of doctors that his withered left leg would prevent him from competing in sports. He participated in football and climaxed his senior year being named All-Conference quarterback. He won the conference high jump championship, setting a conference record and was chosen Sportsman of the Year in Virginia. He opened my eyes and the eyes of others to the realization that many individuals with disabilities achieve success without fanfare or attention. To them the important thing is participation.

Although some sports administrators and medical personnel continue to deny participation in sports to athletes with disabilities, it is very clear that courts consistently protect the disabled athlete by enforcing federal laws. The problem facing sports administrators is how they can inform the disabled athlete about the potential dangers of sports participation and how they can protect their institution and staff from potential litigation in the event of an injury.

After the 1960s and the experience I had with these two men, I had no comparable situation to deal with until the late 1980s when the team physician denied participation in football to a person with one eye and another with one kidney. The doctor told them he would not pass them, but suggested they see their athletics director. We applied the following policy to these situations.

Policy for Individuals With Disabilities

1. Meet with the person with the disability and invite the parents or guardians, spouse, team physician, athletics trainer, and coach to attend.

2. Discuss alternative activities, pointing out the potential danger of participation.

3. If the person decides to participate after he or she is warned of possible danger, keep a record on file of the meeting, discussion, and outcome. Include in the record the individuals who attended the meeting and what was discussed.

4. Require that the individual sign an informed consent agreement that is specific, detailed, and releases the institution and its agents from liability, in the event of injury.

It is my opinion that the protocol listed above will enable people with disabilities to participate in sports activities with full knowledge and consent and provide protection for all concerned.

The *NCAA Sports Medicine Handbook* says this about participation by impaired student-athletes:

> The NCAA Committee on Competitive Safeguards and Medical Aspects of Sports affirms the right of an institution to require joint approval from the physician most familiar with the student-athlete's condition and the institution's specific athletics program in question (and parental consent in the case of a minor), before permitting any impaired student-athlete to participate. Conversely, atypical conditions (handicaps) will be a rightful reason for medical disqualification of a student-athlete by the institution only when those atypical conditions present unusual risk of further damage or disability to the individual and/or other participants.
>
> When handicapped students are identified who are not qualified to participate in the existing programs, this committee urges the member institutions to initiate suitable varsity intercollegiate athletics in the most appropriate, integrated settings possible to meet their needs. Where this is not practicable, suitable programs of other types of athletics should be initiated.
>
> In some instances where the absence or nonfunction of one of a set of paired organs constitutes the specific impairment mentioned above, serious consideration of the risks and benefits of athletics participation must be weighed by the student-athletes, their parents (in the case of a minor), the team physician, and the institution. This discussion, and the subsequent process by which the decision for or against medical qualification to participate is made, should take into account the following factors:
>
> 1. The probability of injury to the remaining organ.
>
> 2. The state of the art in protective equipment and the capability of such equipment to prevent injury to the remaining organ.
>
> When the decision is made to allow the impaired student-athlete to compete, a properly executed document of understanding and

wavier concerning injury to the remaining organ should be signed. (NCAA Sports Medicine Handbook 1986)

The sports administrator should implement a policy that is legally sound and fair for those who have disabilities and want to participate. A copy of a proposed agreement for use is found in Appendix Y.

References

Acosta, R.V., and L. Carpenter. 1986. "The Status of Women in Intercollegiate Athletics: A Five Year National Study." Brooklyn College, CUNY.

American Council on Education. 1975. *Higher Education and National Affairs*. Vol. XXIV, No. 23. Washington, D.C.

Appenzeller, H.T., and T. Appenzeller. 1980. *Sports and The Courts*. Charlottesville: The Michie Co.

Appenzeller, H.T. 1990. Presentation to the North Carolina High School Coaches Association Clinic, Greensboro, North Carolina.

Appenzeller, H.T. 1985. *Sports and Law: Contemporary Issues*. Charlottesville: The Michie Co.

Appenzeller, H.T. 1970. *From the Gym to the Jury*. Charlottesville: The Michie Co.

Appenzeller, H.T. 1975. *Athletics and the Law*. Charlottesville: The Michie Co.

Appenzeller, H., and R. Baron. 1989. *From the Gym to the Jury*. Vol. 1, No. 1. Greensboro, North Carolina

Appenzeller, H., and R. Baron. 1990. *From the Gym to the Jury*. Vol. 1, Nos. 3–4. Greensboro, North Carolina.

Appenzeller, H., and R. Baron. 1991. *From the Gym to the Jury*. Vol. 2, No. 4. Greensboro, North Carolina.

Appenzeller, H., and G. Lewis. 1987. *Sports Executive*. Vol. II, No. 5. Greensboro, North Carolina.

Appenzeller, H., and G. Lewis. 1987. *Sports Executive*. Vol. I, No. 6. Greensboro, North Carolina.

Appenzeller, H. 1987. *Pride in the Past*, Greensboro Printing Co., Greensboro, North Carolina.

Baron, R.L., and H. Appenzeller. 1990. *Risk Management Safety Manual*. Dallas: The Center for Sports Law and Risk Management.

Beasley v. Morton, 564 So. 2d 45 (Ala. 1990).

Bell, G. 1973. *The Achievers*. Chapel Hill: Preston-Hill, Inc.

Bennis, W. 1989. *Why Leaders Can't Lead*. San Francisco: Jossey-Bass Publishers.

Broos, M., Martin, D., and D. Schaefer. 1991. *Sports Emergency Medical Plans*. Greensboro: Guilford College.

Brown v. Wichita State University, 547 P. 2d 1015 (Kans. 1976).

Buttney v. Smiley, 281 F. Supp. 280 (D. Colorado 1968).

Campbell, D. 1991. *Issues and Observations*. Greensboro: Center for Creative Leadership.

The Chronicle of Higher Education. November 27, 1991. Washington: The Chronicle of Higher Education, Inc.

The Chronicle of Higher Education. January 8, 1992. Washington: The Chronicle of Higher Education, Inc.

The Chronicle of Higher Education. January 15, 1992. Washington: The Chronicle of Higher Education, Inc.

The Chronicle of Higher Education. February 26, 1992. Washington: The Chronicle of Higher Education, Inc.

Cramer First Aider. 1984. Gardner, Kansas. Alan Haines Cramer Products, Inc.

The Daily News, 15 June 1991. Morehead City, North Carolina.

DeFranz, A. August 12, 1991. *Sports Illustrated*. New York: Time Magazine Company.

Dixon v. Alabama State Board of Education, 294 F. 2d 150 (5th Cir. 1961).

Dunham v. Pulsifer, 312 F. Supp. 411 (D. Vt. 1970).

Ensor, R. 1987. *Sports Executive*. Greensboro, North Carolina.

Ensor, R. 1990. *The Corporate View Point Towards Sponsoring An Event*. Lyndhurst, New Jersey.

Federal Aviation Administration, Department of Transportation, Office of Public Affairs. 1973. *Look Before You Lease*. Washington, D.C.

44 Fed. Regulations, 416 Manual at 29.

Frederick, G. 1983. *Athletic Administration*. Cleveland: National Association of Collegiate Directors of Athletics.

Garrison v. Combined Fitness Centre, 539 N.E. 2d 1887 (Ill. 1990).

Gleason, T. 1983. *Athletic Administration*. Cleveland: National Association of Collegiate Directors of Athletics.

Greensboro News and Record. 3 June 1984. Greensboro, North Carolina.

Greensboro News and Record. 15 December 1990. Greensboro, North Carolina.

Greensboro News and Record. 30 May 1991. Greensboro, North Carolina.

Greensboro News and Record. 13–14 June 1991. Greensboro, North Carolina.

Greensboro News and Record. 27 July 1991. Greensboro, North Carolina.

Greensboro News and Record. 4 August 1991. Greensboro, North Carolina.

Grove City v. Bell, 104 S. Ct. 1211 (1984).

Guilford College Athletics Handbook. September 1986. Greensboro, North Carolina.

Halbrooks, J. Jan./Feb. 1990. *Marriott Portfolio*. Washington, D.C. Hotel Magazine Network.

Hart, G. 14 March 1983. Presentation to the Twelfth Annual NAIA Athletics Directors Workshop, Kansas City, Missouri.

Horine, L. 1991. *Administration of Physical Education and Sport Programs*. Dubuque: William C. Brown.

Johnson, L. 1970. Presentation to the Western States Conference for Secondary Athletics Directors, Las Vegas, Nevada.

Kinder, T. 1987. *Organizational Management Administration For Athletic Programs*. Dubuque: Eddie Bower Publishing Co.

Kingsley v. Independent School District No. 12, Hill City, 251 N.W. 2d 635 (Minn. 1977).

Knapp v. Whitaker, 577 F. Supp. 1265 (C.D. Ill. 1983).

The Knight Report. 1991. Charlotte: Knight Foundation Commission On Intercollegiate Athletics.

Landry, G. 1989. *AIDS in Sport*. 1989. Champaign: Human Kinetics Publishers.

Levine, P. 1989. *American Sport: A Documentary History*. Englewood Cliffs: Prentice-Hall.

Lewis, G., and H. Appenzeller. 1985. *Successful Sport Management*. Charlottesville: The Michie Co.

Mason, J.G., and J. Paul. 1988. *Modern Sports Administration*. Prentice Hall: Englewood Cliffs, N.J.

Massey v. Persson, 729 S.W. 2d 448 (Ky. App. 1987)

McCormack, M. 1986. *What They Don't Teach You at the Harvard Business School*, New York: Bantam Books.

McGhee v. Miller, 753 S.W. 2d 354 (Tenn. 1988)

Miller v. Cloidt and the Board of Education of the Borough of Chatham, Docket #L7241–62, Super. Ct. of N.J. (1964).

Mueller, F.O., and A.J. Ryan. 1991. *Prevention of Athletic Injuries: The Role of the Sports Medicine Team*. Philadelphia: F.A. Davis Co.

Naisbitt, J., and P. Auburdene. 1982. *Megatrends 2000*. New York: William Morrow and Company, Inc.

NCAA Sports Medicine Handbook. 1986. Overland Park: NCAA.

NCAA News. 24 April 1990. Overland Park: NCAA.

NCAA Study on Women in Intercollegiate Athletics. 1991. "Perceived Barriers on Women in Intercollegiate Athletics Careers. Overland Park: NCAA.

NCAA News. 12 June 1991. Overland Park: NCAA.

NCAA News. 5 February 1992. Overland Park: NCAA.

The National Federation of State High School Associations, Winter 1988. Interscholastic Athletic Administration, Kansas City, Missouri, Vol. 15, No.2.

Neuhaus v. Torrey, 310 F. Supp. 192 (N.D. Cal. 1970).

New York Times, 12 Dec. 1990.

NOLPE Notes. 1970. Vol. 5, No. 1 at 2. Topeka, Kansas.

Palmisano, M. 1990. *College Athletic Management*. Ithaca: College Athletic Administration, Inc.

Parade. 4 August 1991. *Greensboro News and Record*.

Parkhouse, B. 1991. *The Management of Sport*. St. Louis: Mosby-Yearbook, Inc.

Parks, J., and B. Zanger. 1990. *Sport and Fitness Management*. Champaign: Human Kinetics Publishers, Inc.

Poole v. South Plainfield Board of Education, 490 F. Supp. 948 (D.N.J. 1980).

Procedural Plan for Bomb Threats. September 20, 1989. Berkeley: University of California Police.

Public Law 92–318. Education Amendments Act of 1972.

Purdy, R. L. 1973. *The Successful High School Athletic Program*. West Nyack: Parker Publishing Company.

Selleck, G. 15 March 1983. Presentation to the Twelfth Annual NAIA Athletics Directors Workshop, Kansas City, Missouri.

Shahady, E.J., and M.J. Petrizzi. 1988. *Sports Medicine For Coaches and Trainers*. Chapel Hill: UNC Printing.

Shimoyana v. Board of Education of Los Angeles Unified School District, 174 Cal. Rptr. 748 (Cal. App. 1981).

Smallwood, I. 1987. *Sports Executive*. Greensboro, North Carolina.

Smith v. Board of Education of Urbana School District No. 116 of Champaign County, Illinois, 708 F. 2d 258 (7th Cir. 1983).

Stehn v. Bernarr McFadden Foundations, Inc., 434 F. 2d 811 (6th Cir. 1970).

Stevenson v. Wheeler County Board of Education, 306 F. Supp. 97 (S.D. Ga. 1969).

Sullivan, R. 1 July 1991. *Sports Illustrated*. New York: Time Magazine Company.

Uhlir, G. 1987. *Academe*. Washington: Bulletin of the American Association of University Professors.

United Educators Insurance Risk Retention Group, Inc. 1991. *Managing Athletic Liability: An Assessment Guide*. Chevy Chase, Maryland.

University of Lowell Atheltics Handbook. 1989. Lowell, Massachusetts.

van der Smissen, B. 1990. *Legal Liability and Risk Management for Public and Private Entities*. Cincinnati: Anderson Publishing Co.

Vander Zaag, H. 1984. *Sport Management in Schools and Colleges*. New York: John Wiley and Sons.

Vargo v. Svitchan, 301 N.W. 2d 1 (Mich. 1981).

Villalobos, F. 1990. *Journal of National Sports Law Institute*, Marquette Law School, Milwaukee.

Welch v. Dunsmuir Joint Union High School Dist., 326 P.2d 633 Cal. 1958).

Welch, M., M. Sitler, and M.B. Horodyski. 1989. "Should Athletic Trainers Be Concerned about HIV? Guidelines For Athletic Trainers." *Athletic Training.* Vol. 24, No. 1.

Wentworth, "College's Facing Test on Justice," *Washington Post.* 7 September 1969 at BL col. 5.

Woodring v. Board of Education of Manhasset, 435 N.Y.S. 2d 52 (N.Y. App. Div. 1981).

Wright v. Columbia University, 520 F. Supp. 789 (E.D. Pa. 1981).

Part 4

Appendixes

The forms presented in the appendixes are for example only. Each program should design and utilize forms that are appropriate for the needs of their specific program.

Appendix A

Organizational Chart For Athletic Department, Guilford College

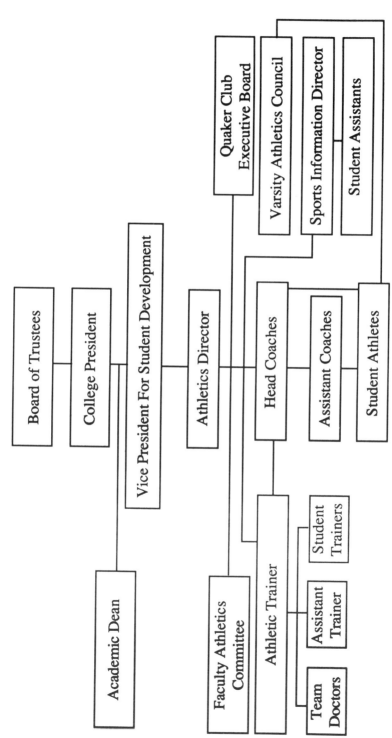

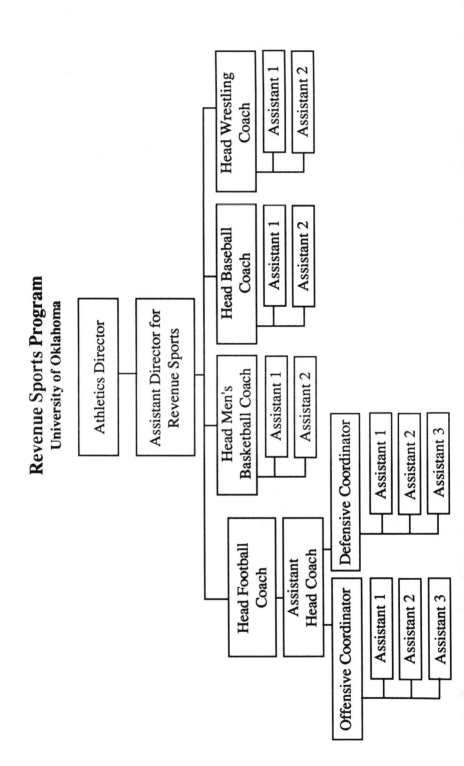

Revenue Sports Program
University of Oklahoma

Departmental Staff Reporting to Athletics Director
University of Oklahoma

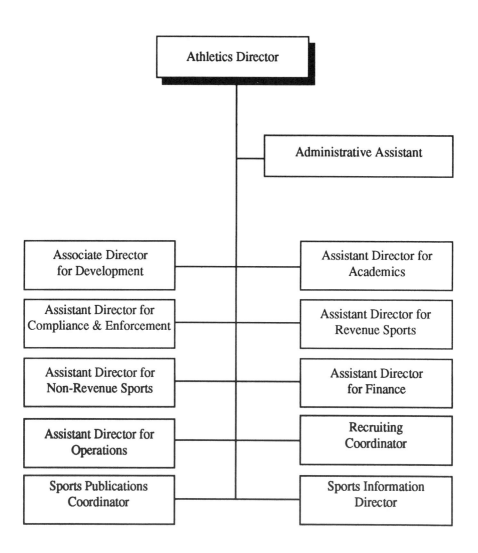

Appendix B

Five Year Plan for Marietta College Athletic Facilities, Equipment, and Staffing
*Impacted by 1986 site plan/12 MI. campaign

Fall 1988 Update

Fieldhouse		Date Comp
Sand and Refinish gym floor	20,000.00	F-87
VHS Equipment	1,500.00	F-87
Wt. Room Equipment	1,500.00	S-87
Training Room-Ice Machine	2,500.00	F-86
Laundry Room-Dryer	1,500.00	F-87
	(1,000.00)	
		S-88
Weight Room-Add nec. Equipment	3,000.00	
Softball Batting Cage	1,500.00	S-86
Laundry Room-Washer	4,000.00	F-86
Pads for Volleyball Standards	400.00	S-88
New Basketball/Volleyball Scoreboard	4,000.00	F-88
*Recreation Lockerroom Renovation	10,000.00	
Laundry Room-Dryer	1,500.00	
Lobby Wall-Rear of Bleacher	5,300.00	S-88
Lobby Plaque Senior Female Athlete	750.00	
Volleyball Standards/sleeve	1,600.00	
Video Equipment	4,000.00	
Weight Room-Replace Carpet	3,000.00	
*Plaque/Case-Female Athlete	500.00	
*Equipment Room/Storage/ Laundry Room	10,000.00	
Laundry Room-Dryer	1,500.00	
*New Fieldhouse Facility	?...	
Varsity Lockerroom Renovationd	10,000.00	
Bus for Travel	38,000.00	

Renovate Offices
Paint Walls/Replace Curtains
Replace all Plumbing
Equipment for Rec Center

Equipment for Rec Center

Outdoor		Date Comp
*Women's Softball Field Developed at Chris Concrete Lot		
Replace Windscreens at Tennis Courts.....1,000.00		F-88
Boathouse-Replace Railings		S-88
-Repair Roof		
(partially done)		S-86

Stadium I.M. Field-top Dress to fill in Holes		
*Soccer-develop Soccer Field on current Marietta Field		
*Tennis Renovate 4 Courts and Add 2 new Courts in Gooserun Area		
New Goal Posts at Stadium 3,700.00		F-87

Outdoor Scoreboard-Soccer/Softball/Lacrosse	
Upgrade Quality of Grass on Varsity Fielkds	
Track-Pole Vault Pit Extension 1,150.00	
Football-Blocking Dummies.................1,200.00	
-Sled Pads.............................. 1,000	

Softball-Infield Tarp
Fifth Street Parking
*Track-Help Financial Campaign of High School
   All-Weather Track
Crew-Insulate Boathouse/Drop Ceiling
   Fix Fascia Board
   Fix Door Facilities

Softball/Soccer Portable Bleachers
*Recreation Center

Renovate Stadium Lockerroom............ 50,000.00

Renovate Stadium Pressbox

Staffing		Date Comp
Part-Time Secretary		F-87
"Grad. Assistant" in Women's Sports		
(Added FT Staff)		

Soccer/Assistant		F-87
Basketball Coach		F-87
Crew Coordinator		F-87

Part-Time Asst. Crew Coach   S-88

Part-Time Coach/Facilities Supervisor

Part-Time Coach/Equipment Supervisor

Facilities/Equipment Supervisor to Replace Part-
   Time (Coaching One Sport)

Part-Time Laundry Person

Appendix C
Athletic Committee Questionnaire

The following questionnaire has been developed to assist the athletic committee in its assigned task of reviewing and clarifying the philosophy and implementation of the athletic program at _____ . Your thoughtful and candid responses will be greatly appreciated.

Background Information
Are you:

Student   —
Faculty   —
Coach   —
Administration   —
Staff   —
Parent   —

Sex: Male __   Female __

(If you are a coach, faculty member, administrator or parent, please go to the section labeled Athletic Director. If you are a student, continue with the following questions.)

What level student are you (1, 2, 3, 4)?
(1 = Senior, 2 = Junior, 3 = Sophomore, 4 = Freshman)   —

Are you a Continuing Education student?   Yes __ No __

Athletic Director
The following question relates to what you think the *Athletic Director* should do.

Please rank the responsibilities of the *Athletic Director*, listed on the next page, in descending order of importance. Assign a value of 10 to the most important item and a value of 1 to the least important item. Some items will not have a ranking. Use each number only once.

a. Supervise the coaching staff and teams   —
b. Conduct athletic staff meetings   —
c. Supervise the budget and system of requisitions   —
d. Coordinate use of facilities, travel, scheduling among
    coaches   —
e. Issue contracts for home contests   —
f. Plan Athletic Banquets
    (Hall of Fame, Annual Athletic Banquet)   —
g. Check on eligibility, physical examinations and insurance
    of all athletes and maintain records   —
h. Crowd control at athletic events   —
i. Direct the Fund Raising for booster club and Athletic
    Program   —

j. Schedule booster club meetings and be ex-officio member
    of every booster club committee —
k. Coordinate intercollegiate programs with Director of
    Sports Studies and Director of Intramurals —
l. Supervise Athletic Advisory Council in monthly meetings —
m. Ex-officio member of Faculty Athletic Committee —
n. Supervise Sports Information Director —
o. Maintain program of publications with groups that
    involve the athletic program —
p. Attend District, Conference and Professional meetings,
    workshops and clinics —
q. Develop an up-to-date athletic policy handbook —
r. Coordinate Academic Advising —

Additional Duties
In addition to the above responsibilities, how much should the
Athletic Director:
(Please mark scale)

Teach:	None		Limited		Full Time
0	1	2	3	4	5

Coach:	None		Limited		Full Time
0	1	2	3	4	5

National and Conference Affiliation
The following National and Conference affiliation options have been
suggested. Please indicate the option you favor by placing a number
in front of the option you prefer (1 indicates strong preference, 3
indicates weaker preference).
Remain strictly in present conference with other teams
playing independently. —
Remain in present conference but foster new conference
affiliations in football. —
Affiliate with the NCAA Division III and join a Division III
conference. —
NOTE: Affiliation with the above conferences suggests the following
       policies on athletic grants:
    • NAIA, implies athletic grants
    • NCAA II, implies a greater number of athletic grants than NAIA
    • NCAA III, implies need-based athletic grants only

Athletics at _____
How do you think the intercollegiate athletic program at _____
effects the "outside" image of the college.

Detracts		No Effect		Improves
0	1	2	3	4	5

Do you think the *men's* intercollegiate athletic programs at _____
should be:

Reduced	No Change	Expanded
0 1	2 3 4	5

Do you think the *women's* intercollegiate athletic programs at ____
should be:

Reduced	No Change	Expanded
0 1	2 3 4	5

Do you think the club sports programs at _____should be:

Reduced	No Change	Expanded
0 1	2 3 4	5

How would you rate parity in athletics at _____:

Favors Women	Parity	Favors Men
0 1	2 3 4	5

For a variety of reasons, _____ is unable to add additional
sports at this time. If, however, the opportunity presents itself in the
future, what intercollegiate sport would you like to see offered that is
not currently offered?

_____

For which of the following groups do you think mandatory Drug
Testing should be implemented at _____ ?

No One Should be Tested	—
Everyone Should be Tested	—
All Students	—
Athletes Only	—

Athletic Facilities

Please rate the following athletic facilities at _____.

Training Room:	Poor	Adequate	Excellent
	0 1	2 3 4	5
Locker Room:	Poor	Adequate	Excellent
	0 1	2 3 4	5
Weight Room:	Poor	Adequate	Excellent
	0 1	2 3 4	5
Gymnasium:	Poor	Adequate	Excellent
	0 1	2 3 4	5
Fields:	Poor	Adequate	Excellent
	0 1	2 3 4	5
Tennis Courts:	Poor	Adequate	Excellent
	0 1	2 3 4	5
Pool:	Poor	Adequate	Excellent
	0 1	2 3 4	5

Office Space:	Poor		Adequate			Excellent	
	0	1	2	3	4	5

Participation in Sports

Are you on an intercollegiate team?   Yes __ No __
[If you are *on an intercollegiate team*, Please go to the section titled Comments on Sports. If you are *not* on an intercollegiate team, Please continue on the next page.]

Have you tried out for a team?   Yes __ No __
    If yes which Sport(s):
        Soccer   __
        Basketball   __
        Lacrosse   __
        Volleyball   __
        Baseball   __
        Softball   __
        Tennis   __
        Golf   __
        Football   __

Did you represent your High School in varsity
athletics?   Yes __ No __
Did you participate in High School club
activities?   Yes __ No __
Did you participate in High School intramural
athletics?   Yes __ No __
Did you participate in other High School
athletics?   Yes __ No __
Considering your abilities and interests, do
you think you had a reasonable opportunity to
participate in an athletic program at _____. Yes __ No __

Comments on Sports

Please enter any additional comments you feel might be useful to the athletic committee.
Thank you for your participation in this survey.

Appendix D
Constitution
Guilford College Quaker Club

Article I — Name
The name of the organization shall be the Guilford College Quaker Club, hereafter called the Club.

Article II — Purpose
The purpose of the Club shall be the promotion and encouragement of athletics at Guilford College. In furtherance of the foregoing purpose the Club shall, among other things and without limitation upon its activities, provide funds to supplement funds otherwise available to carry out the athletic program of Guilford College; engage in activities designed to promote and popularize the athletic program at Guilford College; sponsor banquets and other social activities for student athletes, coaches, press, faculty and others interested in the athletic program at Guilford College; sponsor and present various awards to players, coaches and others who render outstanding services to or in behalf of the athletic program at Guilford College; and otherwise engage in activities which further the purposes of the Club.

Article III — Membership
(a) Members of the Club during each fiscal year of the Club shall be:
1. those persons, firms and businesses who have contributed to the Club the minimum annual contribution fixed by the directors of the Club.
2. the President, Athletic Director, all members of the coaching staff and the Faculty Athletic Chairperson of Guilford College shall be members by virtue of their respective positions.
(b) All members shall be entitled to attend and vote upon any matter of business at any annual or special meeting.

Article IV — Management
(a) The management of the Club shall be vested in a Board of Directors, hereafter called the Board.
(b) The Board shall be comprised of officers, directors and life members.
(c) All Board members shall have the same rights and privileges except where special responsibility is provided by this Constitution.
(d) The Board shall have the power and authority to transact all matters of business not specifically reserved to the membership in this Constitution.
(e) The Board shall meet at least four (4) times a year with at least two (2) weeks prior notice of each meeting being given to Board members.

(f) All business of the Board and committees of the Board shall be conducted after the manner of Friends.

(g) A quorum for transaction of business at any meeting of the Board shall be more than one-third (1/3) of the Board members.

(h) Should an officer or director be absent without cause satisfactory to the Board for three (3) consecutive meetings, it shall be considered the same as a resignation and the position filled in accordance with the provision of this Constitution. After the second such absence the President of the Club shall so advise the individual in question.

Article V — Officers

(a) The officers of the Club shall be: President, President-Elect, Secretary-Treasurer and Past-President.

(b) The President and President-Elect shall be selected in accordance with Article VIII, Board Selections.

(c) The Secretary-Treasurer shall be the person filling the position of Director of Athletics of the College.

(d) The Past President shall be the President of the preceding term.

(e) All elected officers shall serve a one-year (1) term and may be reelected for one (1) additional year.

(f) The President shall preside at all meetings of the Board and of the Club; shall have general supervision over the activities of the Club in carrying out the goals, objectives and policies of the Club as adopted by its Board and membership; shall establish standing committees and appoint, in consultation with officers of the Board, the chairpersons and members to these committees for a one (1) year term; and shall perform such other duties as may be assigned by the Board.

(g) The President-Elect shall act as president at all Board and Club meetings from which the President is absent and shall assist the President in the performance of his duties. The President-Elect shall succeed to the office of President immediately at the expiration of the President's term of office or should that position be vacated through resignation or death. If the President-Elect succeeds to the office of President by reason of death or resignation of the President, the President-Elect shall serve as President during the unexpired term of his predecessor and for an additional term of one (1) year.

(h) The Secretary-Treasurer of the Club, shall be custodian of all records of the Club, record and keep minutes of all meetings of members and directors, be custodian of the Club's funds, and perform such other duties as may be assigned by the directors.

Article VI — Directors

(a) A maximum of twenty-four (24) Directors shall be selected by the Club membership in accordance with Article VIII — Board Selections.

(b) One-third (1/3) of the Directors shall be selected each year to serve a three-year (3) term.

(c) Directors are limited to two (2) consecutive terms. After an absence of one (1) year, they may be elegible for election.

(d) Ex-officio Directors may be appointed by the President in consultation with the Executive Committee for terms not to exceed three (3) years. No more than two Ex-officio Directors may serve at any given time.

Article VII — Life Members

(a) The Board may select life members to the Board.

(b) There shall be no more than ten (10) life members at one time.

(c) Life members do not have to meet the attendance requirement of Article IV, (h).

Article VIII — Board Selections

(a) A Nominating Committee composed of at least three (3) Board members shall be appointed each year by the President of the Board. The Secretary-Treasurer shall be an ex-officio member of the committee.

(b) This committee shall present annually to the Board a proposed ballot of directors and officers for Board approval.

(c) Officer candidates shall come from current Board members.

(d) The candidates selected shall be representative of the membership.

Article IX — Executive Committee

The Executive Committee shall be composed of the President, President-Elect, Secretary-Treasurer, Past President and the chairpersons of all standing committees. When the Board is not in session the Executive Committee shall be empowered to act upon such matters as the Board may delegate.

Article X — Standing Committees

The Standing Committees shall be the Executive Committee, Development Committee, Activities Committee, Hall of Fame Committee and such other standing committees as the President shall from time to time appoint.

Article XI — Club Meetings

A quorum for transaction of business at any meeting of the Club shall be those members attending after due notice. Special meetings of the Club may be called by the Board and may be held upon two (2) weeks advance notice by mail to all members, the notice of such meetings to state the nature of the business to be considered.

Article XII — Quaker Club Fund Drive

Each year the Club shall sponsor and conduct an annual fund campaign which shall be known and designated as The Quaker Club Fund Drive. All contributions thereby obtained shall be paid to Guilford College and shall be added to the *operating budget* of the College to be used for the support of athletic purposes recommended by the Athletic Department and the Quaker Club Board with approval by the College.

Article XIII — Amendments

Amendments to the Constitution shall be made by consensus of the Board after publication of notice to the membership as to the proposed amendment, which notice shall state the date upon which action will be taken by the board. Interested members of the Club shall be given an opportunity to be heard at the meeting of the Board at which action upon such proposed amendment is to be taken. Such meeting shall not be held less than thirty (30) days after the date of publication in which notice of such proposed amendment and meeting of the Board to consider same appears. This Constitution can also be amended by consensus of the members present at any membership meeting if notice of such meeting and the proposed amendment has been given and published not less than thirty (30) days before the date of such meeting.

Article XIV — Effective Date

This Constitution shall be effective upon its adoption by the Board, whereupon this Constitution shall replace the prior Constitution of the Club.

Appendix E
University of Lowell
Policies and Procedures

Appendix F

Football
Team Rules

How do you want people to perceive you? What kind of image do you want to project? We all want people to see us as good citizens, good students, and good football players. Therefore, we should all practice habits that will help us cast the best reflections as individuals representing our families, our college, and out team.

All individual actions that cast bad reflections on our team will be dealt with individually. All steps will be taken to insure the punishment fits the "crime." In most instances, first offenders will be dealt with lightly. Repeaters will certainly face the possibility of suspension from the squad.

In summary, be neat, courteous, respect others, and act in a manner that will draw respect from others. There are three taboos for the football players: Alcohol, smoking, and drugs.

Use your head.

Women's Soccer
Team Rules

1.   Student athletes with a 2.5 GPA or below, all freshman and any other player designated by the coach will be required to sign the academic tutor's notebook (the black book) every Friday by noon and may be required to attend study hall.

2.   Class attendance is required. Players must inform their instructors of any absences due to games and make up all missed work.

3.   All players are expected to attend every practice, on time, unless ill. Notify the coach prior to practice time if you are sick.

4.   If a player is injured, she must notify the coach or trainer. All athletes are required to have a physical exam prior to the season.

5.   All players are responsible for school-owned equipment issued during the season and will be billed through the business office for loss or damage.

6.   Players must be enrolled in 12 hours in the semester they are participating. You must have passed 12 hours the previous semester, if you are a freshman, and 24 hours the previous two semesters (including summer school), if you are an upperclassman.

7.   Student-athletes who violate college, state, or Federal laws are subject to suspension from the team.

8.   Cigarette smoking and the use of illegal drugs is prohibited.

9.   The consumption of alcohol is prohibited during the sports season. Abuse of this rule is subject to the judgment of the coach.

10.   Profanity will not be tolerated.

11.   Be loyal, honest, and respect one another and also the team we play.

12.   Act on and off the field in a manner reflecting human kindness and understanding.

Appendix G

Guilford College Athletic Department
Pre-appraisal Planning

Name _____ Position _____

Coaching experience _____

Yrs. _____Coaching at Guilford _____ Yrs.

Number of assistant coaches:

   Full time _____   Part Time _____   Vol. _____

Performance Objectives

Activity	Action	Priority (Rank)	Completion Date
Recruiting			
Scheduling			
Professional Growth			
Organization			
Execution of Coaching			

Community
Involvement

_____

Other
Objectives

_____

    The performance objectives established above have been discussed and are acceptable to the Coach and Director of Athletics.

_____   _____

Coach of Sport   Director of Athletics

Date _____

Guilford College Athletic Department

Review Conference
(To be completed by Athletic Director)

Name: _____ Position: _____
Years of Coaching Experience: _____
Years of Coaching at Guilford: _____
Number of Assistant Coaches: Full Time: _____
                                    Part Time: _____ Vol.: _____
Number of Students/Athletes at Mid-Season: _____
                                    End of Season: _____
Season Record: _____ W _____ L _____ T
Budget: Under: _____ Over: _____
Career Record at Guilford: _____ W _____ L _____ T
1. Overall Evaluation:

2. Major Strengths:

3. Major Weaknesses:

4. Overall performance since last review conference

5. Performance Objectives Report:
   a. Recruiting

   b. Budget

   c. Public Relations/SID cooperation

   d. Scheduling

   e. Professional Growth

   f. Organization

   g. Execution of Coaching

   h. Other (staff contributions)

6. Potential growth areas:

7. Self-development recognized:

8. Plan of action for next year:

_____   _____
     Coach of Sport   Director of Athletics
Date _____

Guilford College Athletic Department

Student/Athlete Appraisal
(May be used annually and MUST be used bi-annually)

Coach _____ Sport _____

School Year _____ Record: W_____ L _____

Check appropriate box:
☐ Varsity ☐ Junior Varsity Class: ☐ Sr. ☐ Jr. So. ☐ Fr.

ORGANIZATION

	Y	N
1. Were practice times announced at least one week in advance?	___	___
2. Did the coach begin and end practice on time?	___	___
3. Did the coach use a practice plan?	___	___
4. Were the trips announced (time of departure/return at least one week in advance?)	___	___
5. Did you have a squad meeting or communication concerning:		
a. policy on grooming?	___	___
b. policy on alcohol and drugs?	___	___
c. policy on physical education credit?	___	___
d. policy on trip excuses?	___	___
e. policy on awards?	___	___
f. policy on accident/health insurance?	___	___
6. Did you feel the coach was organized?	___	___
7. Is our program competitive in our conference?	___	___

COACHING:

1. Did you feel the coach knew you?	___	___
2. Did you feel the coach knew the game?	___	___
3. Did the coach motivate you?	___	___
4. Did the coach establish good team discipline?	___	___
5. Did the coach demonstrate confidence?	___	___
6. Did the coach motivate the team in general?	___	___
7. Was the coach consistent?	___	___
8. Did the coach enjoy coaching this year?	___	___
9. Is the coach a good communicator?	___	___
10. Is the coach enthusiastic?	___	___

INDIVIDUAL:
1. Did you improve as an athlete?   ____ ____
2. Did you grow as a human being?   ____ ____
3. Will you compete in the sport next year?   ____ ____
4. Did you letter?   ____ ____
5. Did you receive other awards?   ____ ____
6. Did you reach any personal goals?   ____ ____
7. Did the team compete up to its potential?   ____ ____
8. Did your team play too many games?   ____ ____
9. Did your team play enough games?   ____ ____
10. Was your season (including practice) too long?   ____ ____
11. Was your season (including practice) too short?   ____ ____
12. Did you enjoy your season?   ____ ____

COMMENTS:
Describe the strengths of your coach.

Describe the weaknesses of your coach.

List any suggestions you might have to improve this sport program.

Guilford College Athletic Department

Coach's Self-Evaluation

Name: _____ Sports Studies Duties: yes ____ no ____

Position: _____ List of classes this semester:

Years of Coaching Experience: ____ _____

Years Coaching at Guilford: ____ _____

Number of Assistant Coaches: Full Time ____

                                        Part Time ____ Vol. ____

Number of Students/Athletes at   Mid-Season: ____

                                        End of Season ____

Season Record: W ____ L ____ Td ____

Guilford Career: W ____ L ____ Td ____

Budget: Under ____ Over ____ Comments:

What were your overall strengths this year?

What would you like to change about your current job description (if anything)?

If you met some performance objectives, describe how and why you feel that happened.

If you missed your performance objectives on the projected completion date, describe how and why that happened.

How effective do you believe you have been as the coach of your sport and the head of your program this year?

How effective are your recruiting activities?
Are you meeting or exceeding your projected goals?

How can the institution be more supportive of your program?

How can the Director of Athletics be more supportive of your program?

What might aid in your professional development as a coach between now and next year?

_____   _____
Signed   Date

Appendix H

Basketball Operations Checklist

A.   TEAM
____ 1. Method of
        Transportation
____ 2. Where to Park
____ 3. Pass List
____ 4. Entry Door to
        Coliseum
____ 5. Locker Room Entry
        (key)
____ 6. Security of Valuables
____ 7. Post-Game Meal
        Delivery
____ 8. Number of Chairs for
        Bench Area
____ 9. __ Towels, __ Drinks,
        __ Oranges, __ Grease
        Pencils, __ Marking
        Board
____ 10. Recruit Seats
____ 11. Coaches Parking Space
____ 12. Clear Floor Pre-Game-
         Time
____ 13. Starting Line-Up for
         Introductions
____ 14. Coaches Itinerary
____ 15. Goal Protectors
____ 16. Videotaping Location

B.   TEAM EQUIPMENT
____ 1. Parking
____ 2. Personnel Pass List
        (those working game)

C.   TEAM DOCTOR/
     TRAINER
____ 1. Parking
____ 2. Pass List (number of
        medical personnel i.e.,
        trainers, doctors, etc.)

D.   VISITING TEAM
____ 1. Hotel Headquarters
____ 2. Transportation to
        Coliseum
____ 3. Where to Park
____ 4. Pass List
____ 5. Post Game Meal
        Delivery
____ 6. Entry Door
____ 7. Locker Room Entry
        (key)
____ 8. Security of Valuables
____ 9. Clear Floor Pre-Game-
        Time
____ 10. Number of Chairs for
         Bench Area
____ 11. __ Towels, __ Drinks,
         __ Oranges, __ Chalk,
         __ Chalkboard
____ 12. Radio Line Installation
____ 13. Broadcast Location
____ 14. Starting Line-Up for
         Introduction
____ 15. Coaches Itinerary
____ 16. Directions
____ 17. Administrative
         Contact
____ 18. Practice Time __
         Practice Balls
____ 19. Videotaping Location

E.   OFFICIALS
____ 1. Letter to Officials
____ 2. Parking Passes with
        Directions
____ 3. Entry door to
        Coliseum
____ 4. Locker Room Entry
        (key)

_____ 5. __ Drinks, __
Oranges,
__ Towels, __ Chalk,
__ Chalkboard
_____ 6. Security Escort Pre-
and Post-Game
_____ 7. Payment
_____ 8. Programs
_____ 9. Post-Game Meal
_____ 10. Pass List

F. CHEERLEADERS
_____ 1. Transportation
_____ 2. Parking
_____ 3. Entry Door to
Coliseum
_____ 4. Floor Area During
Game Designated
_____ 5. Administrative Table/
Chairs
_____ 6. Cheers/Routines
During Time-Outs
_____ 7. Half-Time
Refreshments-Own
Responsibilities
_____ 8. Post-Game
Responsibilities
_____ 9. Locker Room Location
_____ 10. Towels
_____ 11. Valuables
_____ 12. Check Floor After
Cheers

G. ADMINISTRATIVE AND
OPERATIONAL STAFF
_____ 1. Parking Passes
_____ 2. Admission
_____ 3. Pass List
_____ 4. I.D. Badges

H. COLISEUM
PREPARATION
_____ 1. Floor (cleaned before
game)
_____ 2. Team Chairs
_____ 3. Press and Scorer's
Table

_____ 4. Goals
_____ 5. Scoreboard
_____ 6. Shot Clock
_____ 7. Cheerleader Table
_____ 8. Parking Areas Cleared
(Box Suites/Press/
Operations)
_____ 9. Concession Areas
_____ 10. Restroom Facilities
_____ 11. Traffic Coordination
_____ 12. Seats Behind Bench
_____ 13. Halftime Floor Clean
_____ 14. Press Room
_____ 15. Parking Attendants
_____ 16. Ushers Location
_____ 17. Security, Location,
Reporting Time
_____ 18. Off-Duty Police,
Location, Reporting
Time
_____ 19. Ticket Takers,
Location, Reporting
Time
_____ 20. First Aid Room,
Location
_____ 21. __ PA, __ Intercom,
__ Walkie-Talkies,
__ Outside
Phone Lines,
__ Tape Player
_____ 22. Locker Rooms
_____ 23. Backdoor Attendant
(report time)
_____ 24. Lost and Found
_____ 25. TV Camera Location
_____ 26. Band Seat Location
_____ 27. Print Passes (TV)
_____ 28. Handicapped Parking
_____ 29. Handicapped Entry
_____ 30. Handicapped Seating
_____ 31. __ Backups, __ Clock,
__ Horn, __ nets
__ 45-Second Clock,
__ Backboard
__ Rims
_____ 32. Location of Regular
Student Gate

___ 33. Location of Player
       Comp Gate
___ 34. Location of Press Gate
___ 35. Location of Novelty
       Sales
___ 36. Special Problem Areas
       (ie., Walkway, Post-
       Game Locker Room
       Crowd)
___ 37. All Lights, Bulbs,
       Horns Operational

I.   PARKING
___ 1. Attendants
___ 2. Parking Pass Samples
___ 3. Lot Assignments and
       Instructions
       ___ Lot Entry, ___ Lot
       Exit
___ 4. VIP Passes (honored)
___ 5. Coordination with
       Traffic Police

J.   PROGRAMS
___ 1. Printer
___ 2. Game Quantities
___ 3. Delivery
___ 4. Storage
___ 5. ___ Sellers, ___ Location
       of Sellers, ___ Change
       Aprons
___ 6. Advance for Change
       ($200)
___ 7. Payment Process
___ 8. Seller Coordinator
___ 9. Program Sales Report
___ 10. Number of Programs
       (who delivers)
       ___ Where
       ___ Team
       ___ Visiting Team
       ___ Special Guests
       ___ Press
       ___ Officials
       ___ Scorer's Table
___ 11. Left Over Programs
       Delivered to:

K.   COMMUNICATIONS
___ 1. Walkie-Talkie
       Assignments
___ 2. Installation and
       Location of Intercom
       Phones
___ 3. Public Address System
       (Scorer's Table/Floor)
___ 4. Cassette Player
___ 5. Outside Phone Lines
       ___ AD Box Suite
___ 6. Contact Personnel
       ___ Coliseum (list)
       ___ College (list)

L.   ANNOUNCEMENTS
___ 1. Impromptu
___ 2. Staples (future games,
       half-time, coaches
       show)
___ 3. Special Interest
       (College Sports
       Attractions, game
       scores, individual
       highlights)
___ 4. Coordination of
       Announcements

M.   TICKETS
___ 1. Sales at Game, When,
       Where
___ 2. College Will Call,
       When, Where
___ 3. Visitor Will Call,
       When, Where
___ 4. Player Tickets, Where,
       By Whom
___ 5. Ticket Takers, Where
___ 6. Money Accountability
___ 7. Student Punch
       Numbers
___ 8. Student Entry
___ 9. General Public Entry
___ 10. Handicapped Seats
___ 11. Handicapped Entry
___ 12. Visitor comps Seat
       Location

____ 13. Recruit Seat Location

____ 14. ROTC Color Guard, Seats

____ 15. Half-Time Entertainment Seats (when applicable)

____ 16. Special Promotions

____ 17. Press Gate Entry

____ 18. Women's Player's Ticket Location

N. PRESS ROW

____ 1. Order Phone Lines Through Coliseum

____ 2. Location of Jacks

____ 3. Installation and Location of Intercom Phones

____ 4. Seating Assignments

____ 5. Distribution of Parking and Admission Passes

____ 6. Program Distribution

____ 7. Half-Time Statistics

____ 8. Policy on Drinks

O. PRESS ROOM

____ 1. Order Phone Lines

____ 2. Location of Phone Jacks

____ 3. Installation and Location of Intercom Phones

____ 4. Security

____ 5. Operational, Press, and Administrative Personnel Only

____ 6. Catering

    __ Food

    __ Drinks

    __ Numbers per Game

    __ Begin Serving

    __ End Serving

____ 7. Brochure, Statistical Location

P. HOME RADIO AND PERSONNEL

____ 1. Order Phone Lines

____ 2. Location of Phone Lines

____ 3. Parking Passes

____ 4. Admission to Coliseum

Q. PHOTOGRAPHERS

____ 1. Parking Passes

____ 2. Admission to Coliseum

____ 3. Floor Location

____ 4. Wear Proper Footwear

____ 5. Reserved Locations Along Both Baselines

R. COACH'S TV SHOW PERSONNEL

____ 1. Parking Passes

____ 2. Admission to Coliseum

____ 3. Location (both camera deck above and on floor reserve location)

S. PEP BAND

____ 1. Transportation

____ 2. Parking

____ 3. Entry to Coliseum

____ 4. Seat Location

____ 5. Half-Time Refreshments

____ 6. Game Coordination

____ 7. Warm-Up Area

T. NOVELTY SALES

____ 1. Vendors

____ 2. Concourse Location

____ 3. Commission

____ 4. Sales Report

____ 5. Items for Sale

____ 6. Passes

U.   BACK DOOR PASS LIST
___ 1. Home and Visiting
        Teams
___ 2. Officials
___ 3. Cheerleaders
___ 4. Pep Band
___ 5. Operational and
        Various
        Administrative Staff
___ 6. Half-Time Groups
        Ball Boys, ROTC,
        Equipment Personnel,
        Physicians, (Trainers
        receive passes or
        tickets)

V.   PRE-GAME ACTIVITIES
___ 1. Organization and
        Coordination
___ 2. ROTC Colorguard
___ 3. Spotlight and Operator
___ 4. House Light Operator
___ 5. Alma Mater
___ 6. National Anthem
___ 7. Auxillary Music
___ 8. Team Warm-Ups,
        Introductions
___ 9. Special
        Announcements

W.   GAME IN PROGRESS
___ 1. Ball Boys Coordination
___ 2. Shot Clock Operator
___ 3. Timekeeper
___ 4. Scorer
___ 5. P.A. Announcer
___ 6. Announcements—-
        Program
___ 7. Sound System—
        Volume
___ 8. Announcements—
        Impromptu
___ 9. Media Time-Out
        Coordination
___ 10. Special Problems
        Coordination

X.   HALF-TIME
     ENTERTAINMENT
___ 1. Organization and
        Coordination
___ 2. Parking Passes
___ 3. Admission to
        Coliseum
___ 4. Seat Location Where
        Applicable
___ 5. Necessary Equipment
___ 6. Dressing Rooms
        Needed

Y.   POST-GAME
___ 1. Traffic Flow
___ 2. Parking Lot Lights
___ 3. Press Room
        Administration
___ 4. Floor Security
___ 5. Coaches/Officials
        Escort Security
___ 6. Coaches Interviews
___ 7. Meals for Officials

Z.   MISCELLANEOUS
___ 1. Stopwatch
___ 2. Shotclock Back-Up
        Cards
___ 3. Airhorn
___ 4. Parking Passes Printed
        (Press, Box Suite)
___ 5. Post-Game Storage of
        Back-Up Items
___ 6. Check for Officials,
        Team Meals,
        Guarantee
___ 7. Distribution of Game
        Itineraries
___ 8. Student Signs
        (approval)
___ 9. Special Catering (Box
        Suites, Press Room,
        Assembly Room)

____ 10. Production Sheet/
       Itinerary
____ 11. TV Game
       Adjustments
____ 12. Concessions
____ 13. Security
____ 14. Police
____ 15. Ticket Takers
____ 16. Ticket Sellers
____ 17. Double Header
       Adjustments

Appendix I

Athletics Department
Vehicle Use Form

Driver _____   _____
        (Last Name)   (First)   (M.I.)   (License #) (Exp.)

Departure Date _____   Return Date _____

Departure Time _____   Return Time _____

Destination and
Purpose of Trip _____

_____

_____

Number of Travelers _____   Travel Constituents _____

Approval _____   _____
              (Athletics Director or Dean)   (Date)

Received Keys _____
                (Numbers)

        Credit Card _____   _____
                        (Vendor)   (Card Number)

Responsibility
Statement: I do accept responsibility for this athletics department vehicle
                  and the credit card, if issued, received by me. I understand
                  that only I and other drivers authorized by the college are
                  allowed to operate this athletics department vehicle for the
                  purpose and destination as listed above. Only students, staff,
                  and faculty, of this college or those on official college
                  business are permitted in this athletics department vehicle.

                  _____ _____ _____
                  (Driver's signature)   (Date)   (Time)

Maintenance
Pre-Trip Inspection

Vehicle License No. _____ Mileage_____

Equipment Manager's Use

❑ Head lights_____

❑ Brake lights & brakes _____

❑ Tail lights_____

❑ Turn signals_____

❑ Horn_____

❑ Windsheild wipers_____

❑ Fuel_____

❑ Seat belts_____

❑ Tires_____

❑ Spare tire & jack_____

❑ Cleanliness—inside_____

❑ Cleanliness—outside_____

❑ Other_____

❑ Body damage_____

❑ **Approved for trip** _____ _____
    Equipment Manager's Signature   Date

Maintenance
Post-Trip Inspection

User Comments	User: Please check ☑ If needs attention	Equipment Manager's Use
_____	❑ Headlights	_____
_____	❑ Tail lights	_____
_____	❑ Brake lights	_____
_____	❑ Turn signals	_____
_____	❑ Horn	_____
_____	❑ Windsheild wipers	_____
_____	❑ Seat belts	_____
_____	❑ Tires	_____
_____	❑ Had flat tire-check spare	_____
_____	❑ Brakes	_____
_____	❑ Front end	_____
_____	❑ Steering	_____
_____	❑ Engine ❑ Starting ❑ Stalling ❑ Rough	_____
_____	❑ Transmission	
_____	❑ Heater/defroster	_____
_____	❑ Body damage	_____
_____	❑ Other	_____

General Condition
Comments:_____

Maintenance:	6,000-mile inspection due	❑ Yes ❑ No
	12,000-mile inspection due	❑ Yes ❑ No

_____   _____
Equipment Manager's Signature   Date

Accident Report

Accident: Date _____ Time _____ : _____ AM/PM

Location _____
                    (Address, nearest intersection, mile post)
Description _____

_____

_____

Police Dept.: _____ Officer Name
                                        or Badge No. _____
Property
Damage: Owner _____

Address _____ Phone _____

Driver _____

Address _____ Phone _____

Driver's Licence No. _____

State _____ S.S. No. _____

Automobile _____ Lic. No. _____ State_____
                    Make, Model, Year
Col. Property
Damage   Describe Damage _____

_____

Witnesses: Name _____

Address _____ Phone _____

Owner _____

Address _____   Phone _____

Appendix J

Lander College Department of Athletics
Substance Abuse Policy

Introduction

Recognizing that drug and alcohol abuse among college athletes is of national concern and could endanger the health, development, and well-being of some of the college's student athletes, Lander College Department of Athletics has developed this policy of drug education, testing, and counseling.

The purposes of the Lander College Department of Athletics Substance Abuse Policy are as follows:

a. To provide appropriate substance abuse education for all facets of the Lander College athletic community.

b. To identify those athletes who are involved in substance abuse so that they may receive the professional help and support which they need.

c. To deter athletes from involvement in substance abuse.

e. To convey the message that Lander College believes that the process of chemically-enhanced athletic performance is unethical, and will not tolerate such behavior.

f. To enhance the safety and well-being of Lander College athletes and their opponents.

Substance Abuse Education

Although this document has been subdivided into specific categories for clarity, the Lander College Department of Athletics Substance Abuse Policy is an educational endeavor. The unannounced, random drug testing discussed in this document helps direct specific educational and counseling services to the athletes who need them most.

The Substance Abuse Education component of this policy is designed to provide the athletes with information relative to substance abuse. The major focus is prevention.

The Director of Counseling and his designates will be responsible for planning, coordinating, and implementing the substance abuse education program. Educational techniques could include substance abuse education seminars, guest lectures, and current printed materials relative to substance abuse. The Director of Counseling will contact all persons to be involved in educational program, and provide in-service training when appropriate.

Substance Abuse Counseling

The Director of Counseling will be responsible for coordinating all substance abuse counseling. He shall involve the necessary parties and agencies to conduct the counseling, adhering to the guidelines stated herein. Individual substance abuse counseling will occur 1) after confirmation of a first or second positive drug test, 2) after self-referral by an athlete, and/or 3) upon the request of an appropriate third party. Self or third party referral will not be considered a positive test result. Athletes may also request counseling to assist in dealing with the substance abuse of a third party (e.g., relative, roommate).

Substance Abuse Testing

1. METHODS OF SELECTION FOR TESTING: The selection of athletes for testing will be done as follows:
   a. In keeping with the purposes outlined previously, all varsity athletes, cheerleaders, and student support staff (trainers, managers, etc.) will be subject to testing.
   b. Testing will be carried out on an unannounced basis. Six testing sessions will be conducted during the school year between the dtes of August 15 and May 15.
   c. For testing purposes, the following grouping will be used: Men's Basketball, Women's Basketball, Men's Tennis, Women's Tennis, Men's Soccer, Women's Softball, Cheerleaders, and Student Support Staff. Approximately ten percent (10%) of each group will be randomly selected for testing immediately prior to each of the six test sessions.
   d. In addition to the groups identified above, any athlete who demonstrates behavior indicative of possible substance abuse (probable cause), or having previously tested positive will be subject to unannounced testing at any time.

2. SUBSTANCES TO BE TESTED FOR:
   a. Amphetamines
   b. Barbiturates
   c. Benzodiazepines (valium and similar tranquilizers)
   d. Cannabinoid (marijuana)
   e. Cocaine
   f. Methaqualone (qualudes)
   g. Opiates (heroin and other opium derivates)
   h. Phencyclidine (PCP or "angel dust")

Although athletes will not be tested for alcohol abuse, any athlete convicted of driving under the influence of alcohol or drugs (D.U.I.) as defined by South Carolina state law, or drunk and disorderly conduct will be considered to have had tested positively for substance abuse, and will be subject to the consequences outlined in section 4 a., b., and c. of this document.

3. TEST PROCEDURES:
    a. Each athlete (and parent, if athlete is a minor) will sign a consent form prior to becoming a member of the athletic program. This form will spell out the substance abuse policy, and will indicate the athlete's consent to be tested according to the procedures outlined in the policy as a prerequisite of participation in the athletic program.
    b. The head Athletic Trainer shall be responsible for 1) selecting the dates for testing, 2) randomly selecting the athletes for testing, and 3) notifying the appropriate coaches concerning the specific test date, time, site, and athletes to be tested. It will then be the responsibility of said coaches to insure the presence of said athletes for testing as scheduled.
    c. Prior to testing, the athlete will complete a questionnaire, identifying any drugs he/she is currently taking or has taken within the past three (3) months.
    d. The giving of the urine sample will be directly observed (athlete totally disrobed, facing the observer). The observer shall be an appropriate member of the college's athletic training staff, or an independently contracted medical professional.
    e. The sample collection jar will be sealed with security tape, and along with proper documentation will be placed into a plastic bag, and sealed with security tape.
    f. The athlete will witness the preparation of the sample, and sign the appropriate paperwork, acknowledging that the sample is his/hers.
    g. The sample will be provided to the testing lab according to chain of custody guidelines set forth by the lab.
    h. Upon receipt of the sample by the testing lab, initial testing will be conducted (including confirmatory testing when appropriate), and the remainder of the sample will be frozen and retained according to chain of custody procedures.
    i. In the case of a positive test, the athlete will be given the opportunity to have the remaining portion of his/her sample retested.
    j. Test results will be reported directly to the college's Director of Counseling.
4. ACTIONS RESULTING FROM POSITIVE TESTS:
    a. First Positive Test
        1. Athlete meets with the Director of Counseling, is advised of the test results, and is given the opportunity to have the frozen portion of his/her sample retested.
        2. Athlete is placed on nonrestrictive (no change in athletic, academic, or social status) probation.

3. Athlete agrees to enter into substance abuse counseling for such time as deemed appropriate by the substance abuse counselor involved. Continued participation in the athletic program is contingent upon satisfactory completion of the substance abuse counseling program.

4. Athlete and Director of Counseling sign a contract statement, acknowledging the positive test, the terms of the nonrestrictive probation, and the consequences of a second positive test. Refusal to sign the contract statement will result in immediate dismissal from the athletic program (with loss of athletic grant-in-aid).

5. Any athlete having testing positive will be subject to unannounced testing at any time.

b. Second Positive Test

1. Athlete meets with the Director of Counseling, the Director of Athletics, and his/her coach, is advised of the test results, and is given the opportunity to have the frozen portion of the sample retested.

2. Athlete is suspended from participation in the athletic program for a period of no less than four (4) weeks, pending satisfactory completion of an appropriate substance abuse treatment program (satisfactory completion to be determined by substance abuse treatment professional in charge), and review of the situation by the Director of Counseling, Director of Athletics, and coach.

3. Athlete, Director of Counseling, and Director of Athletics sign a contract statement, acknowledging the second positive test, the terms of the suspension from athletic participation, and the consequences of a third positive test (dismissal from the athletic program, with loss of athletic grant-in-aid). Refusal to sign the contract statement will result in immediate dismissal from the athletic program (with loss of athletic grant-in-aid).

4. Any athlete having tested positive will be subject to unannounced testing at any time.

5. Athlete becomes subject to disciplinary action as outlined in the *Lander College Student Handbook*.

c. Third Positive Test

1. Athlete meets with the Director of Counseling, Director of Athletics and his/her coach, and is advised of the test results.

2. Athlete is dismissed from the athletic program (with loss of athletic grant-in-aid).

3. Athlete, Director of Counseling, and Director of Athletics sign a statement, acknowledging the third positive test and the actions taken.

4. Athlete becomes subject to disciplinary action as outlined in the *Lander College Student Handbook*.

5. FALSIFICATION OF TEST RESULTS: Any attempt to falsify test results by providing false information, altering a urine sample, manipulating test results, or any other conscientious effort to circumvent the process will result in an automatic suspension from participation in the athletic program for a period of not less than one (1) year.

6. SELECTION OF A LAB: An appropriate lab will be selected based upon the following basic criteria:
   a. Ability to provide appropriate initial screening procedures (immuno-assay, thin-layer chromatography, etc.), AND confirmatory testing using gas chromatography and mass spectrometry
   b. Documented accuracy rates with respect to false-positive results
   c. Appropriate chain of custody plan which will minimize the possibility of inaccurate results
   d. Availability of confirmation affidavits from analysts/toxicologists upon request
   e. Convenience with respect to sample storage and transportation, and prompt reporting of test results
   f. Cost

Lander College Department of Athletics
First Positive Drug Test Contract Statement

Student Athlete _____ Sport _____

I HEREBY ACKNOWLEDGE that I tested positive on _____, 19__

for _____.

I UNDERSTAND that the results of this test have been made known only to myself and the college's Director of Counseling.

I UNDERSTAND that I may request that the drug test be repeated using the remaining portion of my original urine sample.

I UNDERSTAND that 1) I am immediately being placed on nonrestrictive probation which means that this first positive test does not affect my academic, athletic, or social status, and 2) my continued participation in the athletic program is contingent upon the successful completion of a prescribed substance abuse counseling program.

I UNDERSTAND that a second positive test will result in 1) immediate suspension from athletic participation for a period of not less than four (4) weeks, pending successful completion of a prescribed comprehensive substance abuse counseling program and clearance by the college's Director of Counseling, Director of Athletics, and my coach and 2) disciplinary action as outlined in the *Lander College Student Handbook*.

I UNDERSTAND that I am free to refuse to sign this statement, but that such refusal will result in immediate dismissal from the Lander College athletic program (with loss of athletic grant-in-aid).

_____   _____
Signature   Director of Counseling

_____
Date

Lander College Department of Athletics
Second Positive Drug Test Contract Statement

Student Athlete _____ Sport _____

I HEREBY ACKNOWLEDGE that I tested positive on _____, 19__

for _____.

I UNDERSTAND that the results of this test have been made known only to myself, the college's Director of Counseling, Director of Athletics, my coach and other appropriate official of Lander College.

I UNDERSTAND that I may request that the drug test be repeated using the remaining portion of my original urine sample.

I UNDERSTAND that I am immediately being suspended from athletic participation for a period of not less than four (4) weeks, pending the successful completion of a prescribed comprehensive substance abuse counseling program, and clearance by the above named individuals.

I UNDERSTAND that as a result of this second positive test, I am subject to disciplinary action as outlined in the *Lander College Student Handbook*.

I UNDERSTAND that a third positive test will result in immediate dismissal from the Lander College athletic program (with loss of athletic grant-in-aid).

I UNDERSTAND that I am free to refuse to sign this statement, but that such refusal will result in immediate dismissal from the Lander College athletic program (with loss of athletic grant-in-aid).

_____   _____
Signature   Director of Counseling

_____   _____
Date   Director of Athletics

Lander College Department of Athletics
Third Positive Drug Test Contract Statement

Student Athlete _____ Sport _____

I HEREBY ACKNOWLEDGE that I tested positive on _____, 19__

for _____.

I UNDERSTAND that the results of this test have been made known only to myself, the college's Director of Counseling, Director of Athletics, my coach and other appropriate official of Lander College.

I UNDERSTAND that, as a result of this third positive test, I am immediately dismissed from the Lander College athletic program (with loss of athletic grant-in-aid).

I UNDERSTAND that, as a result of this third positive test, I am subject to disciplinary action as outlined in the *Lander College Student Handbook.*

_____	_____
Signature	Director of Counseling

_____	_____
Date	Director of Athletics

Lander College Department of Athletics
Substance Abuse Informed Consent Statement

I HEREBY ACKNOWLEDGE that I have received a copy of the *Lander College Department of Athletics Substance Abuse Policy*, that it has been thoroughly explained to me, and that I have been given the opportunity to ask any questions regarding this policy.

I UNDERSTAND the aforementioned policy, and my responsibilities thereto.

I HEREBY CONSENT to have a sample of my urine collected and tested for the presence of drugs in accordance with the Lander College Department of Athletics drug testing program.

I UNDERSTAND that this testing will occur at such time or times as deemed appropriate by the Head Athletic Trainer.

I UNDERSTAND that any urine samples will be sent only to a licensed medical laboratory for actual testing, and that the samples will be coded to provide confidentiality.

I AUTHORIZE the release of my urine testing results to those individuals identified in the *Lander College Department of Athletics Substance Abuse Policy*, and I UNDERSTAND that all results will be made available to me.

I UNDERSTAND that I am free to withdraw this consent for urinalysis testing. However, I UNDERSTAND that should I refuse to submit to testing at the time requested, I will not be permitted to participate in the Lander College athletic program until such time as the Department of Athletics and Lander College shall deem appropriate.

I UNDERSTAND that I am free to refuse to sign this statement, but should I refuse to sign this statement, I will not be permitted to participate in the Lander College athletic program.

I HEREBY RELEASE Lander College, its Trustees, officers, employees, and agents from legal responsibility or liability for the release of such information and records as authorized by this form.

_____   _____
Signature   Date

_____   _____
Signature of Parent(s) or Legal Guardian   Witness
   if Student Athlete is a minor

Lander College Department of Athletics
Drug/Medication Disclosure Form

I HEREBY ACKNOWLEDGE that I am currently taking the following drugs/medications for the reasons indicated:

Drug/Medication	Reason

I HEREBY ACKNOWLEDGE that I have taken (but am not currently taking) the following drugs/medications within the past three (3) months for the reasons indicted:

Drug/Medication	Reason

_____   _____
              Signature   Date

Appendix K

Student Medical History Form

Name of Student: _____
                        Last   First   Middle

Address: _____ Telephone No. _____

_____

Age: _____

Notify in Case of Emergency: _____
                                          Name

                             _____
                                       Relationship

Address: _____
              City   State   Zip

Telephone: _____
                  Home   Business

(1)   List any history of serious illness or injuries (describe and state
       dates of occurrence).

       _____

       _____

(2)   List any prior history of surgery. (Describe and state dates of
       occurrence).

       _____

       _____

       _____

(3)   List any family history of T.B., Heart Disease, etc.

       _____

       _____

       _____

(4)   Please check if you have a history of the following:
  (a)   Asthma   _____
  (b)   Convulsions or Epilepsy   _____
  (c)   Diabetes   _____
  (d)   Fainting   _____
  (e)   Heart Disease   _____
  (f)   Hearing Problems   _____
  (g)   High or Low Blood Pressure   _____

(h)   Heat Prostration   _____
(i)   Hernia   _____
(j)   Menstrual Disorder   _____

(5)   Are you presently under medication? (If so, please name the
       medication):
       _____

       _____

(6)   Are you allergic to medication? _____

       If so, what? _____

(7)   Do you have any other allergies? _____

(8)   Do you wear glasses? _____

(9)   Do you wear contact lenses? _____

(10)   Describe any past athletic-related injuries: _____

       Date _____

       Date _____

(11)   Do you have any present problems or complaints: _____
       _____

The above answers are true and correct to my knowledge.

_____   _____
Student's Signature   Date

Parental Medical Consent Form

I hereby grant permission to the _____
(name of institution) and their duly authorized representatives, to consent to first aid, emergency medical care and all other medical or surgical care they deem reasonably necessary to the health and well being
of my son or daughter.

Also, when necessary for executing such care, I grant permission
for hospitalization at an accredited hospital.

_____

Student's Name

_____

Parent or Guardian's Signature

_____

Date

Emergency Contact Information

Student's Name: _____

Address: _____

_____

Telephone number: _____

Age: _____ Birth Date: _____

Emergency Contact (Name and phone numbers)

1) _____
    (Name)   (Relationship)

    _____
    (Home Telephone)   (Business Telephone)

2) _____
    (Name)   (Relationship)

    _____
    (Home Telephone)   (Business Telephone)

Presently under the following medication: _____

_____

Presently allergic to the following medication: _____

_____

Presently wear contact lenses? _____
Presently wear glasses? _____
Presently a diabetic, hemophiliac or have hearing problems? If so,
please state: _____

Student's signature: _____
Date: _____

Physicians Post Injury/Illness Consent Form

Student: _____

Address: _____

Telephone: _____ Age: _____

Date of injury or onset of illness: _____

_____

Injury sustained in:

_____ _____ _____
Intramurals   Physical   Other
                  Education
                  Class

Sport or activity engaged in at time of injury:

_____

Medical treatment given: _____

_____

Hospitalization required: ____ Yes ____ No

Physician's recommendation: _____

_____

_____

_____
                                        Date

_____
Physician's Name

_____

Signature

NOTE: If a student's illness did not require a visit to a physician, your staff should require a written consent from the parent/guardian prior to permitting the student to return to physical education class or other sport related activities.

Post Injury Agreement

I, _____ , wish to participate in intercollegiate athletics, and more particularly, the _____ (name of sport) program at _____ (name of school). In connection with my participation, I acknowledge that the risk of possible physical harm to me as a result of my participation is increased because of a _____ condition from which I have suffered in the past, and for which I have received medical attention. While there is no immediate danger to me, I am told that my participation in strenuous athletic activities, such as _____ (name of sport) constitutes more risk to me than it does to other athletes, I nevertheless wish to continue my participation in intercollegiate _____ (name of sport). In making this decision, I am aware of the value of intercollegiate athletics in my life, and choose to continue my participation in order to take complete advantage of those values. In weighing the risk to myself of potential injury now and in the future to my _____ , I nevertheless choose to continue in the program and wish to exonerate and save harmless _____ (name of school), its agents and employees, the athletic staff of _____ (name of school), the physicians and other practitioners of the healing arts treating me, from any and all liability as a result of a recurrence of the injury to my _____ , which hereinafter may be claimed as a result of my participation in the program of _____ (name of school).

Date: _____   _____
                                              Signature

_____

Social Security Number   Parent or Guardian

Signature may be that of athlete over 18 years of age; if under 18, please have it signed by parent or guardian.

Appendix L

Sample Physicians Agreement

STATE OF ⎤
⎦

CITY/COUNTY OF ⎤
⎦

THIS AGREEMENT made and entered into the _____ day of _____ 19 _____ , by and between _____ , a school having its principal place of business in _____ , (hereinafter referred to as "School,") and Dr. _____ , a citizen and resident of _____ (hereinafter referred to as "Physician").

WITNESSETH

WHEREAS, School is desirous of obtaining the services of Physician in connection with its _____ program, and

WHEREAS, Physician is skilled in the practice of orthopedic medicine (or other specialty) and is willing to assist School with its orthopedic (or other medical) problems in its _____ program,

NOW THEREFORE, in consideration of the covenants and promises contained herein, the parties hereto agree as follows:

(1) School hereby retains and Physician agrees to be retained on an independent contractor basis by School as School orthopedic (or general medical) consultant in School _____ program for the school year 19 _____ .

(2) Physician will act as consultant with the School's coaches, trainers, students and other personnel with regard to orthopedic (or other) medical problems incurred by students in the School's _____ program. Physician's consulting services shall include the attendance of all of School's games, a schedule of which is attached hereto and incorporated herein by reference, and shall also attend all scrimmages as scheduled from time to time by School, notice of which shall be given to Physician not less than 48 hours prior to such scrimmage. Physician shall also attend all/none of School's other practice sessions, excluding scrimmages, during the term of this agreement.

(3) Physician shall make recommendations to the coaching staff, trainers and other personnel as to the handling of all orthopedic (or

other medical) matters with regard to the students in School's _____ program. Such recommendations shall include prescribing treatment for injuries and other orthopedic (or medical) problems, and recommendations for surgical and other hospital procedures when necessary. All physician charges for such surgery and other hospital procedures are not covered under the terms of this agreement.

(4) As compensation for all consulting services rendered hereunder, School agrees to pay to Physician the sum of $ _____ , to be paid upon the execution of this agreement.

(5) This agreement is to be construed under and governed by the laws of the State of _____ .

IN WITNESS WHEREOF, the parties hereto have executed this agreement in duplicate originals on the day and year first above written.

School _____

By _____

Dr. _____

By _____

Appendix M

Injury Report

INJURY REPORT FORM FROM ATHLETIC TRAINER TO PHYSICIAN

Name: Sport: School:

Date of Report: Date of Injury:

Person Completing Report:

                (Athletic Trainer) (Title) (Phone)

Body Part Injured:

Mechanism of Injury (How? What Happened?)

Physical Findings:
Tentative Diagnosis:
Immediate Care:
Comments:

Follow up: ❏ Physician Visit And/Or X-Rays Recommended
            ❏ Physician Visit Not Recommended

_____   _____
(Athlete's Signature)   (Trainer's Signature)

INJURY REPORT FROM PHYSICIAN TO ATHLETIC TRAINER
Name: Sport: School:
Diagnosis:
Treatment/Rehabilitation Program:

Copy of Specific Program Enclosed: ❏ Yes   ❏ No
Estimated time loss:_____
Follow up: ° Must see me/another physician prior to return to
              practice and/or competition.
         ° May be checked by athletic trainer in lieu of visit to
              physician.
         ° May return to practice and/or competition upon
              successful completion of the treatment/re-
              habilitation program specified above.
         ° May return to practice and/or competition immedi-
              ately with the following modifications
Comments:

_____   _____   _____
(Physician's Signature)   (Date)   (Phone)

Injury Care Recommendation Form

Injury Care Recommendation

Name: Sport:

Date: Injury:

Recommended Care:

❑   May continue regular activity
❑   Should modify activity as follows:

❑   Must see me prior to return to activity:
❑   Other:

                                    _____
                                    (Doctor's Signature)

Appendix N
Insurance Information Form

Parents Complete and Return To:

Athletics Director
Address

Equipment will not be issued until this form is completed and returned to the Athletic Department

Name of Athlete: _____   Sport: _____

College Address: _____   Phone: _____

Home Address: _____   Phone: _____

Father/Guardian: _____   Mother/Guardian: _____

Address: _____   Address: _____

_____   _____

Phone: Home-   Work-   Phone: Home-   Work-

Medical Ins. Co. _____   Medical Ins. Co. _____

_____   _____

Address: _____   Address: _____

Ins. Co. Phone: _____   Ins. Co. Phone: _____

Policy No. _____   Policy No. _____

Is the company or plan listed considered a Health Maintenance Organization (HMO) or a Preferred Provider Organization (PPO)?

Yes _____   No _____

Is your son/daughter allergic to any drugs? _____ Which? _____

List all surgeries, athletic injuries, serious illnesses or hospitalization that your son or daughter has had within the last five years.

1. _____   Date: _____

1. _____   Date: _____

2. _____   Date: _____

3. _____   Date: _____

I hereby authorize _____ (institution) and _____ (insurance agency) to inspect or secure copies of case history records, laboratory reports, diagnosis, x-ray, and any other data covering this and/or previous confinements and/or disabilities. A photostatic copy of this authorization shall be deemed as effective and valid as the original.

Parent's Signature: _____

Student's Signature: _____

I. ADMINISTRATION OF ATHLETIC ACTIVITIES

To provide effective guidance on safety and liability risks, it is important that the institution develop formal operating policies and procedures for all persons involved in the athletic programs. It is also necessary to monitor the implementation of such procedures. Failure to observe institutional safety policies not only increases risk but also increases the exposure to liability suits alleging negligence. The following questions focus on the incorporation of suggested policies into the athletic program.

Safety Responsibilities   YES   NO   NA   Referral

A.   Are safety responsibilities specifically included in position descriptions for all personnel involved in the athletics program, including:

   1.   Administrators
   2.   Athletic directors
   3.   Coaches
   4.   Athletic trainers
   5.   Sports officials
   6.   Support personnel
   7.   Security officers
   8.   Drivers

B.   Do these responsibilities include training and experience requirements?

Athletic Policies

C.   Do specific policies exist regarding possession of alcohol and its serving before, during and after athletic activities? Are they enforced?

D.   Is there a designated person responsible for enforcement of alcohol policy?

E.   Has the institution established a clear policy for pre-game tailgating parties and the presence of alcohol at certain athletic activities such as rugby and hockey?

Goals and Objectives

F.   Are overall safety standards established for all sports and recreation activities? For each sport/recreational activity?

G.   Are individual safety goals, objectives, and activities in each of the following areas reviewed on a regular basis (how often?) and by qualified individuals (who?) to insure a reasonable level of safety for all (employees, students, fans) involved?

   1.   Maintenance of facilities?
   2.   Inspections of playing fields and equipment?
   3.   Intercollegiate athletics?
   4.   Intramural?
   5.   Club sports?
   6.   Recreational/instructional sports?
   7.   Dormitory/residence hall recreation programs?
   8.   Safety training?
   9.   Orientation programs?
   10. Athletic camps and sports leagues?

		YES	NO	NA	Referral

Review and Implementation

H. Is there a regular (how often?) review of safety and liability aspects of athletic programs with follow-up and corrective actions?

I. Are loss records and accident statistics maintained and reported to coaches and athletic management personnel?

J. Does the annual budget request include consideration of resources to improve safety conditions for equipment and facilities? Are such requests prioritized?

Purchasing

K. Is purchasing of athletic equipment centralized and are safety considerations and guidelines included in all bid specifications?

II. ACCIDENT/INCIDENT REPORTING AND INVESTIGATIVE PROCEDURES

It is important that records be created for every incident or accident, and especially those which require medical attention or which result in serious injury. (Serious injury is defined as one which requires at least an overnight hospital stay and/or some surgical procedure). Sound record keeping procedures and documentation of all steps taken in response to the incident enhance the institution's liability protection. The protocol for incident/accident reporting should be developed with the input of the general counsel's office and post incident/accident investigations should also be coordinated with counsel.

Reports   YES   NO   NA   Referral

A. Are "paper routes" for reporting and investigating accidents and injuries established and functioning?

B. Are designated persons trained in proper accident reporting procedures and investigative techniques?

C. Are the accident reports reviewed by the athletic director and the senior administrator responsible for athletics?

D. Do reports include corrective action taken?

E. Are pictures and other visual aids used to aid in identification and documentation of accidents?

F. Are witness statements documented?

Follow-up Actions

G. Is there a process for developing recommendations and for implementing corrective actions?

H. Is there a procedure for an administrator's follow-up with an injured person to ensure that adequate care and response were delivered?

I. Are periodic reviews of accident reports conducted to determine trends, patterns or prominent problem areas?

J. Are medical emergency policies and procedures with all college/ university athletic staff periodically reviewed?

		YES	NO	NA	Referral
K.	Is there an accident/incident review meeting with staff on a regular basis?	____	____	____	_____

III. HAZARD RECOGNITION/SELF-INSPECTION PROGRAMS

Identifying safety hazards and liability risks in advance is critical. Essential to the proactive approach are regular inspections and audits, and continuous review of all accident data. Property and liability insurance companies often can assist in preventative surveys and in the development of recommendations to address priority needs and recognize the effects of use on facilities and equipment.

Inspection		YES	NO	NA	Referral
A.	Are safety inspection programs conducted on a regular (how often?) basis for all indoor and outdoor facilities?	____	____	____	_____
B.	Are safety inspection programs conducted on a regular (how often?) basis for inspection of all equipment?	____	____	____	_____
C.	Are all inspection reports kept on file? Whose responsibility is this?	____	____	____	_____
D.	Are there specific persons trained in proper inspection techniques assigned to conduct safety inspections?	____	____	____	_____
E.	Is old or obsolete equipment disposed of, rather than passed along for use in other activities?	____	____	____	_____
F.	Are corrective actions recommended, prioritized and documented?	____	____	____	_____
G.	Are target dates established for implementation of corrective actions?	____	____	____	_____
H.	Are inspection reports reviewed with a Safety Committee to determine trends or problem areas?	____	____	____	_____

IV. TRAINING

Training is necessary to enable coaches, support staff and participants to be aware of policies and procedures and be able to implement them effectively. Training on safety and liability issues should be incorporated into the regular orientation process.

Areas Requiring Training		YES	NO	NA	Referral
A.	Are all athletic personnel with assigned responsibility for the management and/or supervision of athletic activities trained in the following areas:				
1.	Safety technique training relevant to each sport/activity?	____	____	____	_____
2.	Emergency procedures?	____	____	____	_____
3.	Hazard recognition/awareness programs?	____	____	____	_____
4.	Transportation policies?	____	____	____	_____
5.	Policies on alcohol and drug use?	____	____	____	_____
6.	National athletic governing body regulations?	____	____	____	_____
7.	College/university athletic policies?	____	____	____	_____
a.	Is a policy manual developed?	____	____	____	_____
b.	Is a copy given to all responsible for athletic activities?	____	____	____	_____
8.	Use of emergency equipment?	____	____	____	_____
9.	Accident/incident reporting and investigation?	____	____	____	_____

			YES	NO	NA	Referral
10.	Catastrophic incident management?					
11.	Crowd control/supervision?					

Participant Training

B. Are players/participants trained in the proper techniques of the sporting activity and in the correct use of equipment?

C. Are participants required to sign an "Informed Consent" document?

D. Are players/participants informed about the inherent risks of the sport/ activity in which they are participating?

E. Is a waiver or informal consent document used for high risk club, intramural or recreational sports?

F. Has the informed consent document been reviewed by counsel?

V.   EMERGENCY PROCEDURES

Being prepared is the best prevention of liability arising from emergency situations which require immediate response. While it is impossible to predict when and how an emergency will arise, an institution can develop emergency reaction procedures and train staff accordingly.

Response

YES   NO   NA   Referral

A. Is access readily available to telephones and emergency numbers in the event of any emergency?

B. Are physicians and/or trainers with appropriate training present during intercollegiate contact sports/games?

C. Are appropriate emergency transportation plans in place?

D. Is there an existing directory of all kinds of emergency care provided in institutional facilities, including: appropriate supervision required for emergency care, rehabilitation services, and health care in institutional facilities?

E. Are emergency medical release forms signed and available at all events?

F. Are all emergency care providers identified by profession and outside affiliations where appropriate?

G. Is there an existing policy on designated persons authorized to provide emergency care in institutional facilities?

H. Are persons trained in emergency care required to be present during use of all facilities or equipment?

Qualification and Certification

I. Does a process exist to guarantee appropriate credentials for emergency care providers to include:

	YES	NO	NA	Referral
1. Present or current license?	___	___	___	___
2. Identification of prior record of substandard performance?	___	___	___	___
3. Appropriate levels of malpractice insurance?	___	___	___	___
J. Is documentation of appropriate athlete/participant physical examinations on file before use of facilities and/or equipment?	___	___	___	___
K. Are all students notified as to the coverage afforded them by their student accident/medical/health insurance?	___	___	___	___
L. Is the use of all rehabilitation services under supervision of a qualified physician?	___	___	___	___
M. Does the trainer in charge of rehabilitation services have documented credentials and appropriate experience?	___	___	___	___
N. Are all persons authorized to serve as trainers appropriately trained, credentialed, supervised and insured?	___	___	___	___
O. Does a policy exist as to when trainers will be present at games?	___	___	___	___
P. Does the policy comply with league, national athletic governing bodies (NCAA, NAIA) and legal requirements?	___	___	___	___
Q. Does the institution provide insurance for intercollegiate activities? If so, what type?	___	___	___	___
R. If the institution does not provide student health insurance, does it require evidence of coverage before participation in any sports?	___	___	___	___
S. Who verifies the credentials of emergency care providers and is verification performed on an annual basis?	___	___	___	___
T. Is appropriate notice given and documented as to the limitations of all coverages provided to athletes in all sports?	___	___	___	___
U. Are emergency drills scheduled and conducted regularly?	___	___	___	___
V. Is there equity in the provision and availability of emergency and medical care for both men's and women's sports?	___	___	___	___
W. Do appropriate checks and balances exist separating the making of health care decisions and athletic decisions?	___	___	___	___
X. Are policies developed for contacting relatives of injured parties?	___	___	___	___
Y. Are policies developed for communication between the injured and the college/university?	___	___	___	___
Z. Are unauthorized persons excluded from taping and training rooms?	___	___	___	___
AA. Do student trainers receive suitable training, supervision and insurance?	___	___	___	___
BB. Does policy require trainers to have kits which contain appropriate supplies and access to means of communication in case of emergency?	___	___	___	___

		YES	NO	NA	Referral
CC.	Are suitable liquids provided at all games and practices?				

VI. TRANSPORTATION

More frequently the liability of the college or university is heightened by the risks in transporting athletes from the campus to other locations. Responsibility for the appropriate supervision of all modes of transportation is not significantly decreased by using contractual or private transporters. Supervision of every aspect of transportation is essential, including credentials of drivers, their competency with the specific vehicles under realistic load conditions and the purchasing of vehicles with proper adaptation for foreseeable loads and number of passengers.

		YES	NO	NA	Referral
A.	Is there a written policy on transportation for athletic activities, outlining who can drive and driver qualifications; has it been disseminated to all personnel involved in athletic activities?				
B.	Do contract carriers have appropriate permits and licenses?				
C.	Are certificates of insurance obtained and is the college/university named as an insured?				
D.	Do procedures exist to verify credentials of all persons who drive vehicles in transportation services?				
E.	Is there a policy on allowing personal vehicles to be used for transporting athletes?				
F.	Are there procedures for obtaining authorization for all proposed transportation?				
G.	Are the safety policies of the contract carrier known (i.e., driver qualifications, training, vehicle safety)?				
H.	Are pre- and post-trip vehicle inspections conducted with reports on matters needing maintenance?				
I.	Do these procedures exclude persons with a past record of serious motor vehicle violations, especially driving under the influence (DUI)?				
J.	Are drivers required to pass some form of qualification with each vehicle under actual road conditions?				
K.	Are transportation resources equitable for both men and women athletes?				
L.	Is there a policy on the use of alcoholic beverages on trips?				
M.	Are policies established for accident reporting procedures?				

VII. FACILITIES

Not only is the institution responsible for providing a safe environment in its athletic facilities, but special attention must be paid to those instances where the administration has been notified of a dangerous condition. Failure to take action in a reasonable amount of time (dependent on the condition) can lead to serious claims against the institution. Swimming pools, weight rooms and similar high risk facilities require an even greater degree of attention.

In addition to careful reviews of staffing and orientation programs, this heightened degree of attention would include regular inspections, mandatory reporting systems for all incidents/accidents, review of all reports, and immediate action.

		YES	NO	NA	Referral
A.	Is there a formal annual review of the condition of all sports/athletic facilities for appropriate action to correct unsafe or inadequate facilities?				
B.	Is there designation of responsibility for observing and maintaining safety of all facilities?				
C.	Are there staffing plans for all facilities and are they appropriate to safe use of each facility for all scheduled and informal activities?				
D.	Is there an inventory of sports/athletic facilities used in intercollegiate, intramural, club and recreational/instructional activities?				
E.	Are users required to participate in orientation and safety check-out before first use of facilities?				
F.	Does the design of new or rehabilitated facilities include formal review of safety considerations?				
G.	Are I.D. cards or sign-in sheets used to control admission to the institution's athletic facilities during either regular or off hours?				
H.	Are there special crowd control considerations for all activities?				
I.	Are there appropriate spectator and participant warnings to include informed consent on properly worded signs?				

VIII. EQUIPMENT

In addition to maintaining the athletic facilities, it is necessary to inspect, repair, recondition, and replace equipment. Special attention must be given to high risk equipment such as trampolines and weight machines.

		YES	NO	NA	Referral
A.	Is a formal annual review of the condition of all equipment conducted? Are records maintained?				
B.	Is there a specific designation of responsibility for the maintenance and safety of all equipment?				
C.	Is safety considered in the purchasing and disposal of all equipment? Are records maintained?				
D.	Is an inventory of equipment used in intercollegiate, intramural, club and recreational/instructional sports maintained?				
E.	Are all users required to participate in orientation and safety check-out before first use of high risk equipment?				
F.	Are there any exclusions on the institution's liability insurance policies for specific equipment such as trampolines and weight machines?				

IX.   INTERCOLLEGIATE SPORTS

Intercollegiate sports receive more attention than intramural, club sports, and recreational/instructional sports. Publicity about any shortcomings, accidents, or other incidents are sure to gain local, regional, and possibly national attention. In addition, intercollegiate sports are subject to regulation and compliance with standards set by various governing organizations.

		YES	NO	NA	Referral
A.	Is there a review of compliance with NCAA/NAIA rules and league rules and regulations at least annually?	___	___	___	___
B.	Is there equitable treatment for both men's and women's athletic/ recreational programs (intercollegiate, intramural, club, recreation) in the following areas:				
	1. Equipment?	___	___	___	___
	2. Scholarships?	___	___	___	___
	3. Funding resources?	___	___	___	___
	4. Coaches?	___	___	___	___
	5. Facilities?	___	___	___	___
	6. Transportation?	___	___	___	___
	7. Medical treatment?	___	___	___	___
C.	Is there a procedure for review of all contracts between institutional employees and third parties to avoid conflicts of interest? Are such contracts reviewed by counsel?	___	___	___	___
D.	Is there a provision in athletic contracts with regard to criminal activity and gambling?	___	___	___	___
E.	Is drug testing of intercollegiate athletes carried out only in conformity with detailed protocol?	___	___	___	___
F.	Have contracts with the drug testing laboratory been reviewed?	___	___	___	___
G.	Are the credentials and error rate of any drug testing laboratory documented prior to execution of contract?	___	___	___	___

X.   CLUB, INTRAMURAL, INSTRUCTIONAL/RECREATIONAL SPORTS

Intramural and club sports traditionally involve a larger number of students than intercollegiate sports, but are more informal and perceived to receive less supervision. However, the principles applicable to the care of facilities and equipment and the basic preparation of participants and institution administrators parallel those of intercollegiate sports. Reported incidents/accidents must be reviewed and prompt attention must be paid to any problems with playing conditions.

		YES	NO	NA	Referral
A.	Is there adequate supervision of club, intramural and recreational/ instructional sports? By whom?	___	___	___	___
B.	When appropriate, is each users' proficiency established before participation?	___	___	___	___
C.	Is the adequacy of equipment and safety of facilities documented?	___	___	___	___

		YES	NO	NA	Referral
D.	Does an annual review of all of these sports take place?	___	___	___	___
E.	Is there adequate access to emergency care?	___	___	___	___
F.	Is the use of space and facilities for informal or pickup sports reviewed for safety?	___	___	___	___
G.	Are unsafe activities e.g. "residence hall sports," discouraged aggressively? If so, how?	___	___	___	___
H.	Are off-campus sports trips by institutionally recognized groups appropriately supervised?	___	___	___	___
I.	Are there defined rules of play for intramural sports listed in dorm/ residence hall rules?	___	___	___	___
J.	Are these policies reviewed during the student orientation?	___	___	___	___
K.	Does the college/university distribute pamphlets to students defining these rules, policies, procedures on a regular basis?	___	___	___	___
L.	Are staff members trained in policies?	___	___	___	___
M.	Is there a person responsible for safety issues, including review of accident reports, conduct of safety inspections and coordination with residential life staff for the sports and recreational areas?	___	___	___	___

XI. EMPLOYMENT CONTRACTS

While litigation may be generated more frequently from athletic accidents and injuries, an increasing source of lawsuits come from personnel practices and quite frequently from contractual disputes. It is important to have all contracts reviewed by the institution's counsel. In addition, all athletic personnel with management responsibility should be fully apprised of the institution's personnel policies particularly as to handling grievances and terminations.

		YES	NO	NA	Referral
A.	Are the contracts for all coaching positions reviewed by the institution's counsel?	___	___	___	___
B.	Are contracts for coaches subject to the institution's personnel procedures concerning termination and appeal?	___	___	___	___
C.	Are assistant coaches apprised of any clauses or agreements in the head coaches' contracts that allow for their termination at will?	___	___	___	___
D.	Do contracts clearly specify "perks" such as use of owned or loaned vehicles, permission to operate summer camps as independent contractors, etc.?	___	___	___	___
E.	Are athletic department personnel routinely advised of the institution's personnel policies and procedures?	___	___	___	___

XII. OUTSIDER USE OF INSTITUTIONAL FACILITIES

Many institutions allow outside use of their facilities, either as a community service or on a rental basis, for a fee. When outsiders are allowed to use the institution's athletic facilities, this increases its exposure to athletic-related liability, and must be carefully managed.

		YES	NO	NA	Referral
A.	Is there a clear delineation between "College/University Sponsored" and "Outside Sponsored" use?	___	___	___	___
B.	Does a policy exist detailing conditions under which use of institutional facilities both informally and formally by outsiders will be permitted?	___	___	___	___
C.	If the policy requires contracts for outside use (for both rentals and free use), does the contract state that outsider users assume the risk of activities, and does it specify responsibility for supervising security and public safety during activities?	___	___	___	___
D.	Do contracts for outsider use require certificates of insurance?	___	___	___	___
E.	Is the institution's responsibility for summer and athletic camps, and various types of academic and sports clinics, clearly delineated by policy and contract including insurance requirements?	___	___	___	___
F.	Does the policy specify a particular person who may authorize outside use?	___	___	___	___
G.	Do institutional staffing plans include supervision of public and outsider use?	___	___	___	___
H.	Is coordination with campus security adequate to cover outsider access and use delineated both for informal use, e.g., individuals using the gym, and formal use, e.g., a summer basketball camp?	___	___	___	___
I.	Does a policy exist for dealing with complaints, injuries, and accidents from outside users?	___	___	___	___

XIII. WAIVERS AND RELEASES

Waivers for emergency medical attention are essential to facilitate required treatment, to reduce the level of the medical emergency, and certainly to limit the institution's liability. "Hold harmless" waivers or releases can provide some protection to the institution in the aftermath of an accident where it can be shown that the institution did everything it could reasonably have been expected to have done, and that the participant in the sports or athletic activity knew of the apparent risks and was willing to assume them.

		YES	NO	NA	Referral
A.	Are medical waivers required for:				
	1. Intercollegiate athletics?	___	___	___	___
	2. Intramural?	___	___	___	___
	3. Club sports?	___	___	___	___
	4. Instructional/recreational sports?	___	___	___	___
B.	Is the wording of the waiver reviewed regularly with legal counsel?	___	___	___	___
C.	Do these waivers conform to league rules, NCAA, NAIA, etc.?	___	___	___	___

		YES	NO	NA	Referral
D.	If not all sports participants sign "hold harmless" waivers, then are waivers mandatory for certain high risk sports or recreational activities?	___	___	___	_____
E.	Are Parental Consent Releases obtained for minors?	___	___	___	_____
F.	Are the medical waivers readily accessible in the event of an emergency?	___	___	___	_____
G.	Are waivers required prior to first use?	___	___	___	_____
H.	Are Consent for Medical Care forms on file?	___	___	___	_____

XIV. LEGAL REVIEW

Legal review by experienced counsel can greatly facilitate the reduction of litigation. The most effective counsel will be involved at the key junctures described below.

		YES	NO	NA	Referral
A.	Is legal counsel involved early on in activities, accidents, and injuries that may lead to law suits?	___	___	___	_____
B.	Has legal counsel reviewed coaches' contracts and all other contractual arrangements made between the university and outside groups?	___	___	___	_____
C.	Have arrangements been made for immediate legal services in the event of a catastrophic loss?	___	___	___	_____
D.	Is legal counsel involved in some aspects of the orientation/training of athletic staff, coaches, and those supervising athletic activities?	___	___	___	_____
E.	Has legal counsel reviewed all endorsements to balance safety considerations against income?	___	___	___	_____

XV. INSURANCE

		YES	NO	NA	Referral
A.	Has your Risk Manager or Broker advised you regarding insurance coverage and exclusions for the institution, faculty, staff, students, independent contractors and volunteers in the following policies:				
	Liability	___	___	___	_____
	Property	___	___	___	_____
	Auto and Non-Owned Auto	___	___	___	_____
	Workers' Compensation	___	___	___	_____
	Student Accident/Medical	___	___	___	_____
	Volunteers	___	___	___	_____
	Medical Malpractice	___	___	___	_____
B.	Has the Risk Manager reviewed departmental policies, procedures, handbooks and other publications for risk management purposes?	___	___	___	_____

XVI. ACTION PLANNING

In the process of completing the self-assessment and in reviewing it, certainly a number of priority issues became evident. In this section you will be asked to list a specific number of those problem areas and prepare to address them.

List the most prominent problems that you feel need attention. (You may copy this section if you need more planning pages.)

PROBLEM:_____

Specific Action Steps:

1._____

2._____

3._____

Persons to Contact:

1._____

2._____

3._____

Expected Results:

1._____

2._____

3._____

Expected Date of Results:

_____

Assigned to:

_____

PROBLEM:_____

Specific Action Steps:

    1._____

    2._____

    3._____

Persons to Contact:

    1._____

    2._____

    3._____

Expected Results:

    1._____

    2._____

    3._____

Expected Date of Results:

_____

Assigned to:

_____

PROBLEM:_____

Specific Action Steps:

1._____

2._____

3._____

Persons to Contact:

1._____

2._____

3._____

Expected Results:

1._____

2._____

3._____

Expected Date of Results:

_____

Assigned to:

_____

Appendix P
SPORTS PARTICIPATION FORMS
Student Athlete

I am aware that playing or practicing in any sport can be a dangerous activity involving MANY RISKS OR INJURY. I understand that the dangers and risks of playing or practicing in the above sport include, but are not limited to, death, serious neck and spinal injuries which may result in complete or partial paralysis or brain damage, serious injury to virtually all bones, joints, ligaments, muscles, tendons, and other aspects of the muscular-skeletal system and serious injury or impairment to other aspects of my body, general health and well being.

Because of the dangers of participating in the above sport, I recognize the importance of following the coach's instructions regarding playing techniques, training, rules of the sport, other team rules, and to obey such instructions.

In consideration of _____ (institution) permitting me to practice, play or try out for _____ (institution's) _____ (indicate intercollegiate sport) team, and to engage in all activities related to the team, including practicing, playing and travel, I hereby voluntarily assume all risks associated with participation and agree to exonerate and save harmless _____ (institution, their agents, servants and employees, the athletic staff of _____ (institution), the physicians and other practitioners of the healing arts treating me, from any and all kind of liability, claims, causes of action or demands of any kind and nature whatsoever which may arise by or in connection with my participation in any activities related to _____ (institution) _____ (indicate intercollegiate sport).

The terms hereof shall serve as a release and assumption of risk for my heirs, estate, executor, administrator, assignees, and all members of my family.

I hereby agree to submit any disputes that may arise between myself and _____ (institution), its agents, servants and employees, the athletic staff of _____ (institution), the physicians and other practitioners of the healing arts treating me, and all their agents, trustees, servants and employees, in connection with my activities at _____ (institution), to binding arbitration before three arbitrators, in accordance with the Rules of the American Arbitration Association.

(For contact or collision sports):

I specifically acknowledge that _____ (indicate sport) is a VIOLENT CONTACT sport, involving even a greater risk of injury than other sports.

_____

Student Athlete (Initials)

_____

Student Athlete

_____

Date

Agreement To Participate and Parental Consent Form

Student Athlete

I am aware that participating in any interscholastic sport can be a dangerous activity involving MANY RISKS OF INJURY. I understand that the dangers and risks of participating in _____ (indicate interscholastic sport) includes death, serious neck and spinal injuries (i.e. paralysis or brain damage) and serious injury or impairment to other aspects of my body, general health or well being.

Because of the dangers of participating in the above sport, I recognize the importance of following the coach's instruction regarding playing techniques, training and team rules, and to obey such instructions. I also understand that in order to maintain my eligibility to participate in interscholastic sports I must abide by these instructions, as well as all applicable athletic association, school and team rules.

In consideration of the _____ (School District) permitting me to practice, play, or try out for the _____ (indicate interscholastic sport) School team, and to engage in all acitivites related to the team, including practicing, playing and travel, I hereby voluntarily assume and understand all risks associated with participation and agree to exonerate and save harmless (name of school), their agents, servants and employees and Board of Education, from any and all liability claims, causes of action or demands of any kind and nature whatsoever which may arise by or in connection with my participation in any activities related to the (name of school) _____ . (Indicate interscholastic sport.)

Date: _____

Student's Name: _____ (please print)

Student's Signature: _____

NOTE:
Generally, minors are not legally competent to contractually waive their rights to redress in the event of negligent injury. Although this form may persuade someone to not pursue a claim for injury, it should not be relied on to fully protect you from claims for negligent acts.

Parental Consent

I have read and kept a copy of both the *Agreement to Participate in Interscholastic Athletics* and the accompanying letter from the Athletic Director. Therefore, I understand the potential risks of injury and the responsibilities of my child while participating in the interscholastic sports program.

I hereby grant my permission for my child to participate in _____ (indicate interscholastic sport). I also give permission for my child to receive medical treatment in case of injury during a practice or game.

Parent's Name: _____ (please print)

Parent's Signature: _____

Address: _____

_____

Daytime Telephone Number: _____

Evening Telephone Number: _____

Name and telephone number of person to contact in the event of an emergency if the person above is unavailable:

_____

_____

Date: _____

Agreement To Participate
(Intercollegiate Athletics)

Sport (check appropriate space)

Baseball   _____

Basketball   _____

Cheerleading   _____

Cross-Country   _____

Football   _____

Golf   _____

Tennis   _____

Track and Field   _____

Volleyball   _____

Soccer   _____

Softball   _____

Swimming and Diving   _____

Other   _____

Sample Introductory Letter For Parents of Interscholastic Athletic Participants

Dear Parent or Guardian:

Your child has expressed a desire to particpate in our interscholastic sport program. It is important that you and your child understand the goals of the program and agree to abide by the rules established by the district for the benefit of those who participate both as players, students and representatives of their community.

(1) Interscholastic sports are part of a broad extracurricular program designed to teach students certain skills and reinforce concepts of self worth (achievement), cooperative effort (teamwork), and ethical decision making (sportsmanship).

(2) All participants must receive a physical examination by a school
     physician prior to the start of practice. We will make these ar-
     rangements on a team basis and your child will be notified when
     and where this will be administered. Please consult your physician
     regarding your child's protection against tetanus. If there is a ques-
     tion about your child's eligibility for physical reasons, it will be
     discussed with you.

(3) While the coaching staff and other responsible school officials will
     do everything within reason to protect your child against injury,
     including providing the appropriate equipment, safe facilities and
     training designed to reduce the impact of accidents, injuries will
     occur and on a very rare occasion may be serious and disabling.
     If you are concerned about this possibility you should discuss it
     with your child's coach.

(4) School medical insurance for the medical treatment of sport re-
     lated injuries generally is applicable only after the parents' health
     insurance, if any, has been used. This type of coverage is usually
     excess coverage and generally will not pay the full cost of
     treatment.

(5) Within the first three team meetings the coach will explain the
     attendance policy and training rules and rules for participation.
     In addition to the strict observance of these rules, your child will
     be expected to meet all regular school obligations of citizenship
     and academic achievement.

(6) Not all students who wish to participate in interscholastic ath-
     letics may be able to do so. The size of a team is necessarily limited
     by the availability of supplies, equipment and coaching staff. Cuts
     will be made, when necessary, on the basis of skill development,
     readiness for competition and observance of the rules. No child
     will be permitted to compete until, in the opinion of the coach,
     he or she is ready to do so.
         School equipment issued to your child for participation is his
     or her responsibility and must be returned promptly upon request.
     Reimbursement from the student will be expected for loss or de-
     struction of equipment beyond ordinary wear and tear. We hope
     your child will have a successful and rewarding athletic experi-
     ence. Your support and encouragement of your child will con-
     tribute to that success.
         Enclosed find copies of *The Agreement to Participate* and *Parental
     Consent* forms. Please read the entire contents of the form and sign
     and return one copy and keep the other for your records.

_____

Athletic Director

Appendix Q

Football Roster (Sample Copy)

Name	Agreement to Participate	Physical Examination	Eligibility	Insurance			Scholarship Agreement
				Parental	Form In	Paid	
1.							
2.							
3.							
4.							
5.							
6.							
7.							
8.							
9.							
10.							
11.							
13.							
14.							
15.							
16.							

Trainer: Head Coach: Assistants: Comments:

Appendix R
Recommended List of Equipment and Facility Warning Signs

(1) **Gymnasiumn Rules**
  (a) No food, drink or smoking allowed.
  (b) Workout clothes are required.
  (c) No dark-soled or street shoes permitted.
  (d) No hanging on basketball nets or rims.

(2) **Swimming Pool Rules**
  (a) All persons are required to take a soap shower before entering the pool area.
  (b) Swimwear is required.
  (c) No cutoffs, shirts, or shoes are permitted.
  (d) No masks, fins, snorkels, or foreign objects allowed during open swim, unless approved by a lifeguard.
  (e) No person with communicable diseases, open cuts or wounds will be allowed in the water.
  (f) No running or horse play in the pool area. Walk in all areas around the pool.
  (g) No flips or back dives. Diving blocks are "off limits."
  (h) No smoking, food or drinks in the pool area.
  (i) The only flotation devices allowed are those that are U.S. Coast Guard approved.
  (j) No hairpins or barrettes in pool.
  (k) For safety reasons, there will be no talking to lifeguards except for rule explanations or other safety reasons.
  (l) All swimmers are asked to respect the rights of others to enjoy themselves.
  (m) The staff cannot be responsible for safekeeping valuables. Such items should be locked in your locker or other safe place, or left home.

(3) **Diving Rules**
  (a) Dive straight off the board.
  (b) One bounce only.
  (c) One person on a board at a time.
  (d) No sitting, handstands or cartwheels on the board.
  (e) Be sure the area is clear before diving.
  (f) Exit away from the boards.
  (g) No swimming in diving area.
  (h) Following dives, the diver must swim to the closest ladder, allowing the next diver to dive.
  (i) There are inherent risks of diving that may cause injury.

(4) **Weight Room (both Universal and Free Weights)**

(a) Spotters are required when using free weights.
(b) Familiarize yourself with each individual machine.
(c) Do not bang weights.
(d) Complete exercise and move to next machine—do not rest on equipment.
(e) Workout clothes required (shirts must be worn, shoes required, no street clothes).
(f) No food, drinks, or smoking.
(g) Report any malfunctions to supervisor, attendant or instructor.
(h) Keep fingers clear of weight movement.
(i) Leave the weight room when your workout is completed.
(j) Replace all weights on rack.
(k) Do not remove weights from the lifting area.
(l) Have a productive workout.

(5) **Jogging Track Rules (Indoor and Outdoor)**
(a) Run only within the confines of the designated area (within the taped area).
(b) Run in one direction and in single file only.
(d) Call "track" when overtaking another runner.
(d) Use extreme caution in all entrance/exit areas of the gym, doorways, or steps (people crossing).
(e) No food, drink or smoking in the jogging area.
(f) No excessive speed.
(g) Warm-up and stretch outside the track area.

(6) **Racquetball**
(a) Play with protective eye covering. If you choose not to, you play at your own risk.
(b) Do not look at the ball while it is being hit.
(c) Turn your face away from all shots.
(d) Be sure your wrist straps are always secure.

Appendix S

Sample Accident/Injury Report

I.

(1) Athlete's Name: _____

(2) Sport engaged in at time of injury: _____

(3) Position: _____

(4) Date of Injury: _____

(5) When did the injury occur
    (i.e., practice, game, other): _____

_____

II.

(1) Location of injury:

Head _____	Arm _____	Foot _____
Neck _____	Shoulder ___	Eye _____
Back _____	Leg _____	Chest _____
Face _____	Hand _____	Finger _____

(2) Briefly describe injury: _____

_____

III.

(1) Describe treatment rendered for this injury: _____

_____

(2) List person(s) who administered treatment (i.e., specific
    trainers or physicians, or other staff members: _____

_____

(3) Did the athlete refuse treatment? ❏ Yes ❏ No

(4) Describe any and all follow-up treatments: _____

_____

(5) Was the athlete hospitalized for this injury?
    ❏ Yes   ❏ No

(6) If yes, state name of hospital and nature of treatment: ___

_____

(7) Indicate practices missed: _____

(8) Indicate games missed: _____

Report prepared by: _____

Title: _____

Date report prepared: _____

Appendix T

Spectator Accident/Injury Report

I.

(1) Name of injured party: _____

(2) Address: _____

(3) Age: _____

(4) Sex: _____

II.

(1) Date of injury: _____

(2) Time of injury: _____

(3) Location where accident occurred (level, and section information, if applicable): _____

(4) How did accident occur? _____

_____

(5) Description of injury:

(A) Location (s):

Head	_____	Arm	_____	Foot	_____
Neck	_____	Shoulder	___	Eye	_____
Back	_____	Leg	_____	Chest	_____
Face	_____	Hand	_____	Finger	_____

(B) Briefly, describe injury: _____

_____

_____

(6) Other parties involved (i.e., concessionaires, lessee, other outside contractors): _____

III.

(1) Was first-aid administered?   ❑ Yes ❑ No

(2) If yes, by whom? _____

(3) Describe all action taken in first aid treatment: _____

_____

(4) Were paramedics called? ❑ Yes ❑ No
(5) Were the police called?   ❑ Yes ❑ No
(6) Was the injured party referred to medical assistance?
    ❑ Yes ❑ No

(7) If so, where? _____
(8) Did injured party refuse treatment?   ❑ Yes ❑ No

IV.

(1) Was a parent, guardian or responsible adult notified?
    ❑ Yes ❑ No

(2) If so, name: _____

    Relationship: _____

(3) How did injured party leave the scene of the accident/ injury? _____

(4) To whom was he/she released? _____

(5) Name and addresses of witnesses: _____

_____

(6) Report prepared by: _____

    Title: _____   Date: _____

Appendix T

Sample Witness Statement

I, John Doe, reside at 221 Red Street, and my home telephone number is 555-1212. I am employed by the Red Lake Senior High as a physical education instructor.

On _____, my third period senior physical education class was participating in a softball game. Prior to this class, I inspected the softball field located behind the school building for potential hazards, including rocks, glass, holes, and wet spots. The playing field appeared to be in good condition and free from any identifiable hazards. I documented the results of my inspection in our daily facility checklist. At the time of the class, at approximately 10:00 a.m., the weather was clear and dry. During the class period, I observed Richard Johnson, a student, trip and fall on the basepath midway between first and second base when he attempted to advance to second base on a base hit from a teammate. Mr. Johnson appeared to injure his right leg and the school nurse was summoned to render medical assistance.

The above statement is true and correct to my knowledge.

_____

Signature of Witness

_____

Date

Appendix U
Checklists

Locker Room

Item   **Condition/Remarks**

(1) Showers:
    (a) Lighting
    (b) Drainage
    (c) Cleanliness
    (d) Water temperature and controls
(2) Locker Rooms:
    (a) Location
    (b) Carpet
    (c) How are lockers secured?
    (d) Lighting and emergency lighting
    (e) Towel rack and hooks
    (f) Hand and hair dryers (exposed wires)
    (g) Hot water pipes (leaks/insulation)
    (h) Ventilation, filters and air ducts
    (i) Ground fault interrupter(s)
Date of inspection: _____

Time of inspection: _____

Recommendations: _____

                                       _____

                                       _____

Name of inspector: _____

Signature of inspector: _____

Gymnastics Equipment Checklist

Item   **Condition/Remarks**

(1) Is any equipment open and unsupervised? Location:
(2) Trampoline and Mini Tramp:
    (a) Pads
    (b) Springs
    (c) Canvas

(d) Stability of understructure
(e) Warnings
(f) Rebounders
(g) Blasters
(h) Other devices

_____

_____

(3) Uneven/Parallel Bars:
    (a) Cracks or splinters on bars
    (b) Adjustment Wheel
(4) Balance Beam:
    (a) Base
    (b) Splinters or cracks
(5) Mats:
    (a) Tears and holes
    (b) Cleanliness
    (c) Thickness of Mats - resilience
    (d) Area covered
(6) Pommel Horse/Vaulting Boxes:
    (a) Stability of handles
    (b) Tears on cover
    (c) Stability of foundation
(7) Other: Rings/Ropes/Cargo Nets/Etc.
(8) Floor anchor system:
(9) Equipment storage:
Date of inspection: _____

Time of inspection: _____

Recommendations: _____

_____

Name of Inspector: _____

Signature of Inspector: _____

Weight Room Equipment Checklist

Item   **Condition/Remarks**

  1. Mats and Warm-Up Area
  2. Weight Belts

3. Training Benches
4. Sit-Up Board
5. Free Weight Plates
6. Free Weight Stands
7. Collars
8. Long Bar
9. Short Bar
10. E-Z Curl Bar
11. Stationary Cycle
12. Treadmill
13. Leaper: Real Runner
14. Hip Sled
15. Power Rakes (Isometric Bar)
16. Squat Stands/Stations
17. Leg Press Station
18. Knee Extensions
19. Knee Flections
20. Shoulder Press
21. High Pulley Station
22. Low Pully Station
    a. Chin
    b. Dips
23. Lumbar Extension
24. Neck Machine
25. Other Equipment
26. Lighting

Date of Inspection: _____

Time of Inspections: _____

Recommendations: _____

                                   _____

Name of Inspector: _____

Signature of Inspector   _____

Training Room

Item   **Condition/Remarks**

(1) Temperature
(2) Electric circuits
(3) Thermostat in whirlpool

(4) Ultrasound
(5) Ice machine(s)
(6) Locked medicine cabinets
(7) Ground fault interrupter(s)
(8) Condition of floor surface
(9) File cabinets for student
     records locked?
(10) Private area for consultation
(11) Cleanliness
Date of inspection: _____

Time of inspection: _____

Recommendations: _____

                             _____

                             _____

                             _____

Name of inspector: _____

Signature of inspector: _____

Sample Equipment and Facility Inspection Checklist

Outdoor Playing Fields Checklist

(i.e. Football, Soccer, Lacrosse, Etc.)

Area   **Condition/Remarks**

(1) Field surface condition
(2) Uncovered drains:
(3) Drainage of field:
(4) Presence of unrelated equipment on field:
(5) Debris: Condition of benches and bleachers:
(6) Condition of goals:
(7) Adequate lighting:
(8) Boundaries marked between playing areas:
Date of inspection: _____

Time of inspection: _____

Recommendations: _____

Name of Inspector: _____

Signature of Inspector: _____

Baseball/Softball Field

Area   **Condition/Remarks**

(1) Infield/Basepaths/Mound:
(2) Outfield:
(3) Batting circle:
(4) On-Deck area:
(5) Warning track:
(6) Backstop-screening:
(7) Sidelines:
(8) Drainage of field:
(9) Uncovered drains:
(10) Lighting
(11) Debris:
(12) Presence of unrelated equipment on field:
(13) Benches and bleachers:
Date of inspection: _____

Time of inspection: _____

Recommendations: _____

                              _____

                              _____

                              _____

Name of inspector: _____

Signature of inspector: _____

Track and Field

Item   **Condition/Remarks**

(1) Running Track
    (a) Surface
    (b) Curbing
(2) Discus Circle
    (a) Surface
    (b) Field boundaries visible
    (c) Location
(3) Shotput
    (a) Surface
    (b) Field boundaries visible
    (c) Location
(4) Javelin Throw
    (a) Surface
    (b) Field boundaries visible
    (c) Location
(5) Long Jump/Triple Jump
    (a) Take off board (secure)
    (b) Runway surface (clean & dry)
    (c) Landing board (clean & dry)
    (d) Pit condition
    (e) Location?
(6) High Jump
    (a) Surface
    (b) Landing pit (secure)
    (c) Cross bar
    (d) Take-off runway surface
       (clean, dry, level)
    (e) Mats
    (f) Location
(7) Pole Vault
    (a) Surface
    (b) Take-off box (secure)
    (c) Landing Pit
       (1) Secure
       (2) Mats
    (d) Cross bar
    (e) Location
(8) Equipment
    (a) Lighting
    (b) Storage space
    (c) Ventilation
    (d) Housekeeping
    (e) Locks
Date of inspection: _____

Time of inspection: _____

Recommendation: _____

_____

_____

_____

Name of inspector: _____

Signature of inspector: _____

NOTE:
   The location of field events to the track and spectator seating areas is important for the safety of both participants and spectators.

Swimming Pool and Diving Area Checklist

Item   **Condition/Remarks**

1. Temperature of Water and Air
2. Guard Stands Stable
3. Ladders
4. Chemical Balance
5. Emergency System
6. Diving Boards
7. Warning Signs
8. Other Equipment

Date of inspection: _____

Time of inspection: _____

Recommendations: _____

_____

Name of Inspector: _____

Signature of Inspector: _____

Outdoor Basketball, Volleyball and Tennis Courts Checklist

Item   **Condition/Remarks**

A. Outdoor Tennis Courts
1. Fences (obstructions)
2. Court Surface
3. Nets and Wheels
4. Condition of Court Surface
5. Loose Equipment
6. Lighting

B. Outdoor Basketball Courts
1. Stability of Backboards and Goals
2. Condition of Nets and Rims
   (bent, broken, torn, missing)
3. Ditches for Free Flowing of Water
4. Fence (obstructions)
5. Condition of Court Surfaces
6. Lighting

Date of inspection: _____

Time of inspection: _____

Recommendations: _____

_____

Name of Inspector: _____

Signature of Inspector: _____

Football/Lacrosse/Wrestling Protective Equipment

Participant's Name:

Item	Serial No.	Brand	Condition/Remarks
(1) Headgears			
(2) Face masks			
(3) Mouth guards			
(4) Shoulder pads			
(5) Collars			
(6) Rib protectors			
(7) Bicep pads			
(8) Spine pads			
(9) Hip pads			
(10) Forearm pads			
(11) Wrist/Hand gloves			
(12) Pants			

(13) Jerseys
(14) Shoes
(15) Warning labels in place

Date of inspection: _____

Time of inspection: _____

Recommendations: _____

                                 _____

                                 _____

Name of inspector: _____

Signature of inspector: _____

Appendix V
Maintenance Response Form

1) Date of Maintenance Response:

2) Time of Maintenance Response:

3) Location of Problem:

4) Corrective Measures Taken:

5) Additional Comments:

6 Name of Employee(s) Completing Work:

_____

(Print Name)

_____

(Print Name)

7) Signature of Employee(s) Completing Work:

Date of Inspection: _____

Time of inspection: _____

Recommendations: _____

_____

Name of Inspector: _____

Signature of Inspector: _____

Appendix W
Sample Letter to Person/Organization Regarding the Donation of Protective Equipment

Dear _____ :

In consideration of _____ (organization) donating its inter-collegiate _____ (sport) protective equipment (i.e., helmets, shoulder pads) to _____ (organization), _____ (organization) agrees as follows:

(1) To take full responsibility to recondition the (helmet/shoulder pads) by a NOCSAE cerrtified reconditioner.

(2) Agree to exonerate and save harmless _____ (organization), their agents, servants and employees, from any and all liability, claims, causes of action or demands of any kind and nature which may arise in connection with the _____ (sport) equipment donated by _____ (organization).

_____
(Name of Institution)

By: _____

Receiving Person or Organization

By: _____

Appendix X
Facility Use and Indemnification Agreement

In consideration of the Licensor (School District) entering this Facility Agreement with ⎯⎯⎯⎯⎯⎯⎯ (name) (Licensee), and as a condition of said agreement, the Licensee hereby agrees to indemnify and hold harmless the Licensor, its School Board, and all agents, servants or employees, for any and all claims, lawsuits, or judgments that may come about as a result of the use of the above described facility by the Licensee. This indemnification shall include, and not be limited to, any settlements, judgments or awards by a court of competent jurisdiction, or a board of arbitration. Said indemnification should also include costs for necessary legal representation and out-of-pocket expenses incurred by the Licensor in connection with any action or defense necessary to protect itself under the terms of this agreement.

In addition to the above, the Licensee represents and warrants that it has a policy of general liability insurance in force and effect on the dates of the use of the licensed premises, issued by a liability insurance company licensed to do business in the State of Missouri, and said insurance company will, without any costs or expense to the Licensor, issue a certificate to the Licensor. Said certificate of insurance shall be delivered to Licensee. In addition, said insurance company will agree to give notification to the Licensor of any revocation and/or cancellation at least seventy-two (72) hours before said revocation becomes effective.

It is further agreed that the school district has the **Absolute Right of Cancellation** without liability if the facility is unavailable.

Group ⎯⎯⎯⎯⎯⎯ Accepted: (Name of School District)

By ⎯⎯⎯⎯⎯⎯⎯ By ⎯⎯⎯⎯⎯⎯⎯⎯⎯⎯⎯⎯⎯⎯⎯⎯⎯

Signature ⎯⎯⎯⎯⎯ Signature ⎯⎯⎯⎯⎯⎯⎯⎯⎯⎯⎯⎯⎯⎯

Title ⎯⎯⎯⎯⎯⎯ Title ⎯⎯⎯⎯⎯⎯⎯⎯⎯⎯⎯⎯⎯⎯⎯⎯⎯

Date ⎯⎯⎯⎯⎯⎯ Date ⎯⎯⎯⎯⎯⎯⎯⎯⎯⎯⎯⎯⎯⎯⎯⎯⎯

Facility Use and Indemnification Agreement

Date: _____

Name of group: _____

Address: _____
          Street   City   State   Zip

Contact Person: _____ Title: _____

Telephone: _____

Dates of rental: _____ through: _____

Type of facility requested: _____

Type of activity or sport to be played: _____

Will equipment be needed?   ❑ Yes   No ❑   If so, please list: _____

_____

Number of participants expected: _____

Number of group's staff to supervise participants: _____

Security: _____   Ticket Takers: _____   Ushers: _____

Spectators: ❑ Yes   No ❑   Estimated number: _____

Special details: _____

_____

Will the following facilities be needed?

❑   Concession space
❑   Bleachers
❑   Locker room space
❑   Sound system
❑   Scoreboard
❑   Other equipment   _____

Rate: _____ Other charges: _____

Payment due on or before: _____

Appendix Y
Paired Organ Agreement

I, _____ , wish to participate in intercollegiate athletics, and more particularly, the football program at _____ . In connection with my participation, I acknowledge that the risk of possible physical harm to me as a result of my participation is increased because of my loss of a paired organ (kidney) which I sustained in the past, and for which I have received medical attention. While there is no immediate danger to me, I am told that strenuous, collision type activities, such as football, could render me more susceptible to future problems with my remaining kidney than might normally be expected.

I have discussed alternative activities to participation in football with _____ (Head Football Coach), _____ (Head Athletic Trainer) and _____ the physician who conducted the pre-participation physical examination. I have discussed the situation with my parents and we understand the potential danger of participation in football.

Notwithstanding that, my participation in intercollegiate football constitutes more risk to me than it does other athletes, I nevertheless wish to participate in intercollegiate football at _____ . In making this decision, I am aware of the value of intercollegiate athletics in my life, and choose to continue my participation in order to take advantage of those values. In weighing the risk to myself of potential injury now and in the future, I wish to exonerate and save harmless _____ , its agents and employees, the athletic staff of _____ , the physicians and other practitioners of the healing arts treating me, and the Board of Trustees of _____ from any and all liability as a result of an injury to my kidney which hereinafter may be claimed as a result of my participation in the program of the College, or any treatment by any of the foregoing of any conditions or injuries sustained by me in the past to my kidney. This release is only applicable to any injury that causes harm or damage to my kidney, not to any injury that may occur in the future which is unrelated to my previous injury. I execute this agreement freely, fully intending to be bound by the same.

Executed at _____ , this day of ____ .

Student-Athlete _____

Parent or Guardian _____

Witness: _____

Table of Cases

Index

About the Author

Herb Appenzeller has been a faculty member at Guilford College since 1956 and has had varied responsibilities, including teaching, coaching, dean of students and, for thirty-one years, athletics director. He is known as one of the most distinguished athletic directors in the nation for his dedication to individual development and team cooperation in his student-athletes. His accomplishments as an administrator are a matter of record. He is responsible for turning unsuccessful programs around at four schools. Tangible evidence of his leadership is seen in the development of sports facilities, breadth of the sports programs, and numerous championships on the high school and college level. He guided Guilford College to national titles in men's basketball and women's tennis, and instituted a sports management program that has received national attention. He co-edited *Successful Sports Management*, recognized as a leading text in the field of sport management. He capped his athletics career with the teaching and research responsibilities of an endowed professorship to become Jefferson-Pilot Professor of Sports Management. He is a respected consultant in sports management and athletics in every part of the United States.

For over twenty-five years, Herb has been a scholar in the field of sports law. He has spoken to many groups across the country, including high school and college athletics directors, physical educators, high school principals, educators and sports safety personnel. He has been a board member of the National Association of Sports Officials, the Sports Medicine Foundation of America, and is a special consultant for the Center For Sport Law and Risk Management.

His writings include journal articles, nine books, and contributions to many others. His first book, *From the Gym to the Jury*, was published in 1970. It's also significant to note that Herb's writings have been addressed to educators, not the legal world. His national recognition as an expert and pioneer in sports law has brought honors to him from a number of organizations. Both Guilford College and Chowan College have named him to their sports Hall of Fame. He has also been honored with membership in the athletics Hall of Fame for the National Association of Collegiate Directors of Athletics and the National Association of Intercollegiate Athletics. In 1988 the Safety Society of the American Alliance for Health, Physical Education, Recreation and

Dance (AAHPERD) awarded him its Professional Service Award and in 1988 the North Carolina Alliance for Health, Physical Education, Recreation and Dance (NCAHPERD) recognized him with the 1988 Honor Award. In 1989 he received the Academe/Athletics Award at the International Sports Business Conference in Columbia, South Carolina.